A District Court Jud
born in Brisbane in 1
University of Queen
trar of the Supreme
years later was admitted as a Barrister-at-Law of the Supreme
Court of Queensland. He was Crown Prosecutor for Queens-
land from 1962 to 1972 and in that year became a District
Court Judge, a position he held until his retirement in 1984.
For a short period during 1983 he was Acting Supreme Court
Judge. He has also lectured in law and written several articles.

Born in Brisbane in 1932, Desmond Gibney joined the
Queensland Public Service in 1949 and served in the police
section until 1958, when he was transferred to the Department
of Labour and Industry. He was later seconded for periods of
special duty in both the Premier's and the Treasury Department. He is currently Director of the Division of Administration at the Department of Industrial Affairs in Brisbane.

THE GATTON MYSTERY

JAMES and DESMOND GIBNEY

PENGUIN BOOKS

To our respective wives—Hazel and Nola—
who, throughout the years, have patiently
listened to much debate and discussion
concerning *The Gatton Mystery*.

PENGUIN BOOKS

Published by the Penguin Group
27 Wrights Lane, London W8 5TZ, England
Viking Penguin Inc., 40 West 23rd Street, New York, New York 10010, USA
Penguin Books Australia Ltd, Ringwood, Victoria, Australia
Penguin Books Canada Ltd, 2801 John Street, Markham, Ontario, Canada L3R 1B4
Penguin Books (NZ) Ltd, 182–190 Wairau Road, Auckland 10, New Zealand

Penguin Books Ltd, Registered Offices Harmondsworth, Middlesex, England

First published in Australia by Angus & Robertson 1977
First published in Great Britain by Penguin Books 1989
1 3 5 7 9 10 8 6 4 2

Printed and bound in Great Britain by
Richard Clay Ltd, Bungay, Suffolk
Filmset in Times Monophoto

ACKNOWLEDGMENTS

We owe a special debt to our very good friend, Mr Norman Gulbransen, formerly Assistant Commissioner of Police, Brisbane. His tremendous encouragement was a great stimulus to us and he was the first to read the manuscript.

For permission to reprint copyright material we owe thanks to: Sweet & Maxwell Ltd., London, for extracts from *The Proof of Guilt* by Professor Glanville Williams; Read Press Pty. Ltd., Brisbane, for extracts from *A Journalist's Memories* by Major-General Spencer Browne.

A large measure of thanks is also due to the staff of the following libraries and institutes for their ready co-operation during the period of our research: State Library of Queensland; State Archives of Queensland; John Oxley Memorial Library of Queensland; The Central Library, University of Queensland; The Darling Downs Institute of Advanced Education, Toowoomba, Queensland.

We are very grateful to the following members of the medical profession for their advice and helpfulness to us in enabling us to form our assessment on aspects dependent upon the medical testimony: Dr Merton Thew and Dr R.J. Bovey of Brisbane; Dr Jim McCoy and Dr Bob Morgan of Roma (the latter now of Warwick); Dr Doug Wilson, Government Medical Officer, Brisbane; Dr J.I. Tonge and Dr Alan Davidson of the Laboratory of Microbiology & Pathology, Brisbane. Professor A. Keith Mant, Professor of Forensic Medicine at Guy's Hospital within the University of London, United Kingdom.

In evaluating the significance of "the imprint of cloth and the facsimile" we received great help and assistance from Det. Sgt. Neil Rayward (Scientific Section, Office of the Commissioner of Police, Brisbane) and from Mr D.S. Lecky (Supervising Chemist, Government Chemical Laboratory, Brisbane), and we express our thanks to them.

Our good friend Alan Queale provided us with items of research material as did Mr Eric Drayton Davis of Brisbane. Mr David Rapaport of Toowoomba suggested an avenue of research which proved remarkably helpful. We are very appreciative of the help received.

Of great assistance was the work done for us by Mr Ian Boe, who made reproductions of photographic material originally made available from the John Oxley Memorial Library and by other sources. Mrs P. Hassed of Brisbane and Mrs V. Campbell of Maleny rendered valuable typing assistance when the manuscript was being compiled and afterwards. We are also indebted to "Jeannie", who read our manuscript and made helpful suggestions, and to "Jim", who prepared the sketch of the area in the region of Moran's paddock.

We thank the editor and staff of the *Maryborough Chronicle*, Maryborough, Queensland, for making copies of the newspapers for 1898 and 1899 available to us. We also thank Mr H.W. Nunn, Keeper of Public Records, Public Record Office, Victoria, for the information concerning the conviction and imprisonment of Richard Burgess in Victoria.

As for the others who have contributed in various ways we tabulate our gratitude to them in an alphabetical and not a quantitative order. They are as follows: Mr J.F. Clarke, Judge R.F.J. Cormack, Inspectors Len Gannon and Evan Griffiths and Sergeant Ken Hoggett of the Queensland Police Force, Mrs E. Lacey, Mr Bob Logan (Gatton), Mr Leo P. McCarthy, Mr J.W. Martyn, Mr Keith Noud, Miss Robin Rushbrook, Mr S.H.W. Shand, Mr Rod Stevens and our very good friends—Mr Bill Tew (of Gatton) and his wife, Avilion. Finally, we wish to thank our sister, Mrs Ina Bardsley of Everton Park, Brisbane, who so excellently typed the manuscript and so willingly performed so many other tasks in connection with it. We are most appreciative of her great efforts and for the many helpful suggestions she made.

CONTENTS

My self when young did
  eagerly frequent
Doctor and Saint, and heard
  great Argument
About it and about: but
  evermore
Came out by the same Door
  as in I went.
Rubaiyat of Omar Khayyam, XXVII

INTRODUCTION

One hundred kilometres or so west of Brisbane, in Queensland, on the highway to Toowoomba and almost at the foothills of the Great Dividing Range is the town of Gatton, set amid the lush pastures and rich farmlands of the fertile Lockyer Valley. In the small well-tended cemetery on the outskirts of the town stands an imposing monument bearing the inscription:

IN MEMORY

OF

MICHAEL, Aged 29 Years.

NORAH, Aged 27 Years.

ELLEN, Aged 18 Years.

The dearly beloved children of

DANIEL and MARY MURPHY,

of Tenthill,

who were the victims of a horrible
tragedy perpetrated near Gatton
on December 26th, 1898.

REQUIESCANT IN PACE.

This Monument has been erected by public
subscription to the memory of the
above innocent victims.

This headstone is the sole tangible memento in Gatton today of the tragic events which occurred near the town on Boxing Day in the hot, dry summer of 1898.

The district's oldest residents now have only dim memories of the triple murder which shattered the tranquillity of the rural community of Gatton as the nineteenth century drew to an end. The generation that lived through the events which engulfed the little township on that fateful day is now all but gone. New generations have arisen as the decades have quietly passed and the old wounds have healed.

If faded scars still linger they are tolerably well concealed. Yet, even today, the very mention of Gatton conjures up recollections of the fiendish and shameful murder which, a little over three quarters of a century ago, sent the name of Gatton ringing throughout Australasia and gave the town a lurid and unenviable notoriety.

For its sheer ferocity and the veil of mystery enshrouding it, the murder of the Murphys at Gatton stands starkly apart in the annals of Australian crime. Right from the very outset theories, rumours and reconstructions arose, some of which persist to this very day.

The stunning impact of the Gatton outrage may be gauged from a newspaper headline at the time:

MURDER
Terrible Tragedy.
At Gatton on Boxing Night.
One of the Murders of the Century,
The Worst in Australia.
Two Sisters Ravished and Murdered.
Their Brother Also Killed.
A fiendish crime.
A terrible story.
Full details.[1]

In that same issue of the newspaper, just three days after the events, the report of the newspaper's Gatton correspondent contained the information that:

> Various rumours are in circulation as regards the probable identity of the murderers, and some of them are of such an exceedingly startling nature that I would not dare to even hint at them. I was told tonight by one man that he believes the murderers are still in our midst, and that they were out scouring the country today "looking for themselves".[2]

There have been, in the relatively short history of our country, other crimes of comparable violence. There have been other crimes, never solved, in which seemingly unaccountable circumstances and events have provided a tantalising mystery to titillate the imagination. However, none of these crimes gripped the imagination of the Australian public as did the triple murder at Gatton. Its criminal horror alone incorporated elements which were to secure it a unique place in the nation's criminal history. Those elements were a multiple slaying, the sexual violation of the two women, incredible brutality, and the succession, concurrence and coalescence of seemingly incompatible and inexplicable events and circumstances, all of which gave rise to rumours, reconstructions and competing hypotheses, some of them, as referred to in the newspaper account, being of "an exceedingly startling nature".

In order to enable the reader to gain an accurate appreciation of the events and circumstances leading up to and surrounding the Gatton Mystery it has been necessary for us, in the pages which follow, to outline in some detail such attendant facts and surrounding circumstances as appear to be relevant. However, at this juncture, we will merely state the salient facts, devoid of undue detail.

On Boxing Day, 1898, Michael Murphy, some of his brothers, and his sister Ellen attended a holiday race meeting at Mt Sylvia, a small settlement about eight kilometres south of the Murphys' farm at Tent Hill. The eldest Murphy girl, Polly, also attended the races with her husband, William McNeil. The Murphys, with McNeil and his wife, left Mt Sylvia about five o'clock in the afternoon and arrived back at the Murphy farmhouse at about six thirty. After partaking of the evening meal together at the farmhouse, Michael Murphy and his sisters Norah and Ellen, at or shortly after eight o'clock in the evening, set out in a single horse sulky belonging to William McNeil, to attend a dance which was to be held in the Tarampa Divisional Board's Hall at Gatton. The town was about nine and a half kilometres to the north of the Murphy farm at Tent Hill. On their way to Gatton they passed the sliprails giving entrance to Moran's paddock, which was situated on the eastern side of the road leading from the farm to Gatton, about three kilometres south of the town.

Shortly before the three Murphys arrived at the hall in Gatton, the organisers of the dance had decided to abandon it because "no ladies appeared, or else very few".[3] At about ten past nine the three Murphys arrived at the hall and found it closed. No one spoke to them and the sulky carrying them turned round and drove back in the direction from which they had come.[4] "At about a quarter or twenty minutes past nine" that same evening the three Murphys in the sulky, when "rather more than half a mile [one kilometre] from Moran's sliprails", met their brother, Patrick, who was returning on horseback from the Murphy farmhouse at Tent Hill to the Agricultural College at Gatton where he lived and worked. They all stopped and, after they had spoken together for about three minutes, Patrick proceeded on his way, and his brother and two sisters drove off, apparently towards home. Almost a month later, when describing what had proved to be their final parting in this life, Patrick's actual words were "I saw them start on and I came on into Gatton; they proceeded on towards Tent Hill."[5]

The three Murphys were destined never to see their home again. They had not arrived home by seven thirty next morning and their mother, not unnaturally, grew anxious about them and, at about eight o'clock, their brother-in-law, William McNeil, mounted a horse and went to search for them. He travelled along the Tent Hill road

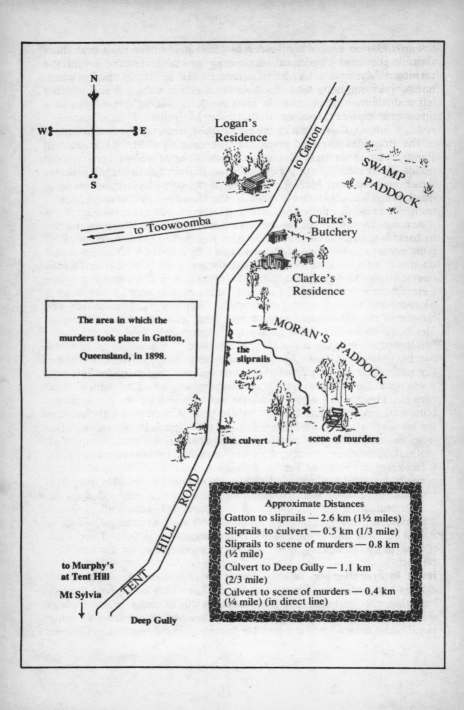

N

W ● ─── ● E

S

Logan's
Residence

to Gatton →

SWAMP
PADDOCK

← to Toowoomba

Clarke's
Butchery

Clarke's
Residence

The area in which the
murders took place in Gatton,
Queensland, in 1898.

MORAN'S PADDOCK

the
sliprails

×
scene of murders

the culvert

TENT HILL ROAD

to Murphy's
at Tent Hill

Mt Sylvia
↓

Deep Gully

Approximate Distances
Gatton to sliprails — 2.6 km (1½ miles)
Sliprails to culvert — 0.5 km (1/3 mile)
Sliprails to scene of murders — 0.8 km
(½ mile)
Culvert to Deep Gully — 1.1 km
(2/3 mile)
Culvert to scene of murders — 0.4 km
(¼ mile) (in direct line)

towards Gatton and, when he reached that part of the road near the sliprails at Moran's paddock, he noticed the wheel tracks of his sulky turning off the road into Moran's paddock. He identified the track as having been made by his sulky because it had a wobbly wheel which left a distinctive track. Shortly afterwards, in Moran's paddock, he discovered the dead bodies of the three Murphys. He immediately rode off into Gatton to notify the police of his discovery, first inquiring at the Brian Boru Hotel as to the whereabouts of the Sergeant of Police. At quarter past nine he informed the Sergeant in charge of police, Sergeant William Arrell, of what he had found and Sergeant Arrell accompanied him to the scene. News of the discovery spread quickly and the township of Gatton was thrown into a state of great excitement; many of the residents went to the scene of the tragedy.

Sergeant Arrell found the bodies of Michael and Ellen lying back to back and quite close together. There was a "heavy bludgeon stick" lying about a foot from Michael's head and it had blood and brains on it.[6] Ellen's skull was smashed on the left side, apparently with a heavy bludgeon, her hands were tied behind her back and her legs were scratched. Her brain was protruding at the back of her head. Michael had his skull smashed in on the right side. Norah's body was lying on a rug at the foot of a gum tree. She also had scratches on her. Her head was smashed in on the left side and she had a cut about fifty millimetres long near the right eye. Her hands were tied behind her back and a leather strap (a hames strap) was tied tightly round her neck. The horse and harness were attached to the sulky but the horse was dead and was lying on the right hand shaft, which was broken. There was a bullet mark on the forehead of the horse. The reins had been brought forward to the horse's head and attached to the bit. The appearance of the bodies, the scratches thereon (apparently from fingernails) and the disordered condition of the young women's clothing tended to indicate that they had struggled desperately for their lives. A post mortem examination confirmed they had been sexually violated. It was subsequently discovered that Michael Murphy had been shot, as a bullet was found in his head.

This then is a brief outline of the factual circumstances of the time and place of the triple murder. In the course of this narrative, we will deal with these and other relevant events in greater detail.

One might reasonably be excused for expecting that the commission of such a crime in such a small locality as Gatton would quickly result in apprehension of the offender or offenders. A writer, in a short review of the Gatton affair in 1936, observed "At first it was held that murder so terrible must with inexorable finger point to the murderer, and it was thought that he would soon be under lock and key."[7] In fact, on the very day the bodies of the Murphys were discovered, a lay magistrate, Mr Robert Ballantyne J.P., went over and spoke to Mrs Murphy who was standing near the bodies of her dead children in Moran's paddock and said to her "This is a sad business." Mrs Murphy clasped her hands and said "Oh Mr Ballantyne, who could have murdered my innocent children?" Mr Ballantyne replied "I am here to try to find that out and I hope to find out before night."[8]

It soon became evident, however, that there would be no early solution, if any at all, to the fiendish crimes. The people of Gatton, naturally enough, were benumbed with horror at the enormity of the happening. A newspaper correspondent, two days after the outrage, reported that

> ... the excitement prevalent in Gatton over the murders is simply indescribable. The town and neighbourhood is thronged with police. Sub-Inspectors Graham, Galbraith, Durham, Sergeant King, and a large body of police and trackers made a thorough search this morning, but nothing important was found, so far as is known. During the whole of the day the keenest anxiety was manifested as regards the receipt of news ... The detectives are very properly reticent on some points, but they admit that the crime was so cleverly planned as to leave scarcely a clue ... It is exceedingly to be regretted that immediately the murder was discovered the paddock was not closed to public traffic. As it is, many hundreds of people visited the scene yesterday before the trackers arrived, thus rendering the chances of tracking the murderers very remote, as the ground is covered with tracks in every direction. The crime was so skilfully carried out that the murderers have left no trace behind them, slaughtering the victims most unmercifully, yet doing it in such a manner as to evade the closest scrutiny of the most skilled men in the Force ... Some contend that whoever killed the Murphys knew them, while others express the opinion that strangers committed the crime ... A few of the police and trackers have just returned, but the same statement is made: "No results so far". People are beginning to call it "The Gatton Mystery" instead of tragedy.[9]

Right from the outset it was apparent to the senior investigating police officers that mystery enshrouded the Gatton tragedy. That much is manifest from the two telegrams which Inspector Urquhart sent to the Chief Inspector of Police, Brisbane, shortly after he had arrived at Gatton on 28 December 1898. The first telegram was sent at 12.15 p.m., only two hours after Urquhart had arrived at Gatton. Its language seems to reflect a mingling of urgency with a sense of frantic futility. The telegram read:

> Circumstances point to premeditation. Details most atrocious. There is so far nothing to lay hold of. Galbraith has done all that could be done. Tracks wholly obliterated by crowds of people who have visited scene. Funeral now on and relatives unapproachable at present. I visit scene

as soon as possible and wait return of trackers and police now out. Please instruct Criminal Investigation Branch warn all ports and railway stations keep close lookout any suspicious characters travelling. While writing this a discharged 380 revolver cartridge has been brought in found on scene close to head of buggy horse. There seems little doubt more than one concerned in outrage. Evidently armed persons and may be heard of in similar way again. I recommend "A" police to be all alert and men to be ready Brisbane when wired for. First-class tracker offered me by resident of Glen Innes to be sent if I wire for him. May I do so if I want. Will work full concert with Galbraith for best results we can reach. If bush work turns out necessary we shall want horses arms and kit which White might hold in readiness to send up if I wire for them.[10]

The second telegram was sent at 1.14 p.m. on 28 December 1898, about an hour after the previous one. It read in part:

Carcass of horse boiled and bullet found corresponding with cartridge case. Paddock scene of murder and adjacent creek searched no result. Two good horses stolen from paddock ten miles [*sixteen kilometres*] from here on night of murders. Now arranging follow them up. Three parties out in different directions and Toomey at local inquiry. Extraordinary mystery about the whole matter.[11]

In the first *Government Gazette* of 1899 it was announced that

His Excellency the Governor, with the advice of the Executive Council, has been pleased to direct that a reward of one thousand pounds (£1000) be paid for such information as may lead to the apprehension and conviction of the person or persons who, at Gatton, on the night of Monday, the 26th December ultimo, murdered Michael Murphy, Norah Murphy and Ellen Murphy, and that a pardon be granted to any person concerned in the crime, not being the principal offender, who may give such information.[12]

Police investigations and inquiries continued throughout January 1899 and we will discuss some aspects of these later. Suffice it at this stage to observe that in those early weeks the police interviewed more than 100 possible suspects.[13]

The police certainly had their hands full. On 18 January there appeared a Press item which related a happening at Gatton the previous night. The item reads:

If the past few days have been dull here, that is as regards anything new happening with the tragedy, certainly there is quite enough excitement reigning in the town now. This feeling is consequent upon the circumstances becoming known that a lunatic, wild, long-haired, unkempt, unwashed and frenzied, is rushing about the district armed with a long knife and breathing awful threats . . . he last night paid a visit to the camp of Mr Emerson, a telegraph line repairer, and took possession of the camp. After a lot of persuasion the fierce looking visitor was induced to leave. He wildly flourished his knife round his head and announced his intention of "cutting the police into mincemeat".[14]

In the same newspaper it was announced that "the police constables who went out yesterday to secure the supposed lunatic have returned. They report that it was unnecessary to arrest the man. He got into a frenzy with several persons, and threatened them. A little persuasion quickly soothed the man." It would seem that "persuasion" was as efficacious a remedy in 1899 as it is now. The same issue of this newspaper indicated that police officers of the Colony of New South Wales were taking an interest in the Gatton affair and were not reluctant to offer advice. The news item is headed "Sydney, January 18" and it reads:

> The members of the Sydney detective force are manifesting deep professional interest in the Gatton case. In conversation with a Press representative yesterday, a well-known member of the Sydney police explained what would be his *modus operandi* in the case. Using a well-known sporting term, he said he would have "bustled" them; the latter pronoun referred to the perpetrators. By this he meant he would have arrested everybody whom suspicion warranted, and he would have done it instantly, and in the excitement and confusion of being apprehended on such a grave charge somebody would be sure to "squeak", and make a confession, perhaps implicating others. This officer expressed the opinion that in view of the serious and horrible nature of the case the police should not have been so gingerly in their tactics. As it was, he considered the Queensland authorities had allowed the matter to get cold which would throw stumbling blocks in the way of justice being vindicated.

It would be interesting to know, and not difficult to guess, just what the future career of this particular "stumbling block" was within the New South Wales Police Force!

On Tuesday, 24 January 1899, the Magisterial Inquiry into the cause of death of Michael, Norah and Ellen Murphy opened at Gatton. The inquiry was conducted by Mr A.H. Warner Shand (Acting Police Magistrate at Ipswich in the absence of Mr Macfarlane, Police Magistrate). Mr Parry-Okeden, Commissioner of Police, Inspector Urquhart, Sub-Inspectors White and Galbraith and Acting Sergeant Toomey were present also. The deposition clerk was Mr J.S. Falconer. The Magisterial Inquiry occupied thirteen actual sitting days during which forty-five witnesses were examined. The deposition clerk wrote 835 pages of depositions totalling not less than 58,450 words.[15] Reports of the evidence given by the witnesses at the Magisterial Inquiry appeared in the Press. These Press reports constitute an important source of information concerning the Gatton

Mystery and the standard of reporting appears to be excellent. The special reporter of the *Toowoomba Chronicle* purported to "append the full notes of evidence, taken at the Magisterial Inquiry, into the cause of death of Michael, Norah and Ellen Murphy, at Gatton on Boxing night".[16]

Another important source of information for our purposes is the evidence given by the witnesses at the Police Inquiry Commission. On 20 July 1899 a Commission was issued to His Honour Judge Noel of the District Court as Chairman, Mr Thomas Garvin (Superintendent of Police in New South Wales), Mr John Sadleir (formerly an inspecting Superintendent of Police in Victoria), Mr F.W. Dickson (Barrister-at-law), and Mr T.O. Unmack. Mr J.W. Blair (later Sir James Blair, Chief Justice of Queensland), then a rising young barrister-at-law, was appointed Secretary to the Commission. The Commission was charged with the responsibility of inquiring into the constitution, administration and working of the Criminal Investigation Branch, the relations between the C.I. Branch and other sections of the Force, and the general organisation, control, discipline and efficiency of the Force.[17] Evidence was taken openly, the representatives of the Press were admitted to all sessions, and full protection was offered to any person who cared to come forward and give evidence. The Commission sat for the first time on 3 August 1899 and the hearing of the evidence was concluded on 13 November 1899. On 29 November 1899 the Commission submitted a Report which, together with the Minutes of Evidence, ran into nearly 700 printed pages of foolscap size. The Minutes of Evidence are of particular significance for our purpose, because the Commission made the handling of the police investigation into the tragedy at Gatton one of the subjects of its inquiry.

We have used the Press reports of evidence given by witnesses at the Magisterial Inquiry,[18] and the Minutes of Evidence given at the Royal Commission (the Police Inquiry Commission) as the principal material upon which to base our portrayal of the events and circumstances surrounding the Gatton Mystery. We have also, to some extent, relied upon various articles and newspaper items dealing with the Gatton tragedy which have been published over the years. We have, however, been quite circumspect and selective in our choice and use of this latter mentioned material, and have only had recourse to it when we have had no reason to doubt its accuracy.

From our very early years we have had an abiding interest in the Gatton Mystery. Our father, his brother and their friends often spoke of it in our presence, and, from the very first, it was a constant source of fascination for us. Throughout the years, however, we have never ceased to be surprised at the inaccuracies in accounts of the matter which sporadically appear and at the various misconceptions of fact in relation to the murders under which many people labour. It is quite evident that many people entertain a distorted and confused understanding of the actual happenings. Indeed, it is mainly on account of this widespread misunderstanding that we have embarked upon this narrative of the mysterious events.

The accounts of the state of the horse at the scene of the murders provides an example of the kinds of falsehood that have developed around aspects of the case. In some printed articles there have been suggestions that not only was the horse belonging to the Murphys shot in the head in Moran's paddock, but also that its body was mutilated and, in some published items, it is actually stated that the horse's throat was cut. Moreover, it is very evident to us that, for reasons which are not readily apparent, many people to this very day believe that the genitals of the horse were cut off. We hasten to say that there is not the slightest basis in fact to support any allegation that the horse was injured in any way other than by entry of a bullet into and through its head.[19] Indeed, one of us, in early 1973, actually interviewed a very old man, Mr Patrick Quinn, who was at that time an inmate of St Vincent's Hospital, Toowoomba. He said he had been at the scene in Moran's paddock on the day of the tragedy and he had helped to load the bodies of the three deceased Murphys into horse-drawn vehicles for transportation to the Brian Boru Hotel at Gatton. He said he particularly made a careful inspection of the dead horse and the sulky at the time and he noticed no blood in or on the sulky, nor did he see anything at all which would lead him to think that any of the deceased had met with an injury while in the sulky. He also stated that he saw nothing to indicate that any of the deceased had been conveyed in the sulky after having been injured at some other place. He was very definite in stating that the only injury to the horse was a bullet wound in its head. He was adamant that the penis of the horse had not been cut or removed and stated that the horse's penis did not appear to have been interfered with in any way whatsoever.[20]

So far as we are aware no detailed outline and factual analysis of the Gatton Mystery has hitherto been published. In 1924, Mr John D. Fitzgerald, Barrister-at-law, Member of the Legislative Council of New South Wales and formerly Minister of Justice and Solicitor-General of New South Wales, published his *Studies in Australian Crime*. He devotes a chapter of his work to "The Gatton Tragedy" and, in the course of thirteen pages, furnishes a short outline and commentary upon it. In his introductory paragraph to the chapter he makes the just and perceptive observation:

The crimes which leave the deepest impression on the human mind are those which remain mysteries. In the absence of a solution man's ingenuity supplies a thousand conjectures, and builds up a thousand probable plots and motives to explain the tragedy. There is a fascination to some minds in speculating upon probabilities and striving to pierce the veil of mystery.[21]

At the time of the triple murders at Gatton, a newspaper commentator said

... almost at our very doors one of the most fiendish murders known in the annals of crime was perpetrated during the very height of the Christmas festivities, and the further details received yesterday show that no more cold-blooded or revolting tragedy was ever consummated in Australia; in fact, it is extremely doubtful if the criminal annals of any country can show a more diabolical tragedy.[22]

After three quarters of a century, it might fairly be observed that it is extremely doubtful if the criminal annals of any country can exhibit a more enduring mystery calculated to excite our curiosity. We have made a somewhat detailed review of the facts and attendant circumstances which give rise to this mystery in our narrative and will shortly present this to the reader. But, just as the distant parts of a landscape —the background—must necessarily be painted in order to furnish an adequate and harmonious setting for the better appreciation and assessment of the main objects in the foreground, so it has been thought necessary, in the next chapter, briefly to sketch the background to the dreadful train of events which occurred at Gatton on Boxing Day, 1898. Throughout the course of the sketching or painting, whether of background or foreground, we have at all times endeavoured to maintain an awareness of that adequate sense of obligation which any writer, who professes to relate facts, owes to the public.

THE PRINCIPAL PERSONS INVOLVED

The victims:
  Michael Murphy
  Norah Murphy
  Ellen Murphy

Other members of the Murphy family:
  Daniel Murphy } Parents of the victims
  Mary Murphy

  William Murphy
  Patrick Murphy
  Daniel Murphy } Brothers of the victims
  Jeremiah Murphy
  John Murphy

  Polly McNeil
  Catherine (Katie) } Sisters of the victims
    Murphy

  William McNeil   Brother-in-law of the victims

The Senior Police Officials and Investigating Police Officers:
  Mr W.E. Parry-Okeden, Commissioner of Police
  Chief Inspector J. Stuart
  Inspector F.C. Urquhart
  Sub-Inspector P.D.F. Galbraith
  Sub-Inspector H.R.P. Durham
  Sub-Inspector J.W. White
  Sergeant W. Arrell
  Acting-Sergeant Michael Toomey
  Detective Robert G. Christie

Those who were subject to surveillance by the police:
  Thomas Joseph Ryan
  William McNeil
  Richard Burgess
  Thomas Day

The Medical Practitioners who gave evidence:
  Dr C.J.H. Wray, G.M.O., Brisbane
  Dr W.H. von Lossberg, G.M.O., Ipswich
  Dr A.W. Orr

1
THE BACKGROUND

GATTON

There has always been some controversy about the origin of the name of the Lockyer Valley town of Gatton. It is said that the western railway line from Brisbane to Toowoomba was surveyed in 1864 by a surveyor named Gatton, and some have contended that this is the source of the town's name.[1] But this obviously cannot be so, because, on 11 April 1855, the site for the village of Gatton was determined by the Government of New South Wales, and, in the relevant notification in the *Government Gazette* of that date, the village is referred to as "Gatton".[2] In 1845 Gatton Park, in the County of Argyle, New South Wales, was a station owned by Mr James Chisholm. It is believed by some that both Gatton Park and Gatton in Queensland could have been named after the village of Gatton, on the banks of the Tweed River, in Roxburghshire, near Melrose in Scotland.[3] But it has also been asserted that it is most probable that Gatton was named after Gatton Park in Surrey, England, where a magnificent marbled Gatton House was built by Lord Monson, whose ancestor had been falconer to James 1.[4]

Gatton has been the commercial centre for many years of the picturesque Lockyer Valley, which is bounded on the west and south-west by the Great Dividing Range, on the south by the Mount Mistake Range and on the east by the Little Liverpool Range. The area was first settled by white pastoralists in the early 1840s. Tent Hill and Helidon runs were leased in 1841.[5] The major difficulty of the early settlers was probably the scarcity of labour; added to this were attendant problems created by lack of transport and a large native population. The railway was surveyed in 1864 and rail communication revolutionised the shape of the township in more ways than one. Gatton was originally surveyed on high ground, but, with the coming of the railway, business tended to move down to the lower level around the railway station. In 1865 the first post office was built and telegraph services were established by 1874.

The 1890s saw the flowering of the agricultural potential of the Lockyer Valley in several different ways. Estates in the area were cut into pastoral and agricultural blocks and sold to settlers at £6 per acre (about half a hectare); an Agricultural and Industrial Society was formed in 1890 and shows were held alternatively in Gatton and Laidley; and the Queensland Agricultural High School and College was opened by the Governor, Lord Lamington, on 9 July 1897. This College was built at Lawes, five kilometres from Gatton on the road to Brisbane, on 685 hectares of land specially selected by the Government. Prior to purchase all the land was thickly timbered and extensive ring-barking and clearing had to be carried out.[6] The College has proved a most valuable institution for the State of Queensland and indeed for the nation. The town of Gatton today is one of the fastest growing small towns in the State. In the last twenty years its population has doubled and is now approximately 4000.

In 1898 Gatton was a little township of approximately 450 people.[7] By that year the Gatton district was fairly closely settled by farmers and pastoralists, mainly of English, Irish and German stock. They grazed herds of beef and dairy cattle, and, on the loamy, alluvial flats of the many creeks, they grew fine crops of potatoes, pumpkins, maize and lucerne. Gatton was at that time like many small towns in the northern Colony—the business community crowded about its tree lined main street, which was wide and unsealed. Gatton then boasted three hotels, a post office, a police barracks, a bank, and the usual collection of merchants and tradesmen. A doctor from Ipswich visited the town each Saturday and Wednesday and a solicitor visited on Mondays. Trains from Brisbane passed through to Toowoomba every day and a coach came in from the nearby settlement of Mt Sylvia three days a week.[8]

Throughout the winter and early summer months of 1898 the weather in Queensland had been extremely dry and, as the year entered its final weeks, the drought stricken Colony was gripped by a massive heat wave. In far western districts temperatures soared. On 17 December 1898, it is recorded that there was "intense heat in country districts; Longreach 119 degrees [48°C] in shade; 117 degrees [47°C] and 120 degrees [49°C] at Isis Downs and Avington respectively. Birds dropping dead from the trees."[9]

On the farms around Gatton the earth was parched and the topsoil crumbled. The stunted crops withered and died. In the paddocks the feed, already sparse, turned brown and tinder dry. The smaller creeks were barely running and the waterholes were drying up. On 17 December 1898, a Gatton correspondent commented:

Business during the past week has been brisker owing to the near approach of Christmas but I am sorry to notice a great falling off in volume of trade as compared with previous years attributable to the dreadful season we are experiencing. Dry winds and a hot sun are destroying every hope we had of obtaining any crops and, as the season is coming to a close, I do not know what is to become of us all.[10]

In such circumstances then were the inhabitants of the Gatton district preparing for the approaching Christmas season. Among those were the Murphys of Blackfellow's Creek, Tent Hill, and it is to them that we must now turn our attention.

THE MURPHYS OF BLACKFELLOW'S CREEK

Daniel and Mary Murphy, the parents of the victims, were Irish immigrants. Daniel arrived in the Colony of Queensland in 1864 in the ship *Mansfield*, and, shortly after landing, he engaged with Messrs Peto, Brassey and Betts to assist in the construction of the railway line from Ipswich to Toowoomba. For some considerable time he worked for the firm in the neighbourhood of Ipswich. About two years later he was married by Rev. Father Brun, of Ipswich. Mrs Murphy had come out to the Colony in the ship *Charlie Palmer*. Shortly after their marriage they moved to a farm on Sandy Creek, (later called Ma Ma Creek), which was about one and a half kilometres nearer to Gatton than the farm at Blackfellow's Creek, Tent Hill, which they were occupying at the time of the tragedy. It was at their farm at Ma Ma Creek that Michael and Norah were born; but the third victim, Ellen, was born at Spring Creek, a few kilometres to the north of Gatton, whither Mr and Mrs Murphy had removed, and where they lived until about mid-1889, when they came to occupy the farm at Blackfellow's Creek, Tent Hill. This farm was about nine and a half kilometres south of Gatton, and had previously been owned by a Mr Norman Rule. While at Spring Creek, Mr Murphy engaged in grazing, and took contracts for roadwork and fencing. For some years after moving to Blackfellow's Creek he also tendered for road and other work; but for some few years before the tragedy he had left that class of labour to his sons, and had confined his own efforts to farming.[11]

By 1898 the Murphy family was well established at the farm on Blackfellow's Creek. Their home was a picturesque little wooden farmhouse on the western bank of the creek, a fine running stream, shaded along its banks by tea-trees and, in places, by beautiful weeping willows. Daniel and Mary Murphy, at the time of the outrage, were both fifty-six years old. Daniel appears to have been a reserved man, slim and of middle height. He wore a full beard and smoked a pipe.

He could neither read nor write. His wife Mary was a robust, strong willed woman of somewhat austere appearance and, in the rearing of her large family, she seems to have been something of a disciplinarian.[12] Both parents were very devoted to their Catholic faith and, along with their sons and daughters, were simple, quiet, hardworking members of the community and they were highly respected by the other residents of the district.

There were ten children in the Murphy family—six boys and four girls. At the time of the triple murder in 1898 their ages ranged from thirty-three years (William) to thirteen years (Katie). The other boys were Michael, Daniel (Jnr), Patrick, Jeremiah and John. The remaining girls were Polly, Norah and Ellen. The only married member of the family was Polly, the eldest daughter, aged thirty-two years, whose husband was William McNeil, a butcher at Westbrook, near Toowoomba. Young Daniel Murphy, twenty-three years old, was a constable in the Queensland Police Force and was stationed at Roma Street in Brisbane. He had joined the Police Force in 1897. Patrick was employed at the Agricultural College near Gatton and lived at the College. William, John and Jeremiah (Jerry) worked on the farm at Blackfellow's Creek where they lived with their parents. Norah and Ellen also lived on the farm with their parents as did Katie, who was still at school.

The three who were to meet their tragic end in Moran's paddock were Michael, aged twenty-nine years, Norah, twenty-seven years and Ellen, who was but eighteen years.

Michael commenced school at the Lower Tent Hill State School on 29 June 1874, when he was five years old.[13] He later attended the Catholic School in Gatton and afterwards attended the Spring Creek School. After leaving school he worked on his parents' farm for a short time and then took on contract work—fencing and road-making.[14] During the shearers' strike of 1891 he was sent out as a special constable, and was considered one of the best men in his company.[15] His activities during his service as a special constable were later to be closely examined in the course of inquiries made into his death; but it was ascertained that no sheds were burned in the area in which he served and he was in no way involved in the Ayrshire Downs affair.[16] Michael's liking for military work caused him to join the Gatton Mounted Infantry. He attained the rank of sergeant and was "universally regarded as the smartest man in it".[17] Michael worked at the Agricultural College near Gatton for a while and, about five weeks before his death, went to work at the Government Experimental Farm at Westbrook. He came down to his parents' farm at Tent Hill on Christmas Eve to spend the Christmas holidays with his family. He had intended returning to his work on the Experimental Farm on Thursday, 29 December 1898.[18] It was said of him that "he was highly esteemed by all who knew him as a genial, kindly young man, faithful in the discharge of duty and exhibiting at all times the most conspicuous integrity".[19] It was also said of him that he "was a quiet, steady, hardworking young man, being a sergeant in the local E Company of Mounted Infantry, and one of the very best and reliable members of that corps. He was a total abstainer, and of quiet and unassuming manners."[20]

Norah Murphy, the second eldest daughter of Daniel and Mary Murphy, was born at Ma Ma Creek in 1871. She commenced her education at the Lower Tent Hill State School on 21 February 1876, when she was only four years of age.[21] Later, when the family moved to Spring Creek, Norah attended the school there with her brother, Michael, and, when she left school, she lived at home with her parents. It appears that she spent most of her time assisting her mother in the home and she led a rather quiet and sheltered life, leaving the farm only occasionally for brief visits to Toowoomba. Once, when she was sixteen years old, Norah spent three weeks in Brisbane where she was employed by a Mrs Bannock. She returned to her parents' farm when Mrs Bannock went to England and she had not been to Brisbane again.[22] It would seem that Norah was much liked by the other young people of Gatton; she attended the dances and other simple recreations staged in the district and occasionally she went horseback riding. So far as is known she had no sweetheart. A chronicler of the time wrote of Norah: "She was a girl who loved her parents and family and her home and was of a kindly and trusting disposition and was respected by all who knew her. There are many in the district who will always keep green in their memory the kindness shown them by the late Miss Norah Murphy."[23]

Ellen Murphy (or "Ellie" as she was affectionately known to her family) was the third daughter of Daniel and Mary Murphy. She was born at Spring Creek near Lake Clarendon in 1880 and attended the school there and later the school at Lower Tent Hill. She left school in 1896 at the age of sixteen years and four months and, until her death, lived with her parents on the farm at Blackfellow's Creek. At school Ellen was a particularly good student. The head teacher of the Lower Tent Hill School, Mr George Wilson, was much affected at the tragic end of Ellen, his former scholar. When he was interviewed at the time of the tragedy, he spoke of her in the highest terms of praise. "Never," he said, "do I remember having had to reprimand her for anything." On being further questioned, he stated that her conduct was most exemplary, and she always applied herself diligently to her lessons. "She was," he said, "under my care in school for a considerable period of time, and I can say that I know she was as good a girl as any parent might wish to have, and, should a prize have been awarded for good conduct on a vote of the scholars, I believe she would undoubtedly have got it."[24] She was exceptionally clever with the needle, and was a constant exhibitor and prize-taker in needlework competitions at the annual shows of the Lockyer Agricultural Society.[25]

Having established the background of the town and family it is time now to consider events closer in time to those which gave rise to the Gatton Mystery. Accordingly, we now move into the foreground.

2
THE FOREGROUND

In 1898 Christmas Day fell on a Sunday. At the Murphy farm on Blackfellow's Creek the family gathered together in a joyful reunion to celebrate the season of peace and goodwill. In the little wooden home Daniel and Mary Murphy were joined by nine of their children. Only young Dan Murphy was absent; he was rostered for duty at Roma Street Police Station over the Christmas holidays and had to remain in Brisbane.

Living at the farm at the time were William, John, Jerry, Norah, Ellen and young Katie. Mrs William McNeil (Polly), the eldest daughter of the Murphy family had also been staying at the farm for some little time past. Polly had left her family's home some eleven years before to live in Toowoomba.[1] About three years before the murders she had married William McNeil and lived with him at Westbrook near Toowoomba, where he conducted a butchery. At the time of the tragedy the McNeils had two children, a bright little girl, three years of age and a boy between five and six months old, who had to be reared by "spoon feeding", a duty which Mrs Murphy had taken upon herself to discharge.[2] Polly McNeil had not been well since the birth of her second child; she had suffered a paralytic stroke in the left side and could get about only with the aid of a stick. She went back to live at her parents' farm. The little McNeil girl had a very affectionate nature and, her mother being an invalid, she became very much attached to her aunt Norah, with whom she had been accustomed to sleep for some time past.[3] William McNeil did not meet any of Polly's family until 17 June 1898. It is apparent that, from that time on, he was on the best of terms with all members of the Murphy family.[4] After his wife went back to the Murphy farm to live McNeil continued to live at Westbrook, but visited his family at the farm every weekend.

On Christmas Eve Michael Murphy and William McNeil arrived at the farm at Blackfellow's Creek. They had driven down the range from Westbrook in McNeil's sulky.[5] McNeil brought gifts for his wife's sisters—a bridle for Norah and a whip for Ellen.[6]

19

So far as is known Christmas Day passed pleasantly for the Murphys. They attended Mass in the morning and undoubtedly enjoyed a happy and a holy Christmas.

While he was in Gatton on Christmas Eve, young Jerry Murphy had spoken to a man named Ted Chadwick (Edward Andrew Chadwick). Chadwick told Jerry that the Gatton girls wanted him to arrange a dance in Gatton for Boxing Night, but he did not say who was coming. He asked Jerry if he would bring his sisters. Jerry promised to try to persuade his sisters to attend the dance in Gatton, but he pointed out that it had already been arranged to hold a dance at Mt Sylvia that same night. On Christmas Day Jerry mentioned to his family the fact that it was proposed to hold a dance at Gatton on Boxing Night.[7]

Quite a few of the Murphy family intended to go to a race meeting to be held at Mt Sylvia on Boxing Day. It seemed likely that it would be attended by a lot of people in the district and it was expected that it would prove to be one of the highlights of the social events of the festive season in that small community.

On Monday, Boxing Day, the weather was fine and hot. At the farm the Murphys prepared for the outing to Mt Sylvia. Ellen and the Murphy boys set off on horseback and William McNeil drove his wife in their sulky.[8] It is often asserted, and not uncommonly believed, that Norah also attended the races at Mt Sylvia that day; but that is not correct—Norah stayed at the farm and looked after Polly McNeil's children. Katie also stayed at the farm. Before the party left the farm for the races, Patrick told Norah to be ready to go to the dance in Gatton that evening.[9] Mr and Mrs Murphy were at their farm in the morning, but later that day went to visit some friends on a farm some distance away.[10]

At the race meeting at Mt Sylvia, Polly McNeil remained in the sulky and Ellen came and stayed in the sulky with her.[11] McNeil and the Murphy boys, it would seem, wandered about speaking to friends and watching the races and Michael ran his horse in two events. After the tragedy they were to be closely questioned by the police (and also at the Magisterial Inquiry) as to their movements at the races and as to the persons they met and to whom they spoke. Apparently the police did not discount the possibility that the brutal crime might have been conceived in the carefree, holiday atmosphere of the race meeting. At the races, when she was in the sulky with Polly McNeil, a young man named Jimmy Ryan asked Ellen whether she was going to the Mt Sylvia dance, and she replied that she was going to the Gatton dance. He appeared to go on with a joke and said "Ah, do go." Ellen replied "Oh, I don't think I will, Jim", whereupon Ryan said "If you come, Mick will be there, if not I will bring him." At this Ellen only laughed, and there seemed to be a joke and Ryan walked away from the sulky.[12]

When William Murphy was at the races he spoke to several acquaintances—Will Connolly, John Tracy and Robert Smith—but no mention was made in his hearing of any of them going to a dance at Gatton the same night. His brother, Michael Murphy, however, told him that he was going home from the races early to go to the dance. William rode home with Ellen and he asked her if she was going to the dance. She said she did not know. He and Ellen arrived home at the farm at half past six and he "turned the horses into the yard".[13] William and Polly McNeil in the sulky left the Mt Sylvia races at about five o'clock in the afternoon and arrived home "at about quarter past six or thereabouts". Those in the house at the time all had tea together—Mr and Mrs Murphy, William and Polly McNeil, William, Michael, Patrick, John, Norah, Ellen, Katie, Polly McNeil's two children and Robert Smith. There appears to have been no mention of the Gatton dance at tea but, after tea, Michael told his mother that he was going to drive the girls in to the dance. Mrs Murphy's reply was both immediate and quaint—indeed, one might almost think she had a premonition, for she answered, no doubt in her rich Irish brogue —"Bother take the dance, stay at home tonight." But Michael said "Oh, we'll go for a few hours as Norah was not out all day."[14] It was apparently with some diffidence that Norah went to the dance without first putting her little niece to sleep. Subsequently, when questioned about this, Polly McNeil said that Norah said "she would rather put my little girl to sleep before she went. I replied 'No, you will be too late, the child will be all-right,' and my husband said 'I will see to it, Norah, you had better go'."[15] Describing this incident, Katie Murphy was later to say "Norah did not wish to go to the dance as one of the children would cry after her. McNeil told her to go and he would look after the little girl."[16] Shortly after the occurrence it was reported that "the little girl cried very bitterly on Monday night because her auntie was leaving her to go to the dance."[17]

Norah and Ellen dressed for the dance and Michael, with McNeil's assistance, harnessed a horse belonging to Mr Murphy to McNeil's sulky. The horse was a brown gelding named "Tom", which was later described by Patrick Murphy as "a stupid animal and deaf, fairly fast in harness, but not free to drive".[18] John Murphy rode away to visit friends at Tent Hill and Jerry rode out to Mt Sylvia to attend the dance there. Patrick Murphy left the Murphy farm on horseback at about eight o'clock. He was returning to the Agricultural College where he worked and lived and where he had to recommence work the following morning. On Christmas Eve Patrick was with his brother, Jerry, when Ted Chadwick informed them that a dance would be held in the

Divisional Board's Hall at Gatton on Boxing Night. Chadwick asked Patrick would he come and Patrick explained that he would be returning to the College "but he would have a look in".[19]

Shortly after Patrick left the farm, Michael set off in the sulky to travel the nine and a half kilometres to the dance with his two sisters, Norah and Ellen. It is thought that he took his father's whip with him.[20] In the sulky was a woollen rug and a mackintosh cape which belonged to Robert Smith and which had been used at the race meeting at Mt Sylvia earlier that day. Robert Smith had come home with the Murphys and slept at their farm that night. Michael and his sisters caught up to Patrick and passed him about one and a half kilometres along the Tent Hill road from the Murphy farm.

As they proceeded on their way to the dance it was necessary for them to pass Moran's paddock, which is situated south of Gatton on the third ridge or hill from the town. The paddock is on the eastern side of the road leading from the farm to Gatton. The sliprails giving entrance to Moran's paddock were on the level top of the ridge which extends for about 150 or 200 metres and then slopes away in each direction, that is, towards the farm to the south and Gatton to the north. That part of the road where the sliprails were situated was known as "Moran's Hill" and it was fifty to one hundred metres south from what was known as "Clarke's butcher's shop",[21] which was a little to the north of the residence of the proprietor, Mr Arthur George Clarke. The residence and butcher shop were on the same side of the road as the sliprails, the eastern side (the right hand side if one were proceeding towards Gatton from the Murphy farm). A bit further towards Gatton and on the opposite side of the road (that is, the western side) was a residence commonly referred to as "Logans". This was the residence of Mr James Logan, an early settler in the Gatton area.[22]

It was about eight fifteen that the trio in the sulky caught up to and passed Patrick on horseback.[23] It was a warm fine night and a brilliant moon shone from a cloudless sky. In his evidence at the Royal Commission, Sub-Inspector Galbraith said "That night was so light— I remember it quite well—that I could read ordinary newsprint by it."[24]

In the township of Gatton, Ted Chadwick and Thomas and Stephen Jordan, the organisers of the dance at the Divisional Board's Hall, opened the hall and lit the lamps. Chadwick then went to see if the girls had come to town for the dance. Besides the Murphy girls, eleven other young ladies had been invited. These were the two sisters of the Jordan brothers, Chadwick's two sisters, two Callaghan sisters and girls named Hennessy, Hay, Crane, Bourke and Quinn. Chadwick found that only about six girls had appeared. Also, at that stage, Simon Laffey, the musician, had not turned up although he was to arrive a little later. Chadwick and the Jordan brothers waited until nine o'clock and, after a conversation with George Callaghan, who was a brother of two of the girls invited, agreed to abandon the dance. At ten past nine Chadwick returned the keys to the caretaker, and, while doing so, saw a sulky drive past with three people in it. Joe Jordan (a brother of Thomas and Stephen Jordan), who was standing near the gate, said "Here are the Murphys now." In his evidence at the Magisterial Inquiry, Chadwick deposed "They turned round and drove back. No one spoke to them. It was nothing unusual for ladies invited to dances not to come." [25]

At "about a quarter or twenty minutes past nine" when "rather more than half a mile [one kilometre] from Moran's sliprails", Michael and the Murphy girls again met Patrick Murphy, who was still riding slowly towards the township. Patrick Murphy reined up his horse and Michael stopped the sulky. Patrick stayed talking there with Michael and the two girls for about three minutes and then Patrick proceeded on his way to Gatton and the sulky carrying Michael and the two girls, in the brilliant moonlight of that Boxing Night, proceeded on towards Tent Hill. The point where the four Murphys met was only about a kilometre from the sliprails into Moran's paddock through which the ill-fated trio were so shortly destined to drive to their doom.

Patrick Murphy was never to see his brother and two sisters again in this life. He could not, of course, at the time have foreseen this. Who, indeed, could ever reasonably have supposed that, among the inhabitants of the Gatton district on that brilliantly moonlit Boxing Night of 1898, there was one in whose feverish mind festered brutal and lustful thoughts so ill-attuned to the spirit of the Holy Season of peace and goodwill? Who, in the quietude and tranquillity of that peaceful and law-abiding community, could ever have foreshadowed, had he been ever so wise, that "upon night so sweet such awful morn could rise"? [26]

3
THE OUTRAGE DISCOVERED

The morning of Tuesday, 27 December 1898, dawned and Michael and his two sisters had not returned to the Murphy farm. Daniel Murphy, who had risen first, noticed that McNeil's sulky was not in the yard. He told his wife, who looked in the girls' room and found that they were not there. There was no sign of Michael either. Daniel suggested that they might have stayed the night at Chadwick's or that the sulky had broken down. Various other surmises were made, but it was not thought that anything serious had happened to them.

At breakfast McNeil asked if it was usual for them to stay out all night and Daniel told him it wasn't. McNeil then suggested that someone should go and look for them and their mother agreed. At about eight o'clock he caught a horse belonging to Norah and rode away down the road towards Gatton.[1] Subsequently, when interviewed by a special reporter, Mrs Mary Murphy said, when speaking of the evening of Boxing Day—

> When the girls left each had a laugh on her face, for Norah, though older than Ellen, was always bright and happy, but quiet. Mr McNeil and his wife and little ones remained at home with the rest of the family, and we all went to bed early; but I did not sleep until after twelve o'clock. I heard that hour strike but I must have fallen to sleep shortly after. In the morning I was anxious, because the girls had not come home as I expected them to return about two o'clock. Mr McNeil was also anxious, because he knew that his trap was an old one and he thought there might have been an accident. The rest of the inmates of the house only laughed at my fears; but at last I induced Mr McNeil to go and look for them and he found them cruelly murdered.[2]

William McNeil was interviewed by a newspaper reporter and he gave the following account of what happened on that Tuesday morning:

> In the morning, finding that the girls and Mick had not come back, the mother got anxious and told me to go and look for them. I started away on horseback and looked carefully for the wheeltracks, because I knew the particular track the wheel would make. One wheel wobbled because of an accident I once had near Helidon. When I got to the

sliprails on the Tent Hill road I saw at once that the trap had turned in there. The sliprails had been placed in position again but bore marks which showed that the trap had been driven over them while on the ground. I did not suspect anything wrong, as I thought they might have turned in there to go to a friend's house. Of course I don't know the locality, as I have been here only a fortnight. Well, I went straight on till I came to the top of the slight ridge and there I saw the cart, and then the bodies came into view. Still I did not think they had been murdered. I thought they were sleeping in the sun. After I got a bit closer I saw the clothing of the girls disarranged and then I could see the ants crawling all over them. I did not go any further, but turned and rode straight into Gatton and told the Police. The one thing which makes me think Mick did not go into the paddock of his own free will was that he was not the sort of man to put the horse over the rails while they were on the ground. He would have moved them to one side unless he was in a hurry. I do not think any of the men camping near him at Westbrook committed the murder, but I don't at all know what to think of it.[3]

Other accounts, more detailed than this, were also given by William McNeil. He was interviewed by a special representative of the *Queensland Times*. A report of that interview reads:

... he noticed the tracks of a vehicle bearing towards the sliprails leading into Mr Frank Moran's paddock.... These tracks, he believed, were made by the wheels of the vehicle which young Murphy was driving on the previous evening, from the fact that the wheel-mark was very tortuous, and looked as though it had been made by a wheel which wobbled about, and one of the wheels on the dog-cart was known to act in this way. Thinking perhaps that his brother-in-law and the two girls had put up for the night in some house that might be near by, he went to the sliprails, which he found intact, pulled them down, and passed into the paddock. On getting into the enclosure referred to he made for the top of a gradual incline, believing that he would there find a house. Finding that there was no dwelling place there, as he had expected, he retraced his steps to the sliprails, and started from that point to follow the wheel-tracks. The direction lay due east for a few chains [*one chain is about twenty metres*], until the top of a spur was reached, when the track following the ridge of the hill, swerved gradually to the south-east and passed through country thickly timbered with wattle trees. For a distance of about half a mile [*one kilometre*] the direction of the wheel-tracks varied between east and south-east until at last they turned rather abruptly to the south, and ran down a slope into a valley. When reaching the termination of the track at a point about 125 yards [*115 metres*] from where it had turned from the spur, to Mr McNeil's horror and consternation, he saw the three missing persons lying dead on the ground, with the horse and trap in close proximity, the animal being also dead.[4]

At the Magisterial Inquiry which commenced at Gatton on the morning of Tuesday, 24 January 1899, William McNeil was the first witness called. After he was duly sworn he deposed to the circumstances surrounding his finding of the bodies of the three Murphys. In what a newspaper reporter described as "the full notes of evidence", McNeil's evidence is recorded in the following terms:

... Came along the road another couple of miles till I reached Moran's slip-panels; ... mean the ones on the right hand side of the road on the Gatton side of the culvert; noticed a wheel track turning in there like mine; it looked like mine because one of the wheels wobbled like my trap; I retraced it down the road a few yards towards Gatton to make sure; I found it after to be mine; I then got off and put down the rails and went into the paddock; the rails were up; got on to my horse at the rails; went into the paddock the direction the track led; did not follow the tracks; left the track, because I expected to meet a house; had never been in the paddock before; there was no road to show there was any house, went about a quarter of a mile [*half a kilometre*] down the paddock straight from the rails over the ridge and down; bore them [*sic*] over to the right and struck a fence to the right; then returned to the rails because I could not see any sign of a house; then examined the wheel tracks again on the road outside the paddock and I felt confident they were the tracks of my trap. I tried to follow the wheel tracks into the paddock; went on foot having got off my horse and got through the rails to inspect the road. I followed the tracks, leading my horse; did not see any other tracks excepting those of my trap and the horse drawing it; the horse was not shod; could not see any tracks of human beings; have been many years in the bush and have frequently followed the tracks of stock; ... followed the tracks about three quarters of a mile [*one and a half kilometres*]; they did not go in a straight direction, they bore to the right all the way; think if I saw a plan showing the sliprails and the place where the tragedy was committed I could point out the route; after following the track in the distance saw three heaps of clothes, one cart, one horse; the horse was lying down; the bodies were all lying on the ground; they were not together; was about fifty yards [*forty-five metres*] away when I first saw them; was still on foot leading my horse; then went down to where they were to within two yards [*two metres*] of them; then saw the one nearest me who was Norah, and she was dead; noticed some ants on her face; her jacket was pulled up to her shoulders and her stays were exposed; her skirts were on but the hooks were undone at the back; they were also pulled slightly up at the back; did not touch her at all; knew she was dead by the ants; she was lying on the right cheek; inclined to be if anything more on her face; saw the back of the corsets; came up on the left side of her and saw her left cheek; she was lying feet inclined to the west; did not walk round her body; could not say exactly what direction the sliprails lay from the spot; did not notice the position of her limbs at the time; saw the other two bodies about eight or ten yards [*six to nine metres*] off; did not go up to them; did not see anything else but the horse and trap; did not notice anything else as regards Norah there; saw them start away; they took a rug, a red cape, a cape of a macintosh (this belonged to Bob Smith and was used when going to the races that day); the next time I saw them was when I came back from seeing the sergeant; saw the rug the first time and Norah was lying on it; it was spread out; after looking at the bodies I left for Gatton; galloped up to Gilbert's hotel, having taken down the top rail at Moran's paddock while sitting on my horse ... went into the bar and saw Charles Gilbert there; I asked him "where was the sergeant"; did not know where the police barracks were and I wanted to report the matter; Gilbert told me where to find the sergeant; then went down to the barracks and told the sergeant what I had seen; the sergeant (Arrell) got his horse and they went back to the bodies; showed him the tracks of my cart as we went along here and there; when we got out there were others followed; some three or four; I looked closely at the bodies when I was there with Sergeant Arrell; recognised them; first went to Norah Murphy, then went to Ellen, and then Michael Murphy; had no difficulty in recognising any of them; did not remain there but went on to Murphy's farm; got there about eleven o'clock; then got a pair of horses and drove Mrs Murphy to the place ...[5]

Mr Charles Gilbert, the licensee of the Brian Boru Hotel at Gatton, was the first person to whom McNeil spoke about the murders. According to Gilbert, McNeil, who was previously known to him, did not know the township of Gatton at all. Gilbert gave evidence at the Magisterial Inquiry. It is recorded that he deposed on that occasion:

William McNeil, between 9 and 10 o'clock, came up to the hotel and said, "Charlie, where is the police station? The three Murphys are lying dead in a paddock. There must have been an accident, as the horse is dead too". He was excited. Witness asked him where it was and he said the second hill from the town, on the left hand side. This was hardly a correct idea, because it was the third hill. McNeil was shown the police station and he rode off. Witness harnessed his horse and started away with men named James, Devitt and Wilson. McNeil and Sergeant Arrell, on horseback, passed them on the way. These were at the sliprails of Moran's paddock when they came up. The sliprails were on the ground, across the entrance. There were wheel tracks turning off the road into the paddock, the turn being gradual. He did not notice that the track "wobbled". They got out of the buggy and the other two dismounted. McNeil was looking at the rails and said when he got there first the sliprails were up, but when he came out he left them down. Witness noticed the rails, and saw that the cart had been driven over them. He could not see marks on the rails. The rails were not lifted up while he was there. The first two rails were about two inches [*fifty millimetres*] apart; the third one was four inches or five inches [*100 to 125 millimetres*] away. The latter was furthest from the road. He looked at the ground between the rails and saw there was no wheel track between the rails, so that the track was broken from the first rail to the last. Sergeant Arrell and McNeil led their horses along the track. They followed the track for about half-a-mile [*one kilometre*] and came upon three bodies, a dog-cart and a dead horse. He recognised the bodies as those of Michael, Norah and Ellen Murphy . . . There were no signs of a struggle near Norah's body, or footprints. The ground was of a soft sandy nature with no grass upon it. Tracks ought easily to be seen upon it. Ellen's hands were tied with a pocket-handkerchief, but her clothes were not disarranged. Michael lay with his back towards her. The conditions gave him the impression that the bodies had been laid there after death. On examining the horse he saw a bullet wound in the forehead. The reins had been pulled through the saddle rings and were lying loose under the animal's head. In the trap there was a waterproof mackintosh, buggy cushion, and a red cloak. In Michael's hand there was an empty purse. A strap was lying across his thigh. He could not swear that the purse showed him was the same as that in Michael's hand. He went all round to see if he could find any tracks, and saw nothing except two or three hoof prints about twenty yards [*eighteen metres*] in the direction of the sliprails from where Norah's body lay. Wilson drew attention to these. They appeared to have been made by a light shoe or a racing plate. The tracks could not be followed; they were made in a clear spot, where a log had been burnt . . . The tracks of the horse struck him as having been made by a horse grazing. He did not think the marks could be made by hoofs recently trimmed and without shoes. He formed the impression that Norah's body had been placed after death where it was. As he drove in his buggy he could discern the wheel tracks quite plainly.[6]

Mr Thomas Wilson, blacksmith, and a Justice of the Peace, drove out to Moran's paddock in Mr Gilbert's buggy that morning. Mr Richard James and Mr William Devitt accompanied them. At the murder scene Wilson noted that the rug on which Norah was lying was "laid out carefully". He said that the top part of her head was over the rug, "but her face was rather sunk into the ground". He said "Naturally you would think there had been a struggle, but there was no sign of any; the ground was not disturbed in any way. We looked very carefully to see if there had been a struggle." When giving evidence at the Police Inquiry Commission on 5 October 1899, Wilson was particularly asked whether there was anything to indicate a struggle there and he answered "Not the slightest." He was also asked whether he came to the conclusion that Michael Murphy and his sisters were killed on the spots where they were lying. To this he answered "Yes, I think they were struck then. I came to the conclusion that they were struck at the places where they were lying because their faces were partly driven into the ground." He was questioned as to whether there was anything to indicate that they had been carried there or placed in those positions, and he replied "I do not think their faces would have sunk into the ground so much if the bodies had been carried there. Their faces were slightly pressed into the ground." He said that was the case with Michael too, but he added "though his face was hardly so much sunk in the ground as the others. Norah's was most in the ground; the side of her mouth seemed to be pretty well sunk in the ground." In answer to an inquiry in that regard he informed the Commission that Michael's trousers were buttoned and he did not think his clothes were disarranged at all. He added that, after it had been established that Michael Murphy had been shot, he came to the conclusion that he had been shot as he was standing there and that he had fallen down to the ground and got the blow afterwards. He said "his hands were behind his back, and one person may have held him while another struck the blow. I was always of opinion that the blow was struck while he was on the ground."[7]

Mr Devitt's evidence at the Police Inquiry Commission was quite brief. He was at one with Mr Wilson in stating definitely that he did not see any signs of a struggle at the scene. He also said that the rug on which Norah was lying was not at all disarranged.[8]

The fourth member of the party which went to Moran's paddock in Gilbert's buggy that morning, Mr Richard James, was a chemist. In the witness box at the Commission he was asked what was the first thing that attracted his notice when he got through the rails. He replied

Not when we got through. Before we got to the rails, I think it was, the sergeant turned round, or else McNeil, and pointed to a wobbly track. We could see it in the distance before us. Then we got near where the cart turned off the road. There is a little rise, and we naturally thought—I thought myself—that if it had been a bolt and three persons were in the trap at the time it would make somewhat the same impression on the soil that our buggy had made in passing over this little rise. I jumped out and noticed that, judging from the impression of the wheel on the soil, the three bodies must have been in the cart at the time of the supposed accident—at the time the cart went into this place. The rails were down at the time. There was some little conversation going on between McNeil and Sergeant Arrell about the position of the rails when McNeil came there the first time. I had got out of the buggy then.

He explained to the members of the Commission that, at the suggestion of Gilbert, they kept to one side of the tracks made by the sulky instead of going in the same course as it had gone. They did this so as to avoid interference with the tracks of the sulky. He said that at first they thought it was a bolt; but Mr Gilbert said it had been no bolt, because no horse could possibly get through this bush without coming in contact with trees. He himself, after they had gone a very little distance, was of a similar view; he considered that no horse could bolt through such closely-wooded country as that without coming in contact with a tree, and very likely smash up and throw the bodies out. Mr James said that, when they arrived at the scene, he saw that Norah's body "was lying with the right side of the face on the ground, partly on the abdomen, which was a little to one side, with the legs straight out, lying on a rug, which evidently had been nicely arranged". He said that the rug was not tossed. He added that, if he remembered rightly, Norah's head was on the ground; he knew the rug did not quite get down to the girl's boots, which were a little off the rug. He described the clothes on the legs as being drawn up to between the ankles and the knees. When he got near the bodies he had not the slightest doubt from the first glance that murder had been done. He said there was blood on the ground and the side of Norah's head lying nearest the ground had made a slight impression in the ground, and there was a lot of blood. He was asked if he saw any marks as if blood had spurted about and he answered "Yes, there was blood on a tree near. She was killed near a tree." He was questioned as to whether he saw any marks of a struggle there and he replied "No, none whatever; and it surprised me very much." He was then asked if he looked for marks of a struggle and he said "Yes, and I could not see the impress of a man's foot or anything. I do not profess to be a tracker, but though I looked as keenly as I could I saw nothing."

Later, in his evidence, James said that there were no marks of a struggle visible about Ellen. He said that Ellen's clothes were not disturbed like Norah's—Norah had a great deal of her bodice torn away, and the string of her corset was very much loosened. He added that Ellen, like her sister, was quite straight and it appeared as if she had been laid out carefully. Mr James was asked "Do you think if people had been struggling there you ought to have seen footprints?" to which he replied "Yes. That is what surprised me very much." He then described the position of Michael's body by saying that it lay on the left side, the knees a little drawn up, and his hands behind his back, about three or four inches (seventy to one hundred millimetres) from each other, and he held a purse in his hand. He saw no marks of a struggle at all about Michael and he could see no footprints whatever in the area. Then the examination of James continued thus:

Q. Did you form any conclusion then as to how they came to be lying there?—Did you think they must have been carried there?

A. My first impression, as I think I mentioned to Inspector Stuart and Inspector Urquhart, was that evidently they had gone there for a picnic. Viewing the bodies and the way they lay—the nonchalant way in which they were found—it was as if they had gone and laid down there for a quiet picnic, finding no dance on.

Q. And there was nothing to indicate to you that there was anybody else there?

A. Not when I saw them first.

Q. What conclusion did you form as to who killed them?

A. I cannot tell you—there were so many conflicting opinions crossed my mind.

Q. You say you came to the conclusion that they had gone to a picnic?

A. No—that was when I saw the bodies as I was approaching, and saw the whole scene—the *tout ensemble*.

Q. When you made your examination you formed the opinion that they had gone there for a picnic?

A. I did not form the opinion. I said it looked as if they had.

Q. After making your examination what opinion did you form as to who had killed them?

A. I cannot say.

Q. As to anybody else being there?

A. I certainly thought someone else had been there.

Q. You could not see any tracks?

A. No. I notice from the report of Mr Galbraith's evidence that he was surprised at the scene of the murder being in such an extraordinary state when he saw it.

Q. Could you see your own tracks?

A. No. I went a day or two afterwards to make a special investigation. I did not walk exactly on the spot which had been disturbed since I had been there before, but to the side where the soil is pretty much the same. I walked along and looked back to see if I could see the impression of my footmarks a second afterwards, but I could see nothing.

Subsequently James was asked by a member of the Commission whether it struck him that Michael's body had been left carefully laid out, that is to say if anyone after the murder appeared to "have laid him carefully out, so as to prevent detection". To this his reply was "All the bodies looked as if that had been done; but the murderer had evidently not taken much trouble to lay out Michael Murphy. I imagine now that he must have been in rather a stooping position when killed, owing to his legs being bent. My own impression is that the man was shot while looking over something."[9]

The Officer in Charge of Police at Gatton, Sergeant William Arrell had, in December 1898, been a member of the Police Force for more than twenty-one years and had been in Gatton for not quite twelve months. William McNeil gave him the information concerning the tragedy at about nine fifteen. Sergeant Arrell immediately saddled his horse and accompanied McNeil to the sliprails at Moran's paddock. Arrell saw the wobbly track of the sulky. He saw that the bottom rail of the sliprails was up, but the other two rails were lying across the entrance. He himself put the third rail down. He was positive that the wheel tracks passed over the rails on the ground. The wheel tracks where the rails were lying were disconnected as if the sulky wheels had passed over the rails on the ground.[10] Sergeant Arrell followed the wheel tracks of the sulky back towards Gatton to see if he could find traces of a struggle or fight, but the sulky appeared to have been drawn without stopping to the rails.[11] Arrell examined the bodies and he said in his evidence at the Police Inquiry Commission "I examined the ground all round where the bodies were lying, to see if I could find any weapon or any sign of a struggle. I made a very careful search, but could not see anything. I could not find any tracks or sign of a struggle . . . there were a lot of dead leaves, broken twigs, and dead branches; but I could see no sign of a struggle." In the course of his evidence at the Commission he was examined by a member and responded as follows:

Q. Did you look for signs or marks to show that there had been a struggle about the place?

A. I made careful search.

Q. And you say there was no sign of struggle?

A. No sign at all.

Q. Did you form any conclusion as to how they happened to be there?—Did you think they were carried there or not?

A. No, I did not think that. I thought they had got the blow on the heads where they lay, because the heads were lying in such a manner that apparently they had been driven into the ground. The blood was all lying about the mouths, and I came to the conclusion that they must have been lying on the ground, and perhaps held in that position while the blow was struck. The bodies had that appearance.

Q. Did you come to any conclusion as to how many it would take to do the thing in that way?

A. Not then; but since I have thought it over. Thinking over it since, I have thought that one man could do it.

Q. Did you look to see at that time if there were any footprints of men?

A. I did.

Q. And you saw no footprints?

A. No.

Q. Was not the ground impressionable?

A. It was not.

Q. It was impressionable enough to track the wheels of the trap?

A. Yes, you could see the track of the trap three chains [*sixty metres*] off, and I followed it into the paddock.

Q. And yet the ground was not soft enough to leave a foot or boot mark?

A. No, I carefully searched and found no footmarks.

Q. Now, did you look carefully?

A. I did.

Q. It was a light, sandy, soil?

A. Yes, it is of a sandy nature, but I do not think it is a good paddock for tracking in.

Q. Are you a tracker?

A. I have had a little experience.

Q. You did your best to find out tracks?

A. I did.

Q. Did you search where the girls were lying to see if there was any struggle—any marks made by the heels of the boots or anything of that kind?

A. No, there was no sign of a struggle.

Q. How far out from the bodies did you go to look for foot tracks?

A. We took a circle round the bodies of, I should say, a couple of hundred yards.[12]

While at the scene of the murders Sergeant Arrell examined the sulky. He found no blood on it.[13] When giving evidence at the Magisterial Inquiry, Sergeant Arrell said that William McNeil only remained about five minutes after they had come to the scene of the killings in Moran's paddock. He said he did not ask McNeil where he was when he first saw the bodies. Nor did he ask him to point out which way he had come. He said it did not at the time strike him as peculiar that there was no appearance of McNeil's tracks along between the wheel tracks. He said if the tracks were there between the wheel tracks he would have seen them; but there were none except those of the horse that drew the sulky. Arrell was then questioned by Inspector Urquhart and answered as follows:

Q. If you noticed that it is peculiar you did not question McNeil? Did you see any footprints about the bodies as if a man had walked up and looked at them?

A. No.

Q. Have you ever had any experience of tracking?

A. Yes; I was three or four months after a black bushranger with four black trackers.

Q. Do you swear there were no tracks?

A. All I can say is I carefully examined, and I believe there were no tracks. I saw none.

Q. Didn't it strike you as peculiar knowing that McNeil had been there before, according to his own statement?

A. Well, yes, it did.

Q. Did you take any steps to test the accuracy of McNeil's statement?

A. No.

Q. Did you question him to see if he was telling the truth?

A. No.

Q. It is difficult to believe you rode from the station to the scene with McNeil without saying something to him. Didn't you ask him for any particulars?

A. No.[14]

4
THE AFTERMATH

Sergeant Arrell waited in Moran's paddock for about twenty minutes or half an hour after he arrived there with McNeil.[1] He then said "As far as I can see there is no trace left here, but if there is a really good black tracker he may be able to pick up some trace or track that we have been unable to find. I will ride into Gatton and wire to the Commissioner of the occurrence and ask him to send a black tracker." He asked the others to remain and protect the bodies. Gilbert and James said they could not, as they had to return to town. Wilson and Devitt agreed to remain. Before leaving the scene Arrell instructed them to stay until he returned, and to allow no one near the bodies or the spot. Wilson, as has already been mentioned, was a "magistrate" (a Justice of the Peace).[2]

Arrell then rode into Gatton and from the railway station wired the Commissioner of Police. This telegram was sent at 10.55 a.m. He asked the telegraph master to send it "Urgent", and, unbelievable though it may seem, was told that the police had no authority to send "Urgent" wires. Actually the police did have authority "under Regulation 6" to send an "Urgent" wire; but Arrell knew nothing about that then—he had received no instructions to that effect. In any event there was no delay in the sending of the telegram because the telegraph master told Arrell that the wire would be relayed immediately, and that it would go to Brisbane as soon as an "Urgent" wire.[3]

Sergeant Arrell did not return to Moran's paddock immediately after sending the telegram to the Commissioner. He waited at the Gatton railway station because the telegraph master told him that the wire would go through immediately and he thought he would get a reply in ten or fifteen minutes.

A telegram was sent by Sergeant Arrell to Sub-Inspector P.D.F. Galbraith at Ipswich at the same time. Sub-Inspector Galbraith was Arrell's immediate superior officer. Arrell waited at the Gatton railway station for "twenty minutes or perhaps half an hour" and as he received no reply from the Commissioner or the Chief Inspector's

35

Office in Brisbane he rode out again to Moran's paddock arriving there at about quarter past twelve.[4]

Meanwhile, of course, William McNeil had reached the Murphy farm at Tent Hill and had imparted the appalling news. When McNeil reached the farm, young Jerry Murphy was cutting chaff with William and John. Subsequently he succinctly described McNeil's arrival in these terms:

> While we were chaff-cutting McNeil rode up looking bad. Bob Smith came up and said that the three had been murdered in a paddock near Gatton. We then went towards the house and met McNeil coming out to them. McNeil said to William Murphy "My God, Bill, such a mess you never saw in all your life."

Jerry Murphy went on to say that McNeil also told them that their hands were tied behind their backs and their heads bashed in in a paddock at Gatton.[5]

William Murphy, when giving evidence at the Magisterial Inquiry said when McNeil came up to the farm after discovering the bodies he was much excited. William asked him if all were dead and he said "Yes, it is something terrible." William said he remembered his mother saying "Oh my God, my poor children." Arrangements were made for Mrs Murphy and McNeil to go to the scene. William, in the meantime, went to fetch his father who was at the farm and who asked what was the matter. William replied that Norah, Ellen and Mike had been murdered. Whereupon his father then asked if they had been shot, and, when he was told the facts, he said he was glad they had attended their church on the Sunday. He also asked if Bill (meaning McNeil) had brought the news. According to William, his father nearly fainted and he had to "hold him up"[6] Shortly afterwards McNeil drove Mrs Murphy to where the bodies were in Moran's paddock and other members of the family also went in. A newspaper correspondent at the time described Mrs Murphy's devotion to her children in these terms:

> In response to a sympathetic expression by a visitor yesterday, Mrs Murphy said: "Though they have murdered their bodies, I thank God Almighty that their souls are still alive in Heaven, where I will see them soon". Mrs Murphy was devoutly attached to her children. When she was informed of the misfortune which had overtaken the three victims, she brought sheets from her home to the scene of the tragedy, and, with her own hands, covered each of the corpses with them. Then, kneeling down in the solitude of the bush, she prayed earnestly for the repose of the souls of those who had been so brutally murdered.[7]

Another correspondent commented:

The members of the Murphy family are as well as can be expected after the fearful shock of last week. Old Mrs Murphy is a very devout woman and rests on the great rock of her religion for consolation. Her chief prayers during the first bitter hours of the tragedy were for the souls of those who had destroyed her children and blasted the happiness of her home. What a sermon that prayer of the grief stricken mother is![8]

On the day the bodies were discovered, Mr Robert Ballantyne, a storekeeper in Gatton and a Justice of the Peace, was informed of the murders after Mr Gilbert returned from the scene. He at once drove out. It has already been mentioned that he spoke to Mrs Murphy at the scene of the tragedy. In making observations in that area he noticed the tracks of a horse leading from the place where the heads of Michael and Norah were towards the sliprails. He followed these tracks for "three or four chains" [*sixty to eighty metres*]. By this time, Sergeant Arrell had arrived back at the scene after sending his telegrams. Sergeant Arrell, according to Ballantyne, ordered the people there off the ground, but they refused to go. He repeated the order but they would not move. Ballantyne then pointed out to these people that "they might be defeating the ends of justice"; but they still would not go. He characterised them as being "very stubborn". Ballantyne described the horse tracks he saw in the paddock as being "those of a small unshod pony hoof". He said he believed he had pointed them out to Sergeant Arrell, but added "there were all sorts of tracks by that time—horses, buggies and German waggons". He said there were many foot-tracks there "but there was one leading from the western side of the sulky to Norah's body. It was a small foot-mark, more like the foot of a woman than a man. It was a peculiar shaped boot, being narrow-toed, but there was no heel mark. It looked as if someone was carrying a heavy weight and had leaned forward." Ballantyne said he was very careful and made a good examination of the ground, especially on the western side towards the fence. He said he saw no appearance of a struggle. Nor could he find any stains on the sulky, which surprised him. He looked at the horse and was under the impression that it had been shot while it was standing still. He was inclined to think the animal had been tied up to a sapling. Referring to the pony tracks he said that if he saw a track by the same pony he would detect a resemblance.[9]

Sergeant Arrell said that when he returned to Moran's paddock after sending his telegrams there were "thirty or forty people close up to the bodies". These he requested to go out of the paddock. They retired a little, but came back again repeatedly, though he remonstrated with them. Mrs Murphy asked him to have the bodies removed and he replied that he would like the bodies to remain where they were until a doctor, for whom he had wired, had arrived. Father Daniel Walsh,

Parish Priest of Gatton, who was standing nearby, said it would be as well to leave the bodies until the doctor arrived. Later on, Mrs Murphy again asked for the removal of the bodies. Mr James, the chemist, who was there then, said the bodies should be removed on account of the sun and the ants. Mr Ballantyne and Mr Clement Wiggins (the latter being also a Justice of the Peace and the justice who gave the order for the post mortem examination and the subsequent order for the burial of the bodies of the victims) also urged the same course. Mr Wiggins said to Arrell "Have you not taken a description of the position of the bodies when you found them?" Arrell said that he had, and the bodies were thereupon removed from the paddock.[10]

The corpses of Norah and Ellen were brought into Gatton by William McNeil. Mr F. Drew, manager of the Tent Hill dairy, brought in Michael's body.[11] The bodies were removed from Moran's paddock at 2 p.m. and they were locked up in a room of the Brian Boru Hotel until Dr William Henry von Lossberg (Government Medical Officer, Ipswich district) arrived on the four o'clock train to conduct the post mortem examination.[12] A number of men helped to remove the bodies from Moran's paddock. Just as Michael's body was to be taken up, Mrs Murphy, who was at the head, lifted the mackintosh that had been placed over the face and said "Who does this belong to?" McNeil said "It belongs to Bob Smith; it was thrown into the trap up at the races yesterday afternoon." Arrell then lifted up portion of the rug under Norah, and noticed dark stains on the underneath part, with dirt about the spot. While Arrell was at the scene of the murders on that afternoon, a man named Andrew Smith handed him a piece of the dead limb of a tree, "about four feet [*1·2 metres*] long and four inches [*100 millimetres*] through. One end was smaller than the other; at the larger end it was knotty, and at that place there were stains of blood." Arrell fitted it into an indentation discovered in the ground near Norah's head, which it fitted exactly. He concluded it had previously been lying in that depression and, on account of some blood and some hair upon it, that it was the weapon with which the wounds were inflicted. It was, he later said, a solid heavy stick of hardwood, but he could lift it with both hands and strike a blow with it.[13]

The carcass of the dead horse was cut up by James Skinner, a carter of Gatton. This was done with a view to obtaining the bullet which had entered the head, but apparently had also penetrated the body. The boiling-down process was carried out at Clarke's butchery under police supervision and a ·380 calibre revolver bullet was recovered. Mr Skinner, on the following day (28 December 1898), found at the scene of the tragedy an empty ·380 cartridge case, covered with blood; it was found near where the horse had been lying.[14]

Dr von Lossberg left Ipswich at 2 p.m. and arrived at Gatton at

4 p.m. on the afternoon of Tuesday, 27 December 1898, having been informed of the murders by Senior Sergeant Johnson of Ipswich, who had received Arrell's telegram addressed to Galbraith. Mr Alfred Robinson, a reporter from the *Queensland Times* of Ipswich, accompanied the doctor to Gatton. Mr Robinson was the first reporter "on the ground" after the Gatton tragedy. Dr von Lossberg and Mr Robinson were met at Gatton by Sergeant Arrell and they went with him to the Brian Boru Hotel. Mr Robinson wished to get an accurate description of the injuries sustained by the victims and he also wished to visit the scene of the murders. He arranged with Mr James, the chemist, who, he believed, was to assist at the post mortem examination, to give him a description of the injuries. Mr Robinson then left for Moran's paddock. When he returned he received from Mr James written notes of the injuries, which, he understood, were dictated by Dr von Lossberg. These notes were read by Mr Robinson to the Commission.[15]

A post mortem examination was carried out on each of the three bodies. Dr von Lossberg's findings are set out in detail in his evidence at the Magisterial Inquiry and before the Commission.[16] We mention here briefly some of the more salient features. The body of Ellen was carried out from the bedroom in which the three bodies had been lying to a back room of the hotel where a post mortem examination was carried out on each body in turn. Ellen's body was inspected by the doctor "in a good light"; he found the face and upper portions of the body were smeared with blood and the brain was protruding on the right side through a fracture. The doctor was of the opinion that Ellen had been dead about twelve to sixteen hours—certainly less than twenty-four hours. The hands of the girl were tied with a handkerchief behind her back. The body showed marks of fingernails, and there were abrasions of the skin on both hands. The skull was fractured in all the principal bones—that is, the frontal bone, the parietal bone and the occipital bones were all fractured. They were all compound comminuted fractures. The doctor then unloosed the hands, and saw that "they were greatly swelled. The nails were black." The doctor was of the opinion that the swelling was due to "the tightness of the bandage". Ellen's clothes were greatly spattered with blood, and the legs were "scratched with fingernails" and smeared with blood. He was of the view that the injuries to the skull had been caused by a heavy blunt instrument. He examined the dead girl internally and found she was not pregnant. He saw what he believed to be fingernail scratches on the thighs, inside the thighs. He said he had not the least doubt about the girl having been violated. He said, in his view, the blood on her petticoat "was caused by the outraging of the girl; it was the effect of resistance. The labia of the vagina was very swollen and scratched.

The finger marks went right through to the anus. The blood came from the scratches on the labia." From her appearance he would have deduced that the girl had resisted violently and he would have expected to see, at the place where she was ravished, marks of a struggle. He said he could say with absolute certainty that she had not been shot. The doctor also mentioned that, when he withdrew his finger after internally examining Ellen, there were undoubtedly signs of semen. He almost certainly would not have had a microscope, but nevertheless was able to say that it was undoubtedly semen.

Dr von Lossberg next examined Norah's body. Her hands were also tied with a handkerchief behind her back. He found in her case a very plethoric state of the face and body—so much so that, before doing anything else, he looked to the upper part of the body, and found a strap quite tight round the neck—so tight that it had stopped the circulation. At the same time he found on her face, near the right eye, a sharp cut—"one which turned out. This cut was about two inches [*fifty millimetres*] long, dividing the true skin. It was made by some sharp instrument—very likely by a knife. It was a clean cut." At the outset of the post mortem examinations he had been shown the big piece of timber, with blood and hair attached to it, which Arrell had taken possession of when it had been handed to him at the scene of the tragedy earlier that day. The doctor was asked whether the injury near Norah's right eye could have been caused by that instrument and he replied "It could not possibly have been made by that." Nor did the doctor think that the injury could have been caused by a fist. Norah's clothes, the doctor found, were more disordered than Ellen's —her clothes, in fact, were torn open from the neck right to the waist. The breastbone, hands, and arms showed a number of fingernail marks, and there were also abrasions on the hands. The injury to the head was about the same as in the case of Ellen, all the principal bones being fractured; but in Norah's case, all the blood-vessels were over-filled with blood, and he took that to be caused by the strangulation. The doctor said that the strap round Norah's neck had been put on before death. It had sunk into the flesh and could not be seen. Nobody had seen it until the doctor had made "a very minute examination. If I had not found it nobody would have known there was a strap round her neck at all." The doctor said he could say that Norah had not been shot. Dr von Lossberg then examined the lower region of Norah and he found, principally on the left thigh, "great numbers of fingernail marks, and they went to the privates and right to the anus— in fact, right to the constrictor anus. The marks were more plentiful than with the first girl. I examined her likewise internally, and found a swelling, but no blood of any kind. The hymen was ruptured. I gave the opinion that she was not in a pregnant state." The doctor was asked whether he would say the girl had been ravished and he answered "Yes, I gave that opinion at the time, and I am still of the same opinion." The examination of the doctor before the Commission then proceeded in the following way:

Q. She was a non-consenting party, struggling to prevent violation, and so received those injuries, in your opinion?
A. That is so.
Q. Would you say there must have been great struggling on her part?
A. I would.
Q. If she was lying on a rug, would you expect to see that rug all tossed about?
A. I would, but I would not expect she would keep on a rug. I would expect that the rug be all disordered, and that she would roll off.
Q. Would you expect the ground to be torn up with the movements of her feet and her struggles?
A. Certainly. She had on a pair of quite new, strong boots, with high heels, and those boots would have made an impression somehow on the ground.
Q. And if the ground was soft and strewn with leaves, would you expect to find it greatly disturbed?
A. I would.
Q. Did you inform Sergeant Arrell that she was outraged, and had struggled violently?
A. Yes; I said she must have struggled more violently than the other girl, because all her hands and face and everything were marked with fingernails. I forgot to say that on the left side of the throat there were the marks of three fingers of the hand just above the strap—a hames strap it was.
Q. Do you think it was possible for one man to have ravished both of those girls?
A. I do not think it was possible at all. I have said from the beginning that I did not think it possible for one man to have done it.
Q. Did you give your opinion to the police?
A. I did.
Q. To whom—do you recollect? Was it to Sergeant Arrell?
A. Yes. I said at the time to the gentleman who was present that it was not possible to outrage the girl, and at the same time to do this tying. If the tying was done after death it would have been another thing; but one man could not possibly tie the hands when alive, and at the same time outrage the girl.
Q. Do you think one man could have outraged both?
A. He could. A strong man could.
Q. Norah was a very strong girl, was she not?

A. Yes.

Q. A man struggling with her on the ground would knock about the ground a great deal?

A. He would; but the girls were not so strong as was represented.

Q. Were they not?

A. Not for farmers' daughters.

Q. Do you not consider from the resistance those girls must have offered, and the force used by the man, that the ground must have been knocked about a great deal?

A. I would certainly expect that.

Q. Were you on the ground at all?

A. No I was not.

The doctor went on to give his opinion that Norah received the cut to the region near her right eye when she was standing up. He considered the man must have been standing close to her—very close to her. He was of the view that it was a downward strike that caused that injury. He considered also that the girls were standing when they received the other injuries to their heads. He believed the girls were ravished before the injuries were inflicted. He was asked "You believe that these girls were ravished before the injuries you speak of were inflicted—the injuries to the head?" and he replied "Yes, I believe so."

Dr von Lossberg then examined the body of Michael Murphy. He said that, when first looked at, Michael Murphy's body represented the same picture, except that his hands were only bent back and not tied. Nor was there any mark on either hand to show that they had been tied, but he had in one hand an empty purse. The doctor said "He had in one hand a quite loose purse, and between the two hands there was lying a strap." The doctor went on to say that, just behind the right ear, there was some blood that extended to the lower jaw and to the neck in a thin film and quite dark and dry. He cleared this blood away. It extended from three to three and a half inches [*seventy-five to ninety millimetres*]. He washed it carefully away, and he found a wound behind the right ear. In his evidence before the Commission Dr von Lossberg said that at the post mortem examination of Michael Murphy he said to the gentlemen present, "Hulloa, there is a bullet wound", and, according to him, nobody said anything to that. He went on to say that he then commenced directly to probe the bullet wound with his finger. He said he went on for a considerable time and "removed a few loose bones from the skull, and felt all at once a very sharp click on one of my nails. I went to a basin and washed my hands in a disinfectant fluid, after which I went on with the examination again. Then I felt a numbness going up my arm, and a swelling of the finger, so I asked the chemist who was present, Mr James, if he would be good enough to probe for the bullet." According to the doctor, Mr James said "Very well", and tried to find it, but did not succeed. Dr von Lossberg continued his evidence by saying "As I felt more and more the effects of the poison I did not proceed further with the examination, but left it in an incomplete state."

The doctor was then asked "What did you get—blood poisoning?" and he replied "I did. I was three months ill, and I have still the effects on my body in blotches on the skin; even my hands show still the marks of abscesses and all sorts of things. I felt regularly ill for three months from the blood poisoning. After that I got the bodies replaced ... I asked the chemist, who is a handy man, to try and find the bullet, but he could not, and then, as I could not go on any more, I got the bodies replaced in the other room where I had found them." The doctor said that the three post mortem examinations occupied about two hours and twenty minutes. He said he was of the opinion that the cause of death of Michael Murphy was that he had been shot. He said that the fractures of the bones of Michael's head (there were fractures of all the principal bones) could have been caused by the piece of timber he had been shown and he was of the opinion that the fractures were caused after death. He said he gave that opinion at the time, and was still of that opinion.[17] The handling of the post mortem examinations by Dr von Lossberg was the subject of considerable discussion and the adequacy of his examination of the bodies of the Murphys was questioned, particularly by some of the senior police officers.

Mr Clement Wiggins was present at the three post mortem examinations. In his evidence before the Commission he verified that Dr von Lossberg had said that he found a hole which struck him as a hole made by a bullet, that he probed with his finger and subsequently requested Mr James, the chemist, to search with his finger. Mr James corroborated these statements also. But Mr Wiggins said that, after probing the hole with his finger, the doctor said "I cannot find any trace of the bullet." Wiggins said that Dr von Lossberg then said "There should be a corresponding hole on the other side for an exit, but there is none." Wiggins then related that the doctor said "I have pricked my finger with a bone, and I feel it a bit sore", and he "washed it in some disinfecting water, and asked James, the chemist, to come and have a try which he did." According to Wiggins, after James had felt about with his finger for a time, he said he could feel nothing, and the doctor then said, "I do not think it is a bullet; it has been caused by the knot on the stick."[18]

In this regard, it would appear not to be without significance that the notes of the injuries of the victims, made by Mr James at the post mortem examination, allegedly at the doctor's dictation, made no mention of a gunshot wound to Michael's head. Those notes, handed to Mr Alfred Robinson (the reporter from the *Queensland Times*), in so far as Michael Murphy is concerned, read as follows:

> Michael, age twenty-nine. Dark hair, light moustache, black coat, waistcoat, and trousers; watch in pocket; empty purse found in hand; blow on head—compound comminuted fracture; parietal and occipital fractured, likewise base of skull.

When Robinson read these notes to the Commission, a member of the Commission said to Robinson "There is nothing about a gunshot wound there?" and Robinson answered, "No, nothing." Alfred Robinson went on in his evidence to say that, when returning in the train to Ipswich with Dr von Lossberg, the doctor said "that while making the examination, there was a wound which he at first thought was a bullet wound, but he said there was no mark or exit, and he came to the conclusion that it was caused by a notch in the stick with which the man was struck."[19]

After the post mortem examinations, the bodies of the victims were washed and laid out by Mrs Caroline Eames, who was assisted by a widow, Mrs Elizabeth Selby. The clothes taken from each of the Murphys were not mixed; they were tied up separately and Mrs Selby handed them to Sergeant Arrell.[20]

Sergeant Arrell did not receive any reply at all to the telegram he had sent at 10.55 on 27 December 1898 to the Commissioner of Police in Brisbane. This telegram was actually sent out for delivery from the Telegraph Office, Brisbane, at 11.52 a.m. and was delivered at the Commissioner's Office in the Treasury Building, Queen Street, at 12.32 p.m. on that day. But, in what was later described as "some unaccountable way", the telegram was not opened till nine o'clock, or thereabouts, next morning. The Chief Inspector said he found it on his table unopened when he arrived in his office on the morning of 28 December. The Commission was later to say "This could not have happened if proper provision had been made for the receipt and opening of telegrams on holidays. This serious omission has, we understand, since been remedied."[21] This matter concerning the delay in opening the telegram was inquired into at some length by the Commission. It undoubtedly militated against a successful police investigation when there was such a delay in having trackers and an investigation team at the scene of the murders. In the result, the Chief of the Criminal Investigation Branch at Brisbane and the man who was to be in charge of the investigation of the Gatton affair, Inspector Urquhart, did not leave Brisbane until seven o'clock on the morning of Wednesday, 28 December. The Commissioner of Police had ordered him to take two men and proceed to Gatton.[22]

Inspector Urquhart's departure was precipitated by news of a telegram received the previous day by young Constable Dan Murphy at the Roma Street Police Station. This telegram, which was sent by Michael Connolly of Gatton at 11.50 a.m. on 27 December, read: "Michael, Norah and Ellen murdered last night. Come at once." Constable Dan Murphy, a brother of the victims, at first thought the telegram a hoax, but later confirmed its veracity by wires to Sergeant Arrell and the telegraph master at Gatton. Dan Murphy obtained leave and departed for Gatton on the five o'clock train in the company of a friend, Constable Joe Murphy, who was no relation.

Although Sergeant Arrell received no reply to his message to Brisbane, he did receive a wire from his superior officer, Sub-Inspector Galbraith, at Rosewood advising that he would make all possible haste to reach Gatton about five o'clock.[23] Sub-Inspector Galbraith was at Rosewood on official business on that day and, at about half past three in the afternoon, he received word about the triple murder, from the telegraph master at Rosewood, who told him that wires had gone through to him and to the Commissioner. The telegraph master told Galbraith "I just heard it going through, but I gathered that two girls and a man were murdered." Galbraith asked him when a train would go up to Gatton and he replied "You have missed the train; there will be no train now till later on in the evening." Galbraith asked him if he would lend him a "bicycle" to go up by the railway, and he said he would; but he advised Galbraith not to go by that means of transport "as the Liverpool Range is rather steep". (Gatton is approximately fifty kilometres west of Rosewood.) Galbraith had with him at Rosewood at the time his little son, aged three years, and he left him at the police station after deciding to go to Gatton on horseback. A Mr George Baines, who knew the country well, accompanied Sub-Inspector Galbraith. Both men were on horseback, Galbraith being mounted on a police horse. They rode over "the back track over the range" and missed their way, so that they did not get to Gatton until about 7.30 p.m. It was no mean feat of cross-country riding in the circumstances, and it is to the everlasting great credit of Percy Dumas Fead Galbraith, First-class Sub-Inspector of Police, that he made such determined and unremitting efforts to fulfil his duty in getting to Gatton as fast as possible.

The Sub-Inspector, who had never been at Gatton before, rode straight down to the police station on his arrival and saw Sergeant Arrell, questioned him with reference to the murders and asked him if the doctor was there. Arrell replied that the doctor was just about to return to Ipswich by the eight o'clock train. Galbraith said, "Come on to the station with me and we will see the doctor, and you can tell me about it as we are going." Galbraith said that Arrell

... gave me the heads in a short time, and what he had heard about the murder. I met Dr von Lossberg at the station. I think I was introduced to him by Mr Baines. I asked him if he had performed the post mortem examination, and he replied "Yes". I said "What was the result, doctor?" He informed me that the heads of the girls were literally smashed in, and the occipital bone was broken. I said to him "Were the girls ravished?" and he said "Undoubtedly they were. The elder girl fought fiercely, as she was covered with scratches." So I said to him, "Have you got any of the semen, doctor?" and he said, "What is the good of my getting the semen? The clothes are literally covered with it."

The doctor then got in the train and the train went away.[24]

In his evidence before the Commission Dr von Lossberg gave his version of his meeting with Sub-Inspector Galbraith at the Gatton railway station. He said:

This is what occurred. I met Mr Galbraith at the station, and he asked me if I had found a bullet. I replied that I had traced a bullet, but had injured myself, and had felt the effects of the poison from the post mortem. I also stated there was a bullet in the head of Michael Murphy, but there was no exit. I advised him to take charge of the bodies at the hotel where I had placed them, and I also gave instructions that the bodies should not be touched before a higher officer of police had seen them. I did not say anything to Mr Galbraith about getting another doctor.[25]

In their report of 29 November 1899, the Commissioners reported:

In regard to the autopsies, we are of opinion that Dr von Lossberg is mistaken in stating that he informed Sub-Inspector Galbraith that he suspected there was a bullet in Michael Murphy's head, as we are convinced that the Sub-Inspector would not, if in receipt of such information, have consented to the burial of the body.[26]

Shortly after leaving the Gatton railway station from which Dr von Lossberg had departed for Ipswich, Sub-Inspector Galbraith went to the Brian Boru Hotel. He went into the room where the bodies were and noticed they were in their shrouds. On learning that the bodies had been undressed by Mrs Selby he asked to see the clothes, and they were brought in to him by Mrs Selby, of whom the Sub-Inspector was later to say, "she was a woman of very good intelligence".[27] He commenced to examine the bodies commencing with Norah. The

Sub-Inspector subsequently said

> I made a much longer examination owing to what I perceived was a
> faulty post mortem examination . . . I then made a proper examination
> for that reason. The bodies of the two girls were lying in one bed, and
> the body of the brother was in another. I then examined the girls very
> carefully. My report will show the result of that examination; but I
> do not suppose you want that. I found certain peculiarities.[28]

Sub-Inspector Galbraith, after examining the bodies, went to the
railway station and sent a wire to Ipswich to Senior Sergeant Johnson
instructing him to send up Constable Doyle and two trackers, if
available, the next morning. The time was then about 10 p.m., and
the reason he mentioned the next morning was that he understood
there were no more trains that day.

Sergeant Johnson acted more promptly than the Sub-Inspector
thought he could, and sent up two trackers during the night with
Constable Murphy, and sent up another constable the following
morning. Galbraith then wired to Constable Perkins at Rosewood
and asked him to come up. He then wired to Sergeant King at Laidley
and requested him to come to Gatton because King knew the district
well, whereas the Sub-Inspector, at that time, had been in charge of
the Ipswich district for only ten days and did not know the country.
It would seem to be a fair comment that, right from when he first
heard of the murders, Sub-Inspector Galbraith acted promptly and
energetically—he took immediate action to get trackers and men
from Rosewood, Laidley and Ipswich.

The trackers arrived in the early hours of the morning and Galbraith
soon had them working in Moran's paddock under the direction of
Acting-Sergeant Murphy. Galbraith himself was examining a suspect
at 2 a.m. on Wednesday, 28 December, and he went to Moran's
paddock at 6 a.m., the black trackers having arrived there before
that hour.

Galbraith was at the railway station when Inspector Urquhart
arrived on the ten o'clock train later on the morning of Wednesday,
28 December. He informed Inspector Urquhart of everything he had
done and of the results of his initial investigations. Galbraith was
subsequently to say "When Mr Urquhart came I felt relieved of the
responsibility of actual charge . . . we then worked together. I took
Mr Urquhart out to the paddock. After we had come back from the
paddock we sent out men to get statements. I think there was a man
sent out to Clarke's, the butcher's shop."[29]

Meanwhile the Gatton community was obviously stunned. Reports
of the day paint the dismal scene adequately. One reporter wrote "the
terrible affair has caused a tremendous sensation; so much so that

all business is paralysed and nothing else is talked of."[30] Another commented

> ... the most mysterious part about the tragic affair is the locality where the awful crime was committed and how the victims—one strong man and two robust women—were taken or induced to go away from the main road through a sliprail and along a dark narrow track to the place where the bodies were found, is difficult to understand. The bodies, which have lain at Gilbert's Hotel, were removed to the Roman Catholic Church on Wednesday—Funeral 11.30 a.m. ... residents of Gatton and the surrounding district could find nothing to talk of all day yesterday, but the atrocious crime committed in their midst on Monday night. Early in the morning folk from surrounding farms and selections wended their way, some on horseback and some in vehicles, to the township, there to await the sad ceremony of the day—the funeral.[31]

Inspector Urquhart considered that Sub-Inspector Galbraith had done all that could be done. The Inspector told Galbraith he would like to view the bodies; but he was told that that was impossible, as they were coffined and the funeral was to start immediately. When giving evidence before the Commission on 29 September 1899, Inspector Urquhart said,

> The next thing I thought of was the clothing the murdered persons were wearing at the time of their death, and in answer to my inquiry he [Galbraith] told me they were in one of the cells at Gatton. I inspected the clothing, and saw things there which were gone into afterwards, but unfortunately with no successful result. There is one very striking matter, which I do not think should be made public even now.

One of the Commissioners then interposed the remark, "Very well, don't mention it." Whereupon Inspector Urquhart said "I should like to refer to my report, which I have with me, and which gives as good an account of the whole business as I can give ... it is compiled from the daily diary I kept and the station diary. It extends to forty-four pages and gives a connected account of the work that was done." The Chairman of the Commission then asked the question, "You tender it as an account of what you did?" and Urquhart replied "Yes. There are some portions which are mere comments." Another member of the Commission then said "You can leave out any parts that you think ought not to be published?" To which Urquhart replied, "I have no objection to any part being published except so far as it may militate against our future success." The Chairman of the Commission then said "You can go through it at your leisure and strike out the parts you think it inadvisable to publish, and then have a copy made of the portion you consider may be published."[32] Although there are ten Appendices to the evidence taken before the Police Inquiry

Commission, the report of Inspector Urquhart, edited or otherwise, does not appear. It is unfortunate that this is so, for it would undoubtedly have made very interesting reading. There is, however, one matter which we know was mentioned in that report of Inspector Urquhart—and we shall refer to that particular matter hereafter with considerable satisfaction.

On the morning of Wednesday, 28 December, crowds of people began to assemble in the township of Gatton. The three bodies had been removed from Mr Gilbert's Brian Boru Hotel to the Catholic Church between seven and eight in the morning. The funeral ceremony in the church at 11.30 a.m. was attended by a vast crowd. The three coffins rested on a long platform down the aisle—they were almost buried in floral tributes of sympathy, many of the wreaths and crosses being most beautiful. The coffins were conveyed to the cemetery in three hearses, and the remains were followed to their last resting place by over a thousand people. The funeral procession was the largest ever seen in the district—it was over two kilometres long and included 357 horsemen and eighty-seven vehicles. The scene at the graveside was most affecting. The brother and younger sister were buried side by side, while the grave of the elder sister was about two and a half metres away. The Rev. Father Walsh officiated at the graveside, and, as he read the burial service a pin could have been heard to drop. Father Walsh then delivered a most impressive and stirring oration. He declared the crime to be

> ... the most atrocious outrage ever perpetrated in Australia, and urged those present to assist the police in every possible way to secure the murderers. His references to the deceased and their bereaved parents were most touching, and ere he had ceased there was not a dry eye in the large congregation. The deep sympathy manifested throughout testified to the popularity of the victims, and the abhorrence of the terrible crime.[33]

Happily, it would seem that the appeal and exhortation of Rev. Father Walsh did not fall on deaf ears, for, shortly afterwards, the following newspaper comment appeared:

> There is one thing I feel it my duty to state as a mark of recognition, and that is the great kindness and assistance given by the Gatton people to the Press representatives. Everywhere we have gone we have met with nothing but the most open handed hospitality. All we have to do is to signify our wants and they are immediately attended to. Horses and vehicles are placed at our disposal free of charge wherever we want to go, the general remark to us being "We will do all we can, in the interests of justice, to help the Police and the Press in the work of hunting down the fiends that have so deeply stained the name of Gatton. We cannot

rest until the murderers are found." That is the general feeling I have met with. The people are only too eager, so far as I have been able to observe, to give all the information in their power and place all their resources at the disposal of the authorities . . . we have met with every possible courtesy at the hands of the Gatton people and our generous treatment will never be forgotten.[34]

One can readily appreciate the feelings of Inspector Urquhart and his men, who so suddenly were confronted with a crime of uncommon magnitude, committed in an unusual location, presenting the most mysterious circumstances, and yielding nothing of real significance in the way of a clue. Notwithstanding his undoubted ability and energetic competence, it must have been with some misgivings that Inspector Urquhart embarked upon the most challenging and difficult task of his career—probably the most difficult criminal investigation which any Australian police officer had, up to that time, undertaken. With the burden of the investigation thrust upon him, he needed the complete co-operation of the public if he were to obtain even a measure of success. He surely must have been grateful for the earnest request of Father Walsh; he certainly must have been gratified at the apparent reaction of the Gatton people in response to it.

5
INVESTIGATION BEGINS

At the time of the Gatton murders, Frederick Charles Urquhart, who was forty years of age, was a Second-class Inspector of Police, in charge of the Criminal Investigation Branch, and subject to the Chief Inspector and the Commissioner of Police. Urquhart was an interesting personality; indeed, he was quite a remarkable man. Born at St Leonard's-on-Sea, Sussex, England, on 27 October 1858, he was the second son of Major F.D. Urquhart of the Royal (formerly Bengal) Artillery. He was educated at All Saints School, Bloxham, and at Felstead Military School, and then served for a time in the Mercantile Marine. Landing in Queensland in 1875, he worked for two years as a drover and book-keeper, and became renowned as an excellent horseman. In October 1878, he joined the Public Service as a line repairer in the Electric Telegraph Department. He joined the Queensland Native Mounted Police as a Cadet Sub-Inspector in April 1882, and was placed in charge of the Great Northern District, embracing the Gulf and Cape York country. Urquhart was the first person to reach the scene of the sinking of the *Quetta* in February 1890 and he spent several days in a boat searching for survivors.[1] During his career, he was twice sent to New Guinea by the Queensland Government. In the execution of his duty he was twice wounded—on one occasion he was speared in the groin by an Aboriginal at Merluna, and, on the other occasion, near Cloncurry, he was struck in the thigh by a quartz tomahawk wielded by an Aboriginal.

He was appointed First-class Sub-Inspector in September 1893, and, in April 1897, he was appointed Second-class Inspector and placed in control of the City Police and the Criminal Investigation Branch. In 1904 he was appointed First-class Inspector and in 1905, Chief Inspector of Police. He was appointed Commissioner of Police on 1 January 1917, succeeding Major Cahill. Urquhart retired from the Commissionership in January 1921, and was then appointed by the Federal Government to the post of Administrator of the Northern Territory, which post he held until 1925. He visited England in 1928.

Urquhart was very widely read and he was a clever writer of verse and prose; he published a collection of bush poems.

Concerning Urquhart, one of his friends, a leading journalist, wrote:

> Another of my friends was F.C. Urquhart, of the police, who was the fourth Commissioner, and later Administrator of the Northern Territory. Urquhart is a bushman and a poet, a very brainy man, and determined. He is an old Northerner, having gone over to the Native Police from the Telegraph Service in 1882. From the Native Police he was transferred or "evolved" into the ordinary "force", and he had there a long and successful career. When he went out on pension he was snapped up by the Commonwealth Government to Administer the Northern Territory. I saw Urquhart at his best in failure. Under Parry-Okeden, and as head of the Criminal Investigation Department, as he then was, he had the main job in seeking to unravel the mystery of the Gatton tragedy of Christmas time in 1898. It is said that the police, in the event of a crime, can only act upon the evidence available to trace the guilty person or persons. That is not correct. At Gatton Urquhart followed out suggestion after suggestion, and clue after clue, without success; but then he would think, strive to reconstruct the whole affair from incentive to the covering up of the line of escape, build up and diligently search theories— but it was all to no purpose, unless it was that a certain man had "done the job". Perhaps it may now be said that Urquhart and I shared the belief that the certain man was guilty; but evidence was against us. Evidence, however, gets a twist at times ... That Gatton story is, perhaps, as vivid in Urquhart's mind as in mine. It was the biggest outside thing while he was chief of the C.I. Department, and it was rough that he could not clear it up. The country rang with it.[2]

Inspector Urquhart, it will be recalled, was taken to Moran's paddock shortly after he had arrived at Gatton a little after ten o'clock on the morning of 28 December 1898. He was accompanied to the paddock by Sub-Inspector Galbraith who had earlier that morning (about six o'clock) examined the murder scene. On this previous occasion Galbraith had stopped and examined the sliprails and the approaches into the paddock, and he said that he had also made "a fairly minute examination of about seven to ten minutes there". It was evident to him that all traces of any particular track were obliterated—that is, there had been, in his opinion, scores of horses over the tracks. He noticed that, on the route which McNeil and Sergeant Arrell had followed down to the scene of the murders, there was a wheel track quite perceptible; it was the wheel track of a buggy. He said "another thing that I noticed at the scene of the murder was that the ground was in no wise disturbed. It was a thing which struck me forcibly."[3]

When giving evidence before the Commission, Inspector Urquhart also said that, when he got to the scene of the murders, the tracks and traces of whoever was responsible were all obliterated. When questioned by members of the Commission he answered as follows:

Q. You state in your report, "I was struck by the ignorance and helplessness displayed by all those who first arrived on the scene of the murders, which undoubtedly led to the utter destruction of most valuable clues, in the shape of tracks, which must have existed, and on that kind of ground should have been read like a book by an experienced eye"?

A. Yes.

Q. Who did you refer to?

A. I referred to everybody who was there. I do not consider there was a man with a grain of common sense amongst them. That is my opinion of them.

Q. Do you mean the police or the public?

A. Everybody. There were magistrates, members of the mounted infantry, police, and the general public, and they did not even think of taking a rail out of the fence to let people go through instead of using the track McNeil's buggy went along.

Q. You had special experience with black trackers?

A. Yes; but this is not a matter of tracking; this is a matter of keeping the crowd off the ground; and I say the tracks should have been read like a book, because when I went there I could read them like a book. I could see where the people had been going all about the place. The ground is an easy ground to track upon.

Q. That is with expert trackers?

A. No; with anybody who had any experience at all.

Q. It is a light sandy soil?

A. It is a light loam, I suppose.

Q. And there is plenty of short grass?

A. No, very little grass. It was scattered and thin.

Q. I think you are speaking after the event?

A. No, I am speaking of the day I went there. I can see the place as I saw it that day as fresh in my mind as if it was here before me. There were footmarks, horsemarks, wheelmarks, all over the place.

Q. Were not those the obliterating marks?

A. Yes; but if I could see those I say that if there had been a tracker there—a man with any pretensions to tracking at all—he must have seen the tracks. The buggy tracks were seen—it is only a light little thing—and if those tracks could be seen why could not the heavy tracks of people stamping about with their feet be seen too?

Q. How do you account for Arrell saying that he searched carefully and did not find tracks?

A. I do not think he could have had experience.

Q. Do you think he looked for tracks?

A. Yes.

Q. Must he not have seen them if they were there?

A. I have seen people who could not see tracks when they were quite plain to me and to trackers. But McNeil saw tracks.

Q. Tracks of the wheel?

A. And he saw them turning off the road casually when not looking for them. But McNeil is a man trained among stock and is a bushman. Unless by some extraordinary method the tracks were obliterated, the tracks must have been there.[4]

In another part of his evidence before the Commission, Urquhart said

> To my mind, the whole thing at first was a matter of tracks. My own opinion is that if I could have been there and have seen the thing as Sergeant Arrell first saw it, and before there was any interruption or complication at all, I believe from the tracks I could have gathered some indication that would have given me some information. What I should have expected to glean was how many were concerned, and in what direction they left the scene. I should have got that much, I do believe; but in saying that I am speaking as a man who has been accustomed to tracks for many years, and could read tracks at one time like a book almost. I do not think Sergeant Arrell has had that experience.[5]

Very early it was generally recognised that mistakes had been made in the handling of the situation at Moran's paddock on the morning and afternoon of 27 December. A reporter from a Brisbane newspaper made the comment

> ... the mistakes made in the early history of the case have, so to speak, covered up the tracks of the murderers, and those who now have the work of tracing them out and bringing them to justice are labouring in the dark, to a great extent ... It may be well here to put plainly before the public what the mistake at the outset was and to note the effect of it ... The sergeant put a guard of four people in the place—people he could trust—not to prevent persons going into the paddock, but to keep the crowd back from the spot where the corpses lay ... the four failed to keep the spot clear and it was overrun. The murderers themselves could have devised no better plan for covering up their tracks.[6]

This report, we rather think, does less than justice to those two persons (not four) who remained at the scene when Sergeant Arrell left the paddock to ride in to Gatton to send the telegram to the Commissioner of Police. We say this, bearing in mind, in particular, the evidence at the Commission of Sub-Inspector Galbraith, who said, in regard to what he had seen early on the morning of 28 December, "Another thing that I noticed at the scene of the murder was that the ground was in no wise disturbed."

Again, we feel that some reports which have appeared have not been fair to William McNeil. It has been written, "McNeil, on discovering the tragedy, galloped into Gatton to inform the police, only stopping on the way to tell the news to all whom he met. This was unfortunate; very naturally, all Gatton and its neighbourhood proceeded to the spot, and obliterated most of the tracks, as well as any evidence of a struggle that might have taken place."[7] We hasten to say that we have not encountered any evidence which might suggest that McNeil, when riding into Gatton, stopped "on the way to tell the news to all whom he met". All the evidence we have is quite to the contrary—it is to the effect that McNeil told only Mr Gilbert, the licensee of the Brian Boru Hotel, of his discovery and the only purpose of his going to Mr Gilbert's Hotel that morning was to inquire as to where the police barracks were situated. Having been told where the police barracks were, he went and informed Sergeant Arrell of what he had discovered in Moran's paddock. We are of the view that another newspaper report at the time did greater justice to McNeil and assessed the situation more accurately and fairly. In part, this report reads:

Throughout the whole of the so-far futile quest for the culprits the police have never failed to lay stress upon the fact that, in official language, "they have been handicapped by a chain of the most extraordinary adverse circumstances that ever baffled pursuers". It is all very well, they argue, to blame the policemen, but had McNeil held his tongue until he got to the police station the paddock would not have been overrun and the tracks obliterated. Things might have ended differently then. To pursue this line of ratiocination further, it is only necessary to assume that had the Murphys been aware that they were to be murdered, they probably would have remained at home on Boxing Night. But to come back to the much maligned McNeil. It must be pointed out that he was a comparative stranger in Gatton, and had to inquire his way to the police barracks. Hence what was more natural than that he should, imprudent as it was from the police point of view, blurt out the errand which caused him to seek police assistance on that hot December morning. Had the whole thing been pre-arranged, the escape of the murderer or murderers could not have been better facilitated. The police now blame McNeil, but the public do and will blame the police.[8]

It undoubtedly was unfortunate that greater precautions were not taken to prevent entry of the crowd through the sliprails into Moran's paddock on 27 December; but it is difficult to blame any one person or class of persons for having grossly mismanaged the situation. It would appear that even Inspector Urquhart might, on reflection, have modified his strongly held earlier view that there was not on the ground that day "a man with a grain of common sense amongst them". For, in a subsequent examination in the witness box at the Commission, he gave the following replies to questions put to him:

Q. Admitting that Arrell had no experience as a tracker, if he had used the ordinary precautions any man holding the position of sergeant should have used when he found the bodies there, could he not have kept the people back for a distance of 100 yards [*ninety metres*] at any rate so as to have preserved those tracks?

A. I am very loth to blame Sergeant Arrell in the matter. There are many things that could have been done. The ground might have been roped off with a clothesline. Another thing—

Q. Our object in asking you these questions is to see whether the promotion of men to the important position of sergeant with charge of a station is just haphazard, or whether due consideration is given to their capabilities?

A. Sergeant Arrell, in my opinion, as I stated in my report, acted as he thought for the best according to his lights.

Q. You said, "The magnitude of the crime bewildered him"?

A. Yes. I think the situation was beyond him, and it might have been beyond another man, too. I should not like to say how I should feel if suddenly called upon to face a tragedy of that magnitude.

Q. And face it alone?

A. Yes.

Q. If he manifestly blundered as no competent man should have blundered, there is something wrong in the system of promotion?

A. Yes; but I think it would be unfair to say that. I think he might have done more, but he did what he thought best. He evidently attached the greatest importance in getting information to Brisbane.[9]

We may say that we consider that to be a fair assessment of the situation; for it could not reasonably be contended, in our view, that Sergeant Arrell, William McNeil or any of the four gentlemen who went out to the paddock in Mr Gilbert's buggy, or Mr Ballantyne, had not "a grain of common sense amongst them"—indeed, we think that ultimately, upon reflection, Mr Urquhart would have conceded this to be an untenable proposition. It is relatively easy for anyone, from the comfort of an armchair, after a protracted period of time and a great deal of thought, to postulate prerequisites for the successful investigation of a crime so unexpected and extraordinary; it is quite another matter, however, for one person alone to be suddenly confronted with such unanticipated and critical complications of human drama. The actions or reactions of those placed under such stress and in such unusual circumstances should not, in all fairness, be "scrutinised with an eye focussed for reproof".[10] It has been most pertinently observed that "After the event even a fool is wise. But it is not the hindsight of a fool; it is the foresight of the reasonable man which alone can determine responsibility."[11]

In addition to those black trackers who had been set to work early on the morning of 28 December, other black trackers came to Gatton. "Norman", a well known Aboriginal tracker from Crow's Nest, arrived on the morning of 29 December. "Paddy Perkins", another Aboriginal tracker was there also. The trackers examined the chain of waterholes in Moran's paddock for the traces of cast off clothing or weapons, but without result. The trackers also examined the ground in the vicinity of the sliprails and they found the head of a heavy hammer and a small riding switch. The hammer head was not stained at all. The two items found, it appeared, were of no significance whatever. Paddy Perkins, it would seem, was also something of an advocate who worked diligently on behalf of his principal client— himself. It was reported, at the time, that "Our old friend Paddy Perkins is in great form, and his well known powers of oratory have impressed some with the belief that he is inferior to none as an expert tracker."[12]

In the early days of the investigation there was no dominant clue indicating the necessity for any particular line of investigation. In such circumstances "teams of police fanned out into the district after a lead to the maniac. They learned quickly that a young man in the district recently had bought a ·380 revolver. He was held on suspicion quickly, but just as quickly cleared. A host of eyewitnesses were able to pinpoint his whereabouts to prove beyond doubt that he could not have had anything to do with the killings."[13]

The police interrogated hundreds of people. A certain Aboriginal was said to be acting in a furtive manner. He was promptly questioned but, paradoxically enough, was quickly cleared of suspicion when it was discovered by a police officer that at the time the murders were committed, he was at a place called Murdering Gully, which was a considerable distance away from Gatton.[14]

A blood-stained pillowslip was found in the Gatton region. This was investigated by the police; it proved to be an unhelpful lead. The police examined persons known to have attended the Mt Sylvia races on Boxing Day. People who promoted the dance at Gatton on the fatal night were also questioned at length. Swagmen were obliged also to undergo the ordeal of intensive interrogation. Regarding them it was reported that "It is noticeable that these men now [*since the murders*] travel in companies, and several whom I have approached state that the whole country for miles around is in a state of alarm."[15]

Dozens of people were asked to give an account of their movements on the night of the murders. It was reported at the time that,

> This ordeal is not pleasant to either examiner or examinee, but it is very necessary, and the police give every consideration to the persons whom they so examine. The man who was questioned today passed through Gatton a few days after the murder, looking for work and carrying a swag. He afterwards secured employment at Murphy's Creek, and there he was found by Sergeant Geary, who brought him down to headquarters. On being questioned after the ordeal he replied "Oh, I don't mind, the police treated me like a gentleman, and paid my fare and gave me three bob." And thus he went on his way rejoicing, bearing his swag with him. The fact of the inquiry being made into the matter of the invitations to the dance, and the circumstances of bringing a man from Murphy's Creek to question him as to his whereabouts, appear to indicate that the police are not depending entirely on sheeting home the charge of murder to the man whose movements they have been following so closely of late. Still, it is just as well not to disregard anything, and above all the police see the folly of a bigoted tenacity to one view, however strong their reasons for suspicion may be.[16]

On Wednesday, 28 December 1898, Mr Archibald Meston, Protector of Aboriginals for South Queensland, was at Fraser Island. At about 11 p.m. in the evening of that day he received a telegram from Chief Inspector Stuart requesting him to send three black trackers to Gatton. Mr Meston had had forty years' experience among Aboriginals. Upon receipt of the telegram he acted most promptly. An hour later, at midnight, he started "with three picked men out of fifty" in an open boat for Pialba. From there they caught the 7.30 a.m. train for Brisbane and left Brisbane at 9 p.m. that same day in a goods train for Gatton. They "reached Gatton practically the same day they left Fraser Island"—quite a remarkable achievement in December 1898.[17]

The three expert trackers sent were described at the time as being "smart, clean, active-looking fellows, one of whom distinguished himself in pursuit of the Kellys and another is the tracker who lately astonished Lord Lamington by following his tracks from Government House across the Domain to the *Lucinda*." Mr Meston himself confidently stated that "these men are in first class working order and will follow any track over any sort of country for any distance".[18] One certainly would need to be in "first class working order" to leave Fraser Island in 1898 in an open boat, between midnight and one o'clock in the morning, then, after a six hours' trip to the mainland, to board a train bound for Brisbane and then to leave for Gatton at 9 p.m. arriving there "practically the same day they left Fraser Island"!

When giving evidence before the Commission Mr Meston said "The three trackers I sent were three picked out of fifty, and one was the best of those that went after the Kellys in Victoria, and one of Sergeant King's favourite men. I was not likely to send any but good men." When asked by a member of the Commission (Mr John Sadleir, a retired Inspector of Police from Victoria, who had been engaged in the hunt for the Kellys) as to the name of the tracker who was in Victoria, Mr Meston replied "Wooranalie, or Barney, as he is known amongst white men. He is a specially good tracker, and the other two were excellent boys and able to track anything anywhere if they got a fair chance and were properly worked." The transcript of evidence of Mr. Meston makes quite interesting reading. Here is part of that transcript:

Q. When did you go to the scene?
A. On Friday.
Q. Three days and a half, roughly, had elapsed?
A. Yes.
Q. Did you put those boys on to try and trace tracks?
A. No. I had nothing to do with the trackers beyond sending them to the Commissioner. I took one of the boys out with me to the scene.
Q. For your own guidance?
A. Yes.
Q. Those you sent were there before you?
A. Yes—the day before.
Q. Did this boy point out anything to you?
A. Yes. The boys all had a very decided theory of their own about who committed the murder and how it was done.
Q. Did they state that they found any tracks?
A. Yes.
Q. All three?
A. Two of them—one of the Fraser Island men and a boy from Crow's Nest named Norman.
Q. What did they tell you, and did you convey that information to any member of the police or officer of police?
A. I understood the information given to me by the trackers of course would be given to the officers of police. I had nothing to do with them; I did not interfere with them in any way; it was merely for my own information that I took the boy out, because I had a very decided opinion of my own.

Q. We want to see whether the police refused to do anything after getting information of any value. Theory is of no particular value unless based on some facts. Did you yourself see any tracks about the scene?

A. One track, which was quite distinct, because it was outside the trodden area.

Q. Track of what?

A. Track of a horse.

Q. There were horses running in the paddock?

A. This was one particular track the boys knew of which had not been interfered with. It was not trodden over at all. It was away; it was back on the ridge; it went from the rails round to the scene of the murder, and round the ridge.

Q. Round the ridge?

A. To the left. As you go on the cart track to the scene, this track was away to the left, round the ridge.

Q. Looking towards Clarke's place?

(*Mr Garvin:* Clarke's place is the other way.)

Q. Did you convey any information to Inspector Urquhart with regard to what you had seen and what the trackers had told you?

A. I told Inspector Urquhart on Saturday who I thought committed the murder, and how I thought it was done, and also called his attention to several significant facts in connection with it; and I told him before leaving: "If you go outside that you will be wasting valuable time and throwing cruel suspicion upon innocent people, and find yourself in a worse position than you were in at the starting point."

Q. Did you ever put anything in writing?

A. I did. On my return to Brisbane I wrote my belief as to how the whole thing occurred, and got it typewritten, and showed it to the Home Secretary, who alone had the right to see it from me, and also to the Commissioner of Police. Outside of that I am not responsible for any statement. I was credited by the public with many statements I had nothing to do with.

Q. Inspector Urquhart says you stated to him, as you were leaving, something to this effect—that you were completely baffled?

A. That is utterly untrue. I never had a shadow of a doubt from the start up to the present time. Mr Urquhart makes some statements in his evidence which are utterly untrue. He says, in answer to question 13870, that I was there a week afterwards. I was there four days afterwards. He was asked whether I gave him any information, and he said, "No. I heard that he announced on the railway platform that he could solve the mystery in twenty-four hours." I did nothing of the kind. I am not in the habit of talking on a railway platform on a subject of that kind in that way.

Q. Or anywhere else?

A. No. All I stated is in my written statement, which I gave to the Home Secretary. He was asked if he thought it would be possible for a tracker to pick up tracks a week after an occurrence, and he said "Such a suggestion would be ridiculous." One of the finest pieces of tracking ever done in Queensland was where the tracks were picked up three weeks afterwards. That was out west from Charters Towers.[19]

Mr Meston went on, in his evidence, to allege that blunders had been made by Mr Urquhart. He said, *inter alia*,

> I pointed out to Urquhart that he was starting in a wrong direction altogether ... When I went there on the Friday, I asked him where was So-and-so and So-and-so at the time of the murders, and he said that they had all proved alibis. He took their statements without hesitation, and took no action on them. He was not even acquainted with human bloodstains. He did not even know that blood dries from the edge to the centre, in a concave form.

Subsequently Mr Meston was examined in this manner:

Q. I want to know what was the theory of your boys?

A. Four of the boys were unanimous in their theory.

Q. What was their theory?

A. That would be hardly fair to make public. The boys were unanimous about one man.

Q. Tell us how their theory led to one man?

A. Well, it involves others.

Q. Well, I won't press you. You indicated that theory to the Minister?

A. Yes. The Minister has it, and I have it.

Q. What action did the Minister take?

A. It was only given to the Minister for his own information.

Q. It was given to the Commissioner, too?

A. Yes.

Q. What action was taken?

A. No action. He did not agree with the theory at the time.

Q. The Minister, the Commissioner, and Mr Urquhart disregarded your theory?

A. Well, they did not act on it. The Commissioner was in doubt as to what action should be taken, but he was very anxious to arrive at the truth.

Q. And yet he disregarded your theory?

A. Yes; he said there was not sufficient evidence to take action on.

Q. You are not helping us with this evidence.

(*The Chairman:* We can see his report.

Witness: I will place my report at your disposal. I may say that the police did all they could. Urquhart's mistake is the whole mistake.

Mr Sadleir: There is no reason for saying that, and we have no evidence in support of that.)

Q. At any rate your theory was not acted upon?

A. No; it is a difficult theory to act upon, except in one particular direction, which can be acted upon now just as easily as then ... I am very sensitive about anything being made public where people are concerned, and, however certain I may feel about it, there is always a doubt, and it is only fair they should have the benefit of it.

Q. Then there is some doubt?

A. I have not the slightest doubt in my own mind—I never had from the beginning.[20]

It would be interesting to read through Mr Meston's report. We have searched the records of the Home Secretary at the State Archives of Queensland in an endeavour to secure this report; but we have not been successful. This is not surprising, because it will be remembered that Mr Meston, in his evidence, told the Commission that he "showed it to the Home Secretary, who alone had the right to see it from me, and also to the Commissioner of Police",[21] and that "The Minister has it, and I have it ... It was only given to the Minister for his own information."[22]

Mr Meston, of course, was not the only one to propound a theory. In those three or four days after the discovery of the bodies the murders appear to have been practically the sole topic of conversation. A reporter wrote,

The townspeople can still talk of nothing else than the outrage and if the murderers were arrested and brought into Gatton now while the excitement is at fever heat, the Police would have all they could do to protect them and prevent their being summarily dealt with by the residents. The idea that the outrage was committed by persons well acquainted with the country is growing and the general opinion now is that the murderers will be found not far from Gatton. The township presents much the appearance of a military camp. The Murphy family is well known to the Under Secretary for Agriculture as a steady, respectable family, the younger members having done nearly all the fencing in connection with The Agricultural College.[23]

Another newspaper reporter offered the comment,

During today many hundreds of persons went out to visit the scene of the tragedy, and, isolated as it is, the wonder is how the victims came to

62

drive into such a place. Of course, speculation is very rife over the matter. Some are of the opinion that when the victims proceeded along the main road that night they were met at the top of the hill near the sliprails and were decoyed into the paddock, while others hold the opinion that they were "bailed up", gagged, and brought in by force. Suffice it to say that the track was a most difficult one, and the position being so far from any residence, and off the main road, must have been most carefully planned out beforehand ... It was a strange coincidence that the legs of the three victims were pointing due west ... What, however, local residents cannot understand is how the vehicle and its occupants could have been got to the spot where they were found without leaving any other traces than the wheel tracks. The paddock is fairly thickly timbered with wattle bushes, and, as one party put it, it would be rather difficult to drive along the ridge in the day time without coming into contact with stumps or bushes, not to speak of performing such a feat at night time. Last Monday night, however, was a beautifully clear moonlight one, and the surmise is that the horse must have been led along, in the paddock, by someone, who picked his way as he proceeded, as best he could. The spot where the bodies were found, although fully half a mile [*one kilometre*] from the sliprails where the vehicle entered the paddock, is not more than a distance of twenty to twenty-five chains [*400 to 500 metres*] from the main Blackfellow's Creek road in a direct line ... From all that can be gathered it would seem that lust was the first motive which prompted the committal of the crime and that other disastrous consequences followed.[24]

Another published newspaper comment reads, "Excitement still continues, which is accentuated by the impression which generally prevails that the murderers are in our midst and probably among those loudest in their manifestations of mingled grief and indignation."[25]

The New Year came and a Gatton newspaper correspondent wrote,

Today, although it is New Year's Day, the joy which should have prevailed was absent. Gloom and sadness reign in its stead. At the Anglican and Congregational churches touching reference was made to the terrible event of last week. A largely attended memorial service was conducted by Mr Purnell in the Congregational Church.[26]

A special reporter of a Brisbane newspaper commended the efforts of the police in searching for clues and assured the public that "no stone is left unturned, no exertion is spared; careful, thoughtful men are at work, quietly and patiently following every point and every clue, and the people who look to the Police Department to unravel the tangled skein must be patient."[27] The special reporter of this Brisbane newspaper had a very high regard for Inspector Urquhart. Concerning him he wrote:

Inspector Urquhart is a splendid bushman, as good a tracker, possibly, as any of the Aboriginals employed, and an officer of indomitable energy. But, to my mind, it requires more than a bushman or a tracker or even the most complete human bundle of energy in the universe to handle this case. It requires a judge of human nature, a man of strong reasoning power, and generally high mental attainments. Those qualities Inspector Urquhart possesses, and with them an intense though quiet earnestness and tenacity of purpose ... time will, I am confident, show that the system of working out the mosaic of a complete case is vastly ingenious ... Today, I have managed to get some idea of the work being done here, and can assure the people of Queensland that it is on lines which do credit to the mental calibre of the principal officers concerned. There need be no anxiety on that score.[28]

When the Commissioner of Police sent Inspector Urquhart to Gatton he gave him no instructions but merely told him "to go up and see what was the matter".[29] Urquhart was, however, definitely appointed to take charge of the investigation on 5 January 1899. On that date, the Commissioner of Police issued a memorandum together with a "Plan of Action" which is Appendix No. 9 to the evidence taken before the Police Inquiry Commission. That memorandum and "Plan of Action" are as follows:

APPENDIX NO. 9.

Gatton, 5 January 1899.

Re the Gatton Murder.

So far the police are not in possession of information of vital importance; nevertheless, I am, as I believe are all my officers, hopeful of a successful issue. It is clear to me now, however, that to arrive at this, much time and patience will be necessary, and much arduous work will have to be willingly and intelligently carried out by the police officers and men detailed to operate under the direction of Inspector Urquhart. I am thoroughly alive to the immense difficulties that surround the mystery, and, although I am aware that at the very outset all was not perhaps done that might have been done by the local sergeant, I thoroughly appreciate the excellent manner in which the work was set about by Sub-Inspector Galbraith, and in which it has been since carried on by those acting under the direction of Inspector Urquhart, in whose hands the case is placed, and in whose ability and energy I have the fullest reliance. To facilitate the inspector's work I have created a temporary district, to be called the "Special District," the charge of which is assigned to Inspector Urquhart. The boundaries of the "Special District" and the Sub-districts within the same are shown on the maps marked and initialled by me.

W.E. PARRY OKEDEN, Commissioner of Police.

Rough memo. of "plan of action" is attached, but of course the inspector in charge may have occasion at any moment to depart from the lines laid down. I have such confidence in his judgement and discretion that he is, in emergency, empowered to act as he deems best.

Gatton, 5 January 1899.

Plan of Action.

Wire if necessary for maps and plans of district showing—

Gatton, Tent Hill, Laidley, Helidon, &c., cut up with four sub-districts, Inspector Urquhart in charge of case and district, headquarters at Gatton. Sub-Inspector White, Sub-Inspector Galbraith, Sub-Inspector Durham, each to have charge of sub-districts, say, one with Helidon or Laidley headquarters (White), one (Galbraith) Tent Hill, one (Durham) Laidley or Helidon headquarters.

Inspector to detail certain men for headquarters (Gatton), and such men and trackers as he considers requisite for each sub-district. Six picked good men to be drawn from police in colony at once to be added to strength here to facilitate work.

1. Quilter.　...　...　2. Wyer.　...　...　3.
4.　...　...　5.　...　...　6.

System of procedure to be that already adopted and now working—namely, careful examination by police officers of all persons in the district, each police officer of course working within the district assigned to him. Each officer to be supplied at once with clear "outline of case" up to date so far as known to police, together with suspicions entertained and with names and particulars or circumstances likely to be of assistance in unravelling the mystery.

All statements to be forwarded daily, or oftener if necessary, by mounted constable or other sure means to headquarters. Each officer will keep the "outline of case" carefully written up, and, in separate book, all suspicions, statements, or evidence against persons interchanging with each other every opportunity; all matters requiring quick or careful investigation or clues to be followed up. General reports of course to go to headquarters, so that the inspector may be seized at all times with every detail of consequence. Another clerk will at once be supplied to headquarters to enable the inspector to keep level with the work. The shorthand clerk and typist now here will of course remain at headquarters. The inspector in charge of the case, Mr Urquhart, is relieved from the necessity of reporting to me, as I shall keep myself up to date by frequent visits to headquarters, and by receipt of such particulars as the inspector may from time to time find time to give me.

W.E. PARRY OKEDEN, C.P.

The investigating police carried out their plan with energy. It has been reported that

Every tramp on the road within a hundred miles was arrested, interrogated—and released. Most respectable persons were interrogated, for everyone was under suspicion ... the clues were few; but they were carefully followed ... search was made for a whip which Michael Murphy had in his possession when starting out in the sulky, but it was never found; and after a careful search of the paddock the throatlash of the dead horse was found about thirty chains [*600 metres*] from the scene of the murder... The police, however, exhausted all the resources without avail... the fact is recorded that they examined over a hundred suspects, and visited no fewer than 1051 families. All they were able to bring forward was a theory which may be taken side by side with the rumours... it was not substantiated, and so did not solve the mystery, but it caused the arrest and examination of a likely suspect, who was in the vicinity on the night of the murder.[30]

That "likely suspect" was one Richard Burgess. We shall, at a later stage in the pages which follow, examine in some detail the facts relating to him.

It is evident that the police often worked under very difficult climatic conditions. On 18 January 1899, one newspaper reporter in Gatton wrote,

Terrific heat has prevailed here during the past two days. Yesterday the thermometer recorded 103 degrees [*39°C*] but today it reached 108 degrees [*43°C*]. The heat has been distressing enough to anybody, but it must have been doubly so to the police who are engaged in the active search operations. Those who are carrying on their investigations in the ranges must be experiencing a very trying time. The work put in by Sub-Inspector Galbraith and his capable body of men—Detective Adam Johnson and Constables Balaam, Perkins, Doyle, Gorman and Ward and the tracker Barney yesterday was of such a character as to almost thoroughly exhaust them.[31]

The energy of the police is indicated by the fact that, by 20 January 1899, over 3000 written statements had been taken by them in connection with the case.[32]

Moreover, there was a complete check of firearms by the police. In his evidence before the Commission, Inspector Urquhart said, "I gave very particular instructions about the rifles. I sent out men all over the district, and they went to every place and man, and had to bring in a description of every firearm, its calibre, whether they had one borrowed or whether they had sold one. That will be all there in detail."[33] The Inspector was asked by a Commissioner whether he could say whether the cartridge which had been found at the scene of the murders came from a revolver or rifle and he said,

That cartridge could be fired either from a revolver or a sporting rifle. I am inclined to think that it was fired from a sporting rifle. If it had been fired from a revolver, no empty cartridge case would have been found on the ground, because there is no necessity to unload the chamber of a revolver, whereas to fire a second shot out of a sporting rifle it would be necessary to extract the shell before the second shot could be fired.[34]

66

The police were plagued with letters from "astrologers, dreamers, palmists and others giving particulars of how the crime was committed, and how the police should work to discover the perpetrators". As at 19 January 1899, there were 639 letters on the "Astrologers' File" at police headquarters. A journalist friend of Urquhart reported an absolute gem—he wrote:

> From every part of Australia came suggestions—some valuable, some weirdly tinctured with occultism, and some just silly. Urquhart had some sense of humour. He showed me one day a letter which said: "Take a divining rod, and follow it, prayerfully, silently, and it will lead you to the very spot where the criminals are hidden, and it will point to the ringleader." We secured a divining twig, and followed it. It was a very hot, dry day, and it led us to Fred English's bar![35]

6
SOME CURIOUS CIRCUMSTANCES

The investigation of the tragedy brought to light various attendant circumstances, some of which were of a rather singular nature. The peculiarity of some of the unexplained, and seemingly inexplicable, features of the crime furnished fertile fields for rumour, reconstruction and theorizing. Over fifty years ago it was stated that "Rumours arose, and are still current, which would lift the crimes to a plane of grim passion comparable to the themes of Greek or Shakespearean tragedy —*Oedipus* or *Lear*. And to this day the tribe of newspaper correspondents is apt to break out at unexpected moments with new suggestions and facts made to fit them."[1] With the passage of half a century little has altered. We are no nearer to understanding the enigma. The mystery is as baffling as it ever was.

Attempts to unravel the tangled skein are as fascinating as they ever were. In passing, we have already referred to some of the unusual features encountered, such as the fact that the bodies appeared to have been carefully laid out and that the feet of each body pointed due west; also that there was an absence of tracks near the bodies and the ground nearby showed absolutely no sign that a struggle had taken place. But there were other curious circumstances which we will now proceed to outline.

THE CIRCUMSTANCES UNDER WHICH THE VICTIMS ENTERED MORAN'S PADDOCK ON THE FATEFUL NIGHT

These circumstances, of course, have never been established. However, they have exercised the minds of many people and have been the subject of much debate which has given rise to various theories. We have already referred to the description of the wheel tracks of the sulky given by those who observed them near the sliprails shortly after the discovery of the bodies.[2] A newspaper special reporter at the time wrote "I have interviewed all those who saw the track of the cart on the road and leading into the paddock, and they are unanimous in the opinion that the cart went right in, and the track showed no indication that it had stopped right up to the scene of the murder."[3] The same reporter two days earlier had reported:

Perhaps the most intricate problem which is perplexing persons is how the victims and the vehicle were got off the road—whether decoyed by some device, or stuck up in advance, or how? As against the latter theory, it is pointed out that there is not the slightest sign of a struggle on the road or at the sliprails. Mr McNeil, who first found the tracks, is positive that the wheels of the vehicle which conveyed them did not even stop directly in front of the sliprails, but turned off the road towards the rails at a long angle several yards away. This renders the matter more perplexing, although some think that the male victim was stunned nearer Gatton and the vehicle then driven by the murderers on to, and through, the sliprails. If so it could not be much nearer, inasmuch as people going into Gatton passed and saluted them on the road as the victims were driving homeward, and it being a clear moonlight night, saw them plainly. The whole affair is involved in the most inextricable mystery, and as one person remarked to me today, "Some people think it simple; but its apparent simplicity makes the problem more difficult for solution." It would take a "Sherlock Holmes" to unravel the threads.[4]

In the course of giving evidence at the Police Inquiry Commission on 2 October 1899, Inspector Urquhart was asked by the Chairman of the Commission how he eliminated from his mind "the peculiarity of Michael Murphy and his two sisters going voluntarily into that paddock". To this Urquhart replied "I have never held that they did go voluntarily. I never shall believe that they did." He was then asked "What train of inquiry would that put you on if they were involuntary visitors?" and he answered "That did not put me on any train of inquiry, but the idea that presented itself to my mind as against their going in voluntarily was that they went in under compulsion—that they were stuck up on the road by an armed man and compelled to go in."[5] When McNeil gave his evidence at the Commission he was also questioned by the Chairman and other members as follows:

Q. Was Michael Murphy a coward?
A. I do not think so.
Q. Do you think he went there voluntarily?
A. I think he was coaxed in.
Q. You do not agree with Inspector Urquhart that he was forced in?
A. I do not.
Q. (*By Mr Sadleir*) What do you think?
A. I think they were coaxed in.

Q. (*By Mr Dickson*) In what way?

A. By a hoax that some assistance was wanted down the paddock.

Q. What for?

A. There are a lot of reasons that might be given. They would probably be told that a man was hurt and wanted some assistance.

Q. And that would take them all down there?

A. Yes.[6]

THE MAN AT THE SLIPRAILS

The police investigation revealed that, on Boxing Night, 1898, a man was seen near the sliprails of Moran's paddock. Great efforts were made to establish the identity of this man.

Arthur Booking, aged eighteen years, when giving evidence at the Magisterial Inquiry, said that he passed Moran's sliprails at about 7.45 p.m. on Boxing Night and he saw a man standing there. He described the man as being strongly built. He said the man wore dark clothes and a dark felt hat pulled down over his face.[7]

Mrs Margaret Carroll, a widow, conducted a fruit shop in Gatton in December 1898. On Boxing Day of that year she attended the races at Mt Sylvia in order to sell fruit there. Her son John, who was thirteen and a half years old, accompanied her, as did a person by the name of Mary Callahan. Mrs Carroll and her son returned to Gatton from Mt Sylvia in the evening, in a cart. They came along the Tent Hill road and reached Moran's paddock about 8.30 p.m. Michael and his two sisters, on their way to Gatton, came up in their sulky and passed Mrs Carroll and her son. When the Carrolls were near Moran's sliprails the Murphys were in front of them. Mrs Carroll, when giving evidence at the Magisterial Inquiry, said that she saw a man standing on the left side of the road (opposite the sliprails) as the Murphys passed. Mrs Carroll said that this man stood looking after the Murphys and then he came towards her cart and passed it. He did not speak. She said that this man had a small parcel in his hand and he wore a soft hat with the brim pulled down all round. She described him as being a stout man of medium height and said that he was wearing dark clothes.[8] Young John Carroll also gave evidence at the inquest. He virtually corroborated his mother's testimony. He said that he noticed that Michael Murphy had a whip. He deposed that the man at the sliprails was wearing a grey slouch hat and a blue coat or shirt.[9]

Both Mrs Carroll and her son gave evidence before the Commission. On that occasion she said "We were coming in from the Mount Sylvia races, and when we were near the sliprails, the Murphys were in front of us, and a man was standing in the road. Both carts were close

together, and my son said, 'That is Clarke's man'." She was asked
by a member of the Commission, "Are you quite certain that when you
passed the sliprails your boy said to you, 'That is Clarke's man'?"
and she answered "Yes. I thought it was somebody from Gatton who
might want a lift, and I said to the boy, 'That is a man on foot,' and
the boy said, 'Yes, it is Clarke's man'." Again she was asked by the
member of the Commission "You are quite sure of that?" to which she
replied "Yes, that is exactly what happened." She was then asked
"Did the boy tell you the man's name?" and she responded "I do not
know that he knew his name."[10] The transcript of young John Carroll's
evidence before the Commission reads as follows:

Q. What age are you?
A. Fourteen, last June.
Q. You were with your mother coming home from some races on
the night of the murder?
A. Yes.
Q. The Murphys were ahead of you?
A. They were.
Q. What time at night was that?
A. A little after eight, but not much after.
Q. The Murphys and you were going into Gatton?
A. Yes.
Q. How far ahead of you were they?
A. Not much further than the length of this room.
Q. You saw somebody?
A. Yes.
Q. Did you say anything to your mother with regard to it?
A. Yes. After we passed him my mother said, "There is a man";
and I said, "Yes; that is Clarke's man."
Q. How did you know it was Clarke's man?
A. I thought it was by the clothes and hat he wore.
Q. Where had you seen him?
A. I had seen him several times in the cart.
Q. What was he?
A. He was working for Mr Clarke.
Q. (*By Mr Dickson*) Had you seen him often before driving in the
cart?
A. Pretty often.
Q. (*By the Chairman*) Was it a fine night?
A. A moonlight night.
Q. Did you tell the police?
A. Yes. I told Sergeant Arrell and McNeil that I saw the man.
Q. What did they say?

A. I forget.
Q. Did you tell them whom you saw?
A. They did not ask whom I saw.
Q. You did not give his name?
A. No. I did not know his name.
Q. You did not say it was Clarke's man?
A. No.
Q. Did you at any time tell the police that you saw Clarke's man?
A. When I was giving my evidence.
Q. How long afterwards was that?
A. I do not know.
Q. (*By Mr Garvin*) When you passed with your mother, and before your mother asked you who it was, did you think at the time who the man was?
A. I was not taking any notice.
Q. How did you know then?
A. I just looked up in passing.
Q. How close were you?
A. My mother was on the side of the cart next to the man, and he walked right up close to the cart.
Q. Did you get a good look at him?
A. I did not take much notice of him.
Q. How did you identify him as Clarke's man?
A. I noticed his clothes and hat.
Q. (*By Mr Unmack*) Did you know him by his figure?
A. Yes, and by his clothes.
Q. (*By Mr Garvin*) Have you ever thought over the matter since?
A. Yes.
Q. Are you still of opinion that it was Clarke's man?
A. Yes.
Q. Could you identify him?
A. I would know the man.
Q. You think there is no possibility of being mistaken about him?
A. I do not think so.
Q. (*By Mr Sadleir*) Did you identify any other man as the man who was there?
A. I did not identify Burgess. I said he looked something like the man.
Q. Did you say that he was the man?
A. No. I said Burgess looked something like him.[11]

"Clarke's man" was one Thomas Day who was employed by Mr Arthur George Clarke, the butcher. He was a stranger to Gatton and was only employed by Clarke for about four weeks. Day was interviewed by Sergeant Toomey on 30 December 1898. The man "Burgess" referred to by John Carroll was a convicted criminal named Richard Burgess. He came under the close scrutiny of the investigating police and, at one stage of the investigation, he was strongly suspected of the murders. The evidence relating to Day and Burgess will be outlined in detail at a later stage of this narrative. The activities of each, at the relevant time, are worthy of careful examination.

A person named Thomas Drew also saw a man at the sliprails that evening. Drew, a butcher, was an employee of Michael Donoghue. When giving evidence at the Magisterial Inquiry he said that he was returning to Gatton on Boxing Night from the races at Mt Sylvia. He was in the company of his employer, who was "under the influence of drink". Drew deposed that, on reaching "the culvert" (a channel under the Tent Hill road approximately 480 metres south of Moran's sliprails) at about nine o'clock, he heard a revolver shot, and saw a flash about "fifteen or twenty chains" [300 to 400 metres] ahead—at a spot between the quarry and Moran's sliprails. According to Drew "the flash went upwards". Drew, continuing his evidence, said, that on reaching the top of the hill, they met a man near the sliprails, a little further towards Gatton than where the flash was seen. This man was walking towards the town. Drew did not see the man's face. Donoghue said, "Good night", but the man made no reply. Drew looked back and saw the man, when they were three and a half metres past, make "a kind of stagger". Drew did not notice if the man carried anything, nor did he connect him at the time with the shot which was fired. Everybody resident in the district within a radius of fifteen kilometres was known to Drew; but the man that he met near the sliprails appeared to be a stranger, and unlike anyone he knew. According to Drew, the next person they met was a Miss Florrie Lowe, and after that they met the three Murphys "in a small trap, opposite Logan's house. Donoghue spoke and Michael replied." Drew and Donoghue arrived at Gatton at ten minutes to ten o'clock.[12]

Miss Florence Lowe was at the Agricultural College at Gatton on Boxing Day. In the evening she left on horseback for her parents' home at Deep Gully (which is approximately 1125 metres south of "the culvert") at 7 p.m. She went through Gatton at 8.40 p.m. and met Mrs Carroll "near O'Cleary's". As she continued on her way home she next met Pat Murphy on horseback. Then she met Michael Donoghue and Thomas Drew at Sandy Flats. She then saw Sergeant Arrell and Michael Connolly "on the hill all making for Gatton". Florence Lowe reached Moran's sliprails at 9.15 p.m. She saw there a man who came towards her. He was in the middle of the road, but moved over and passed on her right hand side at a distance of about three metres. He muttered something but she could not say what. She did not think he had a beard. He had dark clothes and was wearing a slouch hat.[13]

It is apparent then that of eight persons who passed along the road by Moran's sliprails on the night of Boxing Day, 1898, five testified that they saw the man at the sliprails. Though Mr Donoghue was understandably not called to give evidence, it seems likely that he also saw the man, for he is alleged to have said "Good night" to him. On the evidence of these witnesses it would seem that the man was seen at the sliprails on four occasions between 7.45 p.m. and 9.15 p.m. A part of the mystery, of course, is that while these people saw the stranger, the Police Sergeant, William Arrell, who was in the vicinity of the sliprails a short period of time before Florence Lowe, said he did not see any person at the sliprails.[14] Yet Miss Lowe saw Sergeant Arrell and Michael Connolly, and they saw her. Also they saw the three Murphys who were on their way back from Gatton, just as Drew and Donoghue saw them. Moreover, at the Magisterial Inquiry, Patrick Murphy described how Michael and his two sisters in the sulky passed him at 8.15 p.m. as he slowly rode along the Tent Hill road into Gatton. He then went on to say "Sergeant Arrell and Michael Connolly came along at Deep Gully and rode about a chain [twenty metres] behind me. The next person I met was Florrie Lowe. I met her at Logan's Hill, about 200 yards [180 metres] on the Gatton side of Logan's house. She was on horseback, going out towards Tent Hill. I passed her. I next met my brother and sisters in the dog cart coming back in the direction of Tent Hill; that would be about a quarter or twenty minutes past nine in the evening; they stopped and so did I and we spoke to each other; where we met was rather more than half a mile [one kilometre] from Moran's sliprails. I stopped talking with them for about three minutes. I saw them start on and I came on into Gatton; they proceeded on towards Tent Hill."[15] So it is evident that Patrick Murphy passed Moran's sliprails shortly before Florence Lowe reached them—yet he makes no mention of having seen any man at or near the sliprails.

Where was the man at the sliprails when Patrick Murphy and Sergeant Arrell passed there? It is possible, of course, that the man temporarily withdrew himself from observation as Patrick Murphy and, shortly afterwards, Sergeant Arrell and Michael Connolly came along past the sliprails. It seems unlikely that the five witnesses were deceived and that they actually saw nobody. Their testimony as to the man's general appearance (his hat and his clothes) substantially coincides. Their evidence, when examined, bears, it is submitted, the ring of reality. And what is more, one of the witnesses, the boy Carroll, said he had seen that man before "several times in the cart" and he also said he had seen him "pretty often" before, driving in the cart. The evidence of these witnesses is of a positive nature and, notwithstanding the evidence of Sergeant Arrell that he did not see any such man there, and the failure of Patrick Murphy to mention seeing any man there, we are, on the apparently available evidence, led to the conclusion that the five witnesses were both truthful and substantially accurate in regard to their observations. Even if the man did not consciously seclude himself when Patrick Murphy and when Arrell and Connolly passed the sliprails, it is by no means beyond the bounds of possibility that Patrick Murphy and then Arrell and his companion omitted to see a man who, at the particular time, was acting unobtrusively. In this regard the following observation is apposite:

> Still less are mere omissions to be considered as necessarily casting discredit upon testimony which stands in other respects unimpeached and unsuspected. Omissions are generally capable of explanation by the consideration that the mind may be so deeply impressed with, and the attention so riveted to, a particular fact, as to withdraw attention from concomitant circumstances, or prevent it from taking note of what is passing. It has been justly remarked that, "upon general principles, affirmative is better than negative evidence. A person deposing to a fact, which he states he saw, must either speak truly, or must have invented his story, or it must have been sheer delusion. Not so with negative evidence; a fact may have taken place in the very sight of a person who may not have observed it; and if he did observe it, may have forgotten it."
>
> Negative evidence is therefore regarded as of little or no weight when opposed to affirmative evidence of credible persons.[16]

There is nothing to suggest that the five witnesses were other than credible persons. Accordingly we have accepted them as such. In the circumstances, perhaps the omission of Patrick Murphy and of Sergeant Arrell and his friend to observe the man at the sliprails might well be ascribed to Patrick's mind being preoccupied at the time with the depressing prospect of recommencing work on the morrow, and to the Sergeant and his comrade being deeply engrossed in reflecting upon and discussing their punting endeavours of the day. We feel that there was a man at the sliprails that evening and we believe that he, to use the words of Mrs Margaret Carroll, "stood looking after the Murphys" as they drove into Gatton that night. We consider it most likely that this very man encountered the Murphys near the sliprails on their way home that evening. Where did this man come from? Whither did he go? What subsequently became of him? Who was he? Varied and sustained efforts were directed to finding answers to these questions. There can be but little doubt that those answers constitute the key to the lock on the door behind which lies the secret of the Gatton Mystery.

WAS THERE BLOOD ON THE SULKY?

It will be recalled that earlier in this narrative it was mentioned that one of us had interviewed a Mr Patrick Michael Quinn in early 1973. He had been at the murder scene in Moran's paddock the day that the bodies were discovered there, and he actually assisted in loading the bodies of the victims into vehicles. He had said that he particularly made a careful inspection of the dead horse and the sulky, and he found no blood in or on the sulky, nor did he see anything at all which would afford a basis for inferring that any of the deceased had met with an injury while in the sulky. Mr Quinn also stated that he saw nothing to indicate that any of the deceased had been conveyed in the sulky after having been injured at some other place.[17] It might also be remembered that earlier in this account we referred to the fact that, in his evidence at the Magisterial Inquiry, Mr Ballantyne deposed that he could not find any stains on the sulky when he examined it in Moran's paddock.[18] In his evidence at the Magisterial Inquiry, Sergeant Arrell corroborated Mr Ballantyne's evidence in this regard and his evidence was also in accord with what Mr Patrick Quinn subsequently told one of us in 1973.

It is, therefore, a curious circumstance that, when giving evidence before the Commission, Sergeant Arrell expanded on what he had formerly said at the Magisterial Inquiry in regard to his examination of the sulky. Part of the transcript of his evidence before the Commission reads as follows:

Q. Did you examine the cart to find traces of blood?
A. Yes.
Q. Were there any?
A. Not that I could see. I examined the trap again, and I saw a little tint of blood.
Q. (*By the Chairman*) How did you know it was blood?
A. I thought it looked like blood.
Q. Was there any examination of that?
A. No.
Q. Did you point it out to your superior officer?
A. Yes.
Q. (*By Mr Unmack*) Where was the cart all this time?
A. In the paddock.
Q. Was anybody watching it?
A. Yes, a constable.
Q. When did that constable turn up on the scene?
A. About five o'clock the same evening.[19]

This evidence would appear to be not only an expansion upon what he said at the Magisterial Inquiry, but it would seem to be at variance with what he said on that former occasion. The report of his evidence at the Magisterial Inquiry reads, in part:

> Sergeant Arrell, continuing his evidence, said that he thought the bodies had been dead for about twelve hours. He next examined the trap, which was about six yards [*five and a half metres*] away. He found no blood on it. He searched for tracks or weapons . . . [20]

We can find no record at all of Sergeant Arrell, while in the witness box at the Commission, being referred back to his previous inconsistent statement in this respect. Apparently what he had previously said at the Magisterial Inquiry was overlooked. It is a surprising discrepancy in his two sworn accounts of the matter and it tends to heighten the mystery.

THE SCREAMS AND THE SHOTS THAT WERE HEARD

Two witnesses who gave evidence on the opening day of the Magisterial Inquiry were Louisa Theuerkauf and Catherine Byrne. Their evidence at the Inquiry was reported as follows:

> Louisa Theuerkauf deposed: Am a domestic servant living with my brother at Deep Gully, about nine miles [*fourteen kilometres*] from Gatton; at Christmas time was employed at Mr Clarke's, a butcher, at Gatton, who resides on the Tent Hill road; know Moran's paddock on the left hand side of the Tent Hill road going from Gatton; the sliprails of that paddock are about half a mile [*one kilometre*] from Clarke's house; Mr Clarke's paddock is separated from Moran's by a road; can see Moran's paddock from Clarke's house; remember Christmas day last, but was in Gatton on Christmas evening; walked home from Gatton that evening; remember the Monday following, Boxing Day; did not come into Gatton that evening; stopped at home at Mr Clarke's; went to bed at nine o'clock; looked at the clock on the wall and saw it was that time; went to bed and was lying awake for about an hour or so; heard the clock strike ten; they keep four cats in the house; they are all Toms; after I heard the clock strike ten got out of bed because the cats were in the kitchen; got up to put them out; put the cats out through the back door of the kitchen; the door faces towards Moran's paddock; when I was at the door heard a shot go off; the sound of the shot came from towards Moran's paddock; heard two shots; there was not much time between them; they went quickly, about a couple of minutes; heard two screams; the sound of the screams came from the same direction; heard the screams about two or three minutes after the last shot; the screams were not of a child; more like a lady's scream; the wind was not blowing at the time; it was a still night; the screams

I heard were in the same tone of voice; the first scream was the loudest; heard the word "Father" only; that was all I heard; heard the word "Father" called on each occasion; heard the screams; did not hear too plain, but am sure it was the word "Father"; stood at the door and listened for about ten minutes; did not wake anyone up and tell them what I heard; went to bed; heard nothing else during the night.

To the Bench: Heard the screams come from Moran's paddock, below the hill; could not say how far away it was; did not tell anyone in the house what I had heard because I did not think of it.

Catherine Byrne deposed: Am a single woman residing with my parents at Lower Tent Hill; know Moran's paddock on the Tent Hill road; know where the sliprails are; they are on the left-hand side going towards Tent Hill; remember last Boxing Day, 26 December; it was a Monday; on the evening of that day I was at home; my home is about a mile and a quarter [*two and a half kilometres*] from the sliprails; have often walked that way so am well acquainted with the distance; between half past nine and ten o'clock of that evening was sitting on the back verandah of the house, which faces towards the Tent Hill road and Moran's paddock; was sitting there about half an hour or more by myself; when I got up from my seat on the verandah, I went inside the house; that was about ten o'clock; while I was sitting on the verandah I heard screams which were loud at first and afterwards died away; the screams came from the direction of Moran's paddock; also heard the report of a firearm coming from the same direction; the screams and the report of the firearm were very close together; that would be about half an hour or so before I went inside; took no notice of the screams and report at the time; thought it was either children at play or young people going along the Tent Hill road singing out. Judge the time was correct by the train arriving while I was on the verandah; that would be the half past nine train; the night was a calm one; there was only my father in the house with me. I went to bed and said nothing about it.

To the Bench: Could not tell the difference between a revolver and a rifle shot. The sound was pretty loud and quick.[21]

THE "IN MEMORIAM" NOTICE AND THE CHIN STRAP OF THE HORSE

A matter calculated to arouse curiosity was the discovery in Moran's paddock of what soon became known as the "In Memoriam" notice and a strap. These two items were found by a supernumerary constable, James Portley, who was performing duty at Gatton at the time. On 31 December 1898, he found

... a strap with a buckle at each end and a piece of paper—a cutting from a newspaper which he took to be the *Queensland Times*. The cutting was a memorial notice about a girl named May Cook who died at Gatton. He marked the paper and handed it over for safe keeping. He found the articles near an ironbark tree on the right hand side of the track from the sliprails to the scene of the murders and about thirty-three and a half chains [*670 metres*] from the scene.[22]

It is reported that at the Magisterial Inquiry Katie Murphy deposed that

... about twelve months before the murders, by request of Norah, she cut out of a paper a memorial notice of the girl Cook. This remained on the dresser for about two months, and she then put it into a box in her room, and never removed it afterwards. About six months ago she missed it. (Witness described the memorial notice, and identified that shown to her as similar to the one she cut from the paper. This piece of paper was found at the scene of the murder.)[23]

When giving evidence before the Police Inquiry Commission, Sergeant Toomey was questioned concerning the "In Memoriam" notice. The relevant part of the transcript of his evidence reads as follows:

Q. There was a piece of paper found tied up in a strap?

A. It was an "In Memoriam" notice. No doubt it belonged to the harness of the horse which carried the victims to the paddock. It was an "In Memoriam" notice about a person who died in the district. I questioned everybody about this notice, and they all said they knew nothing about it, but they knew the girl referred to in it. On the day of the inquiry Katie Murphy said: "I forgot to tell you that Norah cut the notice out of the paper." She said it would be nice to have, and that she had put it into a box in Norah's room. She also said: "It is not there now, and it was not there when the victims were killed."

Q. How far was this paper found from where the bodies were found?

A. About 800 yards [*730 metres*].

Q. In what direction?

A. Towards the sliprails.[24]

In a newspaper article written not long after the murders a special reporter referred to the finding of the "In Memoriam" notice of the girl May Cook who had died on 27 December 1896. Part of this article reads

This young woman had been a resident of the Gatton district, and it may have been pure coincidence, after all, that the anniversary of her death occurred a few hours after the brother and two sisters were enticed into and murdered in Moran's paddock, where the newspaper cutting was found. Press and public alike were kept in profound ignorance of this singular find, but, while the police have traced out those responsible for the insertion of the advertisement, they have signally failed to account for the presence of the cutting where it was picked up.[25]

The police may have failed to account for the presence of the "In Memoriam" notice in Moran's paddock, but another special reporter came forward with an ingenious explanation. He wrote:

Since one of the matters which the police had desired to keep secret has been made public (I refer to the discovery of the chin strap of Murphy's horse and the cutting from the *Queensland Times* of an "In Memoriam" notice of a young girl who died on 27 December 1896) no objection can now be taken to the stating of the facts in regard thereto ... These articles were lying a few yards on the right hand side of the course along which the vehicle was taken and about 309 yards [*280 metres*] or so from the sliprails. The strap, it was ascertained, was the chin strap of the harness on the horse which the victims drove on the fatal night. How it got to the place where it was picked up is, so far, of course, only a matter of surmise. It has been said that it points to the murderer or murderers having left by the route along which they entered the paddock and that the strap was dropped there by one of them. That might or might not be so. It is just possible that on the journey into the paddock one of the girls might have made a bolt for liberty. Were it so she would most likely have been pursued. Her pursuer possibly had the strap at the time, and, on securing the girl and finding that the strap had a buckle on each end, he might have discarded it for the girl's own handkerchief with which he tied her hands. It is easy to conceive that in the excitement of the moment, the strap, if it had fallen to the ground, would be forgotten, and the "In Memoriam" notice might possibly have been drawn from the girl's pocket with the handkerchief. It is known that the Misses Murphy were on friendly terms with the young girl to whom the "In Memoriam" notice referred.[26]

POST MORTEM EXAMINATION OF THE BODY OF MICHAEL MURPHY— EXAMINATION OF HIS CLOTHES

Dr von Lossberg, it will be recalled, performed a post mortem examination on the body of Michael at the Brian Boru Hotel on the afternoon of the day the bodies were discovered. Ever since that examination there had been rumours that Michael Murphy had been shot. William McNeil adhered stoutly to the theory that his brother-in-law was shot while he was in the sulky and he stated openly that there was a wound behind the ear which he believed was caused by a bullet, or else by a pointed stick. The authorities sought the consent of the Murphy family to an exhumation of the bodies with a view to finally establishing whether or not Michael had been shot. It was reported that "The Rev. Father Walsh undertook to obtain the necessary consent of the relatives, and did so with rare tact, breaking the intelligence to Mrs Murphy in his kindly sympathetic manner."[27]

Therefore, at three o'clock on the morning of 4 January 1899, a special train conveying Dr Charles James Hill Wray, the principal Government Medical Officer in Brisbane, Dr von Lossberg, the Government Medical Officer at Ipswich, and Sub-Inspector White arrived near Gatton. The train did not come right into Gatton. It pulled up between the Agricultural College station and Gatton. A vehicle was in readiness and, just as day was dawning, the party from the train proceeded to the cemetery, accompanied by the Commissioner of Police (Mr Parry-Okeden), and Sub-Inspector Galbraith. The three bodies were then exhumed, only the officials being present and a second post mortem examination was made. A bullet was found in Michael's head.

At the Commission, it was suggested to Inspector Urquhart by a member, "Do you not seem to have been unfortunate in the post mortem arrangements?" to which the Inspector answered "Exceedingly unfortunate."[28]

Dr Wray gave evidence at the Commission and his view was sought as to the thoroughness of the first post mortem examination. Part of the transcript of his evidence reads:

Q. (*By Mr Garvin*) Can you say, if a proper and careful examination had been made in the first instance, that the bullet would have been found?
A. Yes.
Q. Should such an examination have been made?
A. I made it afterwards. Had the search for the bullet been made in the first instance it would have been a very clean job, but it was a very dirty one at the second examination.
Q. (*By Mr Sadleir*) But should not a professional man have made such an examination in the first instance?
A. Yes. If anything prevented him he should have called in assistance.
Q. It was a very important omission?
A. It was a very important post mortem.[29]

Dr Wray was questioned concerning the heads of the two Murphy girls and then about other matters. This portion of the transcript of his evidence is as follows:

Q. What examination had been made of their heads?—Can you say

whether a complete post mortem examination had been made of
their heads?

A. No.

Q. Was the scalp removed in their cases?

A. No.

Q. Were you able to form any opinion as to the weapon by which
they had met their death?

A. It was a heavy blunt instrument.

Q. Could you say that there were any projections on the instrument
that had left a mark upon the scalps?

A. No. I say that about the same force was used in each of the three
cases, and it was unnecessary force. I am of opinion, also, that it
was an ambidextrous man who inflicted the blows—that is, if the
position in which Michael Murphy was found, as described to
me, was correct. A right-handed man could not have inflicted the
wound on Michael Murphy.

Q. Would it not be possible if the man had been standing on the
other side?

A. Of course, I am only going by the position described to me. I put
the man in that position, and he could not have received the
wound on the right side from a right-handed man. The girls were
struck on the left side.

Q. (*By Mr Garvin*) Could he not have received it from a right-handed
man delivering the blows from behind him?

A. No, not according to the position described.

Q. (*By the Chairman*) Did you inform any police officer of that
opinion of yours?

A. I think I gave that in evidence at Gatton.

Q. At the time you formed that opinion, did you tell any police officer?

A. Yes; I told Inspector Urquhart. I could not say positively that
I did not also tell Mr White.

Q. The reason I ask, of course, is that they would then search for a
man known to be left-handed as one of the probable murderers?

A. Yes, that was my opinion—that the man could use right and left
hand as well. I gave that opinion in my evidence; and that the one
weapon was used, by one man, in each of the three cases, with
about the same force, and with unnecessary force.

Q. (*By Mr Garvin*) Would a man receiving that first blow be knocked
down?

A. Yes; that one blow would kill him.[30]

The clothes worn by Michael Murphy and his two sisters at the time
of their deaths were examined by Dr Andrew William Orr M.D. and
it would appear that analytical tests were made of certain stains on the

clothing of the two girls and that such tests may have also been made of a stain "just inside the fly" of Michael's trousers. Dr Orr's evidence before the Commission was as follows:

Q. (*By the Chairman*) You are not a Government medical officer?
A. No.
Q. A general practitioner?
A. Yes, if you like.
Q. Are you a specialist?
A. Yes, I suppose so.
Q. You made an analytical test of the stains found on the clothing of two girls who were murdered?
A. I did.
Q. Do you form any conclusion from the results of that test as to whether or not the girls had been violated or ravished?
A. Well, I found semen on the clothes of both girls.
Q. Was there more on the clothes of one than there was on the clothes of the other?
A. I had more difficulty in finding semen on the clothes of the older girl than I had in finding it on those of the younger.
Q. Did you form any conclusion from that as to whether there was more on the younger girl than on the older?
A. No, I did not think of it; I was not asked for an opinion on that point. I was simply asked to find out if there was any semen on the clothes.
Q. Did you come to any conclusion for the aid of the police as to whether or not there was more than one man concerned?
A. The police did not want to know that from me.
Q. (*By Mr Garvin*) They did not want to know that point?
A. No, the point never came up.
Q. (*By Mr Sadleir*) You do not suggest any concealment by anybody?
A. Concealment?
Q. Yes?
A. Of what?
Q. You said the police did not want to know that?
A. Well, they did not ask me, and I suppose if they had wanted to know they would have asked me.
Q. (*By Mr Dickson*) Is it possible to distinguish the semen of one man from that of another?
A. I do not know. Perhaps the Almighty could do it.
Q. I am asking you if it is possible?
A. I could not do it.
Q. Well, that is the answer, is it not?
A. No, you asked me, "Is it possible?"

Q. (*By the Chairman*) The police did not ask you any questions definitely, except to find out whether there was semen on the clothing of the women?

A. Yes, there were certain things asked me definitely. When I was told I would be called here, I saw the Commissioner, and he distinctly gave me to understand that there were certain points he does not want mentioned—that he does not want to come out.

Q. They are still under consideration?

A. They are still, I suppose, under consideration.

Q. (*By Mr Sadleir*) Speaking as a specialist, is it quite possible to distinguish human blood from the blood of mammals—say from sheep's blood?

A. It is said you can do so.

Q. Can you do so?

A. It is said you can do so by measuring the size of the corpuscles; but if the blood were dry the corpuscles would probably be broken up, and would lose their form, and you would no longer be able to do so.

Q. Once the blood was dry you would no longer be able to do so?

A. No.

Q. A day or two would be quite sufficient to dry up blood?

A. Yes. With respect to the semen, I found it on the two garments of each of the girls, and on Michael Murphy's trousers.

Q. (*By the Chairman*) You heard Dr Wray's evidence, and that he did not think it likely in the case of Michael Murphy that there had been an involuntary emission of semen at death?

A. Yes.

Q. Do you agree with that opinion?

A. I do not know. I asked Dr Wray the same question myself.

Q. You cannot form an opinion?

A. No. I should not imagine it was. I do not see any particular reason. In fact, I am inclined to think it had occurred at that time, as if the shirt was down it would not occur where it did occur. The place where it occurred was just inside the fly; it was quite distinct.

Q. Did you form any conclusion from that?

A. No. He might have had—

Q. You did not tell the police you had formed any conclusion upon that?

A. No.

Q. (*By Mr Dickson*) Do you know that it is possible to detect blood-stains 100 years old?

A. I do not know. I have not lived 100 years yet.

Q. No, but you might have examined stains 100 years old?

A. I have not had that good fortune. What is the authority—is it the

Strand?

Q. Perhaps you would not know it, but Dr Tidy is the authority for it—did you ever hear of him?

A. The *Strand*—yes, I have heard of Dr Tidy.[31]

Part of the transcript of Dr von Lossberg's evidence before the Commission reads as follows:

Q. (*By Mr Dickson*) Did you examine the private parts of Michael?

A. I have seen the penis.

Q. Did you notice anything about it?

A. No.

Q. Did you notice any trace of semen about it?

A. No; I must say that I did not examine the parts to see if there was semen about. I had only a glance at them, but I saw that there was a swelling of the prepuce.

Q. (*By the Chairman*) In the case of death from a gunshot wound is the emission of semen a common thing in the male?

A. It happens in cases.

Q. But is it a common thing?

A. I dare say it is, but I have not experience enough to give an absolute opinion on that point.

Q. (*By Mr Dickson*) Have you ever known of any cases of death by gunshot where at the time of death there has been an emission of semen?

A. Yes, I have seen that.

Q. (*By the Chairman*) So that it would not have surprised you if semen had been found in Michael Murphy's trousers?

A. It would not. But understand this: I could not go on any further with my work. I ceased with my work there. You put yourself in my position, doing three post mortems one after the other on a hot December day in a narrow room only a few feet wide, with all those people round; and standing there, feeling the effects of the poison, you are not inclined and you cannot look for all those things. I had never taken the clothes off Michael Murphy. I had not taken his pants off, but they were open in front, and I could see that the prepuce of the penis was swelled. I had to leave the operation of the post mortem in an unfinished state.

Q. How did you account for the prepuce of Michael being swelled?

A. I did not account for it.

Q. Did you form any opinion about it?

A. I did not.

Q. You did not express any opinion?

A. No.

Q. (*By Mr Garrin*) What would cause it?

A. It could be caused by a great many things. A violent connection is a very common cause of it. Through violent connection this swelling frequently takes place, but it could be caused by a blow or anything else.

Q. (*By Mr Dickson*) From the way in which you saw Michael had been killed, would you have expected to find an emission of semen?

A. I might. I say I would. But, as I say, I did not examine that.

Q. I am not asking if you examined that, but if in that case you would have expected to find it?

A. Yes, I would certainly have looked for an emission of semen.[32]

At a later stage of his examination in the witness box at the Police Inquiry Commission, Dr Wray was questioned and answered as the following extract from the transcript indicates:

Q. Do you think the persons struck were standing up when they were struck?

A. I do not think so. I think they were down.

Q. Sitting up or lying down?

A. Lying down.

Q. (*By the Chairman*) You disagree with Dr von Lossberg. He thinks Michael Murphy was in an erect attitude, sitting or standing up when he received the bullet wound?

A. I do not say about the shooting; I say he was down when he got the bash on the head.

Q. Will you tell me if it is customary, or if you would expect to find an emission of semen in the case of a man killed by a bullet wound in the head?

A. No.

Q. Do you know of any cases of that kind?

A. No; I never heard of it. It is said to follow strangulation—hanging —but it does not always.

Q. You never heard of it in the case of death by a bullet wound?

A. No.

Q. You see, Dr Orr proved semen on the trousers of Michael Murphy?

A. Yes.

Q. You would not expect that to be an emission the result of a bullet wound?

A. No.

Q. Or that it would result from the other wound?

A. No.

Q. (*By Mr Dickson*) Would you expect to find it after a battering of the skull?

A. No; in my opinion Michael Murphy did not require any blow on the head. It was evident that the murderer wanted to make sure there was no life remaining, and he gave them all the same.

Q. You only expect to find it after hanging and not after battering of the head?

A. I do not expect it. I say it is said to be found after hanging, but it is not always found.

Q. Do you know what is the reason?

A. No; I do not.[33]

This medical testimony in regard to the seminal stain alleged to have been found "just inside the fly" of Michael Murphy's trousers is rather interesting. We have given a deal of consideration to the circumstance and we have discussed it, over several years, with various medical practitioners, one of whom is Dr J.I. Tonge, Director of Queensland's State Health Laboratory and Institute of Forensic Pathology. Dr Tonge has had many years' experience in the conduct of forensic autopsies and in the interpretation of findings. After careful consideration, we have come to the view that the finding of such a seminal stain is not of significance. The knowledge of medicine was relatively meagre until towards the last decade of the nineteenth century; the limitations of surgery were also great until that time. Be that as it may, it seems to us that the evidence of Dr Wray, to which we have referred, is, even by modern medical standards and experience, capable and worthy of being treated as reliable.

In an interview with Dr Tonge he told us that "it is well recognised that involuntary emission of semen can occur or has been observed to occur in cases of judicial hanging, suicidal hanging and accidental hanging. Never, however, have I observed it or have I seen it reported in association with a gunshot wound."[34] Dr Tonge's view was that the presence of such a stain, at such a time, and in such a place would have little significance. He instanced various ways in which such a stain could be produced and referred, *inter alia*, to an investigation by Professor A.K. Mant, Professor of Forensic Medicine at Guy's Hospital within the University of London. Professor Mant conducted a series of 500 consecutive post mortem penile swabs from the bodies of males aged between sixteen and eighty-one years. In 1962 he published his findings, which were to the effect that semen was found in the penile urethra in seventy-five per cent of those 500 cases.[35] Dr Tonge did not discount the possibility that a seminal stain, such as was apparently encountered in the case of Michael Murphy, could result from a gradual release, in ordinary circumstances, of minute quantities of seminal fluid. In answer to our inquiry, however, as to whether extreme terror would be likely to cause an involuntary emission of semen the doctor said that he thought "it would be most unlikely".

It might also be mentioned that Dr Tonge did not treat the swelling of the prepuce of the penis of Michael Murphy as being significant—he said that, after eighteen hours it could well have been a post mortem change and, therefore, of no consequence at all.

We have since had the privilege of meeting Professor Mant personally and discussing these matters with him. He is generally in accord with the views expressed by Dr Tonge; but, in the course of the discussion we had with the Professor, he advanced his own view as being that "the presence of semen or spermatozoa on the tip of the penis is a regular post mortem finding in sudden death from *any* cause".

During our meeting with Professor Mant we referred to the evidence before the Royal Commission by Dr Andrew William Orr to the effect that, in the then state of medical knowledge, it was impossible "to distinguish the semen of one man from that of another". The Professor explained the great advances made since that time within the field of exclusion serology. He said, in effect, that, with modern grouping techniques (in regard to seminal fluids), it is now possible to exclude a particular person from a number suspected of being the author of a specific specimen of semen—the one excluded being of a different group.

KISMET—THE ALLEGED APATHY AND INDIFFERENCE OF THE MURPHY FAMILY

At the close of the Magisterial Inquiry at Gatton on 24 March 1899, the presiding Magistrate, Mr A.H. Warner Shand, made a statement, which was reported as follows:

> Mr Shand said he could not allow the proceedings to close without remarking upon the extreme apathy shown throughout by the blood relations of the victims of the tragedy. With the exception of Dan they appeared to have taken no steps in the matter at all nor had they offered to assist in the search in any way even by the loan of horses of which they appeared to have plenty. They had given their evidence too in a reluctant and contradictory manner, excepting Mrs McNeil, whose evidence had been given with readiness contrasting well with the other members of her family. The family appeared to accept it all as kismet and had decided to bury the whole matter. Such conduct he considered beyond all comprehension and precedent. He had himself been accused by one of them of pressing the family because he called them to give evidence and assist in the work of unearthing the murderers. In conclusion he desired to congratulate the Police Department on having such

an officer as Inspector Urquhart who had conducted this protracted and anxious inquiry in such a patient and assiduous manner.[36]

This statement by the Magistrate was the subject of comment the following morning in a Brisbane newspaper. Part of the comment reads:

Mystery is still the last word to be said in connection with the awful tragedy which took place at Gatton three months ago. The magisterial inquiry just concluded only makes the darkness deeper; though the strange reticence of the Murphy family must add to the general feeling that something lies close at hand in the way of explanation if one could only reach it. A word of warning may perhaps be timely just here. Our very eagerness to get at the truth may incline us to give undue weight to circumstances which are capable of explanation in quite other terms than suspicion would suggest. Mr Shand has commented severely upon the way in which some of the evidence was given before him, and with apparently good grounds. Yet it is not difficult to conceive that panic, rather than knowledge of facts that ought to be revealed, has been behind the evident reluctance of the Murphy family to reply to the questions of Inspector Urquhart. Looking at the matter as dispassionate onlookers, we may conclude that something has been kept back. Yet, putting ourselves in the places of people who lack knowledge of the world, whose thoughts have never travelled very much beyond Gatton, and whose senses have been dazed by a triple murder more horrible in its details than any the colony has known, and it may be dimly realised that an unreasoning fear of, and an unaccountable aversion from, publicity have made them impossible as witnesses. Perhaps something is being concealed which has nothing to do with the murders, but which the Murphys in their panic are determined shall not be known. Half a dozen theories could be made which would reconcile their behaviour with panic-stricken ignorance. We urge this view because the temptation to believe the worst of people is always present in complications such as the one that has occupied the public mind and attention so long. And the same call for calm and dispassionate judgment may be made on behalf of the police.[37]

We hasten to say that we are completely in accord with the sentiments expressed by the writer of this newspaper article in so far as he pleads for understanding for the Murphy family. Indeed, after having carefully scanned reports of the evidence allegedly given by members of the Murphy family before the Magistrate at the Magisterial Inquiry, we feel obliged to remark that the reported evidence bears no clear indication of their alleged reluctance to give evidence; nor does it indicate that they gave their evidence "in a contradictory manner". In saying this, we are, of course, well aware that we were not present at the Magisterial Inquiry, and that Mr Warner Shand presided at that Inquiry—we readily concede that he had the very great advantage of seeing and hearing the witnesses and of being able to observe their manner and demeanour. We must confess, however, that, if the Murphys did give their evidence "in a reluctant and contradictory manner" to an extent that it was noticeable, we would have expected that such reluctance and contradiction would be reflected in the reports of that evidence. But that, as we have said, is not so; in fact the opposite appears to be the case. From a reading of reports of the proceedings it seems to us that those conducting the Inquiry, who were so very familiar with court procedure did not, at all times, show that patience and understanding which reasonably should have been shown to people, who, never having been in a court before in their lives, were obliged to go through the ordeal of being questioned in public concerning a happening the recollection of which must have been so painful to them. Following are just a few instances as illustrations of this lack of understanding of the witnesses' positions.

John Murphy, giving evidence at the Magisterial Inquiry, had deposed to William McNeil and Michael Murphy arriving at the Murphy farm on Christmas Eve. He then stated, after questioning, that McNeil had brought a bridle for Norah and a whip for Ellen. It is reported that Inspector Urquhart (who was examining the witness Murphy) said to him "It is absurd the way we have to get these things out of you."[38] Urquhart also questioned John Murphy, who was only sixteen years old, as to which members of the family attended church on Christmas Day, and, when the youth replied that he could not remember definitely who went to first Mass and who went to second Mass, Urquhart told him that it was absurd for him to answer questions in that manner.

In another instance, in his evidence at the Inquiry young Jerry Murphy said that McNeil came back to the Murphy farm with news of the murders and said to William Murphy "My God, Bill, such a mess you never saw in all your life." Jerry Murphy then said he could not remember what else was said. Inspector Urquhart is reported as having then said "Try and remember, Murphy, because this is of great consequence to everybody." Jerry Murphy then said he did not remember who McNeil said found them. After being asked a series of questions by Inspector Urquhart, the examination continued in this fashion:

Q. Did your mother say anything before she left to go to the scene of the murder?
A. She said "Whoever did it didn't mean it for my children."
Q. Did you see Mrs McNeil that day?
A. Yes.
Q. Do you remember anything she said?
A. No.

90

Q. Have you always a blank memory like this?

A. It is not bad, but I cannot remember at a time like this.

Inspector Urquhart: It is just the time you ought to remember.[39]

Another instance of what might be considered petulance occurred when Mrs Murphy was recalled on 24 March 1899, to give evidence at the Inquiry. The incident is reported as follows:

> Mrs Murphy was recalled. She asked what she was wanted for as she had already given her evidence.
>
> *The Bench:* You have been subpoenaed to give further evidence.
>
> The witness was sworn.
>
> *Urquhart:* Did you kiss the book?
>
> *Witness:* Yes, what else would I do.
>
> *Urquhart:* Did you?
>
> *Witness:* Yes.
>
> Witness then went on to depose how she put Mrs McNeil to bed on the night of the murders.
>
> *Urquhart:* What side did you put her?
>
> *Witness:* She always slept on the front of the bed.
>
> *Urquhart:* Don't fence with the question. What side did you put her?[40]

In regard to this incident two observations might be made. First, it is not, and was not in 1899, necessary for a witness being sworn on the Bible or Testament to kiss the copy of the book by way of assent. This was commonly done; but it was not a legal prerequisite to the administering of an oath. The person to whom the oath was administered was "bound by the oath administered provided the same shall have been administered in such form and with such ceremonies as such person may declare to be binding".[41] In any event, Mrs Murphy apparently did kiss the Bible as was the custom. She showed, it would seem, no indication that she would not submit to authority or formality. It would appear that Inspector Urquhart was rather over watchful of her in this regard. The second observation which might be made is that it seems to us to have been unnecessary to accuse her of "fencing" with a question. The fact is that Mrs Murphy was barely literate, and the notion of her "fencing" with questions in a witness box when being examined before a Magistrate is preposterous, if not ludicrous. One might reasonably think that Mrs Murphy's knowledge and understanding of "fencing" was confined to what she had heard from her husband and her sons concerning ironbark posts being sunk into the ground—the younger members of the Murphy family "having done nearly all the fencing in connection with the Agricultural College".[42] The feelings of Mrs Murphy, and the extent to which she was upset by what had befallen her, may very well be gauged from a reading of the transcript of her evidence before the Commission. Part of that transcript is as follows:

Q. We are inquiring, Mrs Murphy, into the general conduct of the Police Force and we understand that you wish to tender some evidence to us regarding the unfortunate occurrence that took place at the end of last year. Will you tell us what you want to say?

A. I want to say that I was accused of keeping something back.

Q. By whom?

A. By the police and by the man who was on the bench.

Q. We have nothing to do with the gentleman who was on the bench. Who accused you of that?

A. The police; I don't know who they were.

Q. Was it an officer of police?

A. They did not say it out plainly, but they wanted to make me say something that I did not know anything about.

Q. In what manner?

A. Bringing me in here and accusing me of something of which I did not know, and saying that I knew more than I wanted to say.

Q. Do you remember the exact words they used?

A. I don't remember what they said, except that I knew it was a family affair.

Q. Do you make a general accusation against the police?

A. Yes, against a few of them—against the inspector who was on the bench and who accused me of that.

Q. No inspector was on the bench.

A. He was in the Court.

Q. We all know you were very upset at the time, Mrs Murphy, but you are making serious accusations, and we should like to try and indicate the individuals that you are accusing of accusing you of keeping something back which might have led to the identification of the criminal.

A. I think it was Mr Shand who accused me of that, because I saw it in the paper.

Q. He is the Police Magistrate?

A. Yes, and there were members of the police there as well.

Q. Do you remember where the police were stationed who accused you of this?

A. They were here about Gatton. They were the detectives and Mr Urquhart. He came to me and wanted to make me say something that I did not know about.

Q. (*By the Chairman*) In what way did he try?

A. By asking me several things that happened that night—what I said to my children and what they said to me; where my husband was; when he went out and when he came in; and they made him take off his boots, so that they might examine them. I never saw anything like it.

Q. All you complain of is the way in which Inspector Urquhart talked to you?

A. Yes, and for saying that I kept something back, which I did not. I can declare before my God that if I knew half a word that would show who the guilty parties were I would speak it. You would think I was something unnatural the way I was persecuted by the police. My heart was sore and broken enough without them bothering me.[43]

One can readily appreciate the immense emotional trauma which Mrs Murphy experienced in the death of three of her children in such dreadful circumstances on the one evening. On top of this, she had to cope with questioning by newspaper reporters who came to her home, and with the subsequent interrogation of herself, her husband and her family by police investigators. Later she was examined in the witness box at the Magisterial Inquiry and subsequently before the Commission. She had been through a most painful and trying experience. It indeed must have been an ordeal for her to be so closely questioned by the police and to have realised that the thoroughness of the police investigation meant that even her husband would have to remove his boots so that they could be examined. No doubt Mrs Murphy also knew that, following upon Mr Ballantyne's evidence at the Magisterial Inquiry in relation to tracks of "a small unshod pony hoof" allegedly seen by him in Moran's paddock, a pony belonging to the Murphy family was brought into Gatton the very next day to enable its hoof prints to be compared with those said to have been seen by Mr Ballantyne.[44]

The police, of course, had their duty to perform and they were obliged to consider every aspect. Apart from Mr Ballantyne's evidence, they had also to take into account the evidence of Louisa Theuerkauf, who said that on that Boxing Night of 1898 she distinctly heard shots and screams of "Father, Father". That is admittedly a circumstance to be weighed. But, even assuming the accuracy of Miss Theuerkauf's observations in regard to the words she alleged she heard used, this seemingly unusual feature does have a ready explanation. For surely it is by no means unreasonable to suppose that a young single girl, in the transport of extreme terror, might well be likely to call for her father—her paternal protector from childhood. All in all, when all the circumstances are examined (including the circumstance that no one at the Murphy farm that evening could reasonably have predicted that the dance at Gatton would be cancelled), it seems to us that Miss Theuerkauf's evidence is by no means as significant as it first might appear. One thing that strikes us as being strange is that apparently not one of the Murphys was asked at the Magisterial Inquiry whether Mr Murphy was addressed by his daughters as "Father". There is not the slightest thing to indicate that Miss Theuerkauf was doing other than giving truthful evidence at the Inquiry. It is, however, interesting to note that in early January 1899, a Gatton correspondent of a Brisbane newspaper reported "I have run down the story that the domestic servant in the employ of Mr Clarke, near the scene of the murder, heard screams on the night of the murder. The girl undoubtedly made the statement and it was reported in the *Courier* in the early accounts of the tragedy; but now she has somewhat modified her statements and it is doubtful whether she heard any screams at all."[45] We have no means, of course, of knowing what was in her original statement. Nor is any indication given as to what extent she was alleged to have modified that statement.

Inevitably tension was created by the fact that the perpetrator of the Gatton crimes had not been discovered. This tension was heightened by the earnest endeavours of the investigating police officers to obtain a significant clue at all costs. It is not unnatural for them to have felt frustrated and surprised that such a terrible crime could have been committed in such a small community without any real indication as to who was the perpetrator. Such unaccountable circumstances are calculated to generate suspicion that vital information is being withheld.

In retrospect, it is evident that everyone connected with the investigation was endeavouring to act very properly and fairly. But at the time there were surely moments when there was not complete rapport between the examiners and those being examined in the witness box. An instance of this was when Daniel Murphy (senior) was being questioned at the Inquiry before the Magistrate in relation to his belief that McNeil went to bed at about 9.30 p.m. on the night of the murders and did not go out afterwards. Mr Murphy was a man who could neither read nor write, and he was questioned and answered as follows:

Q. What reason have you for thinking he did not go out afterwards?
A. I never saw him go out afterwards.
Q. How do you know he never went out?
A. He usually goes to bed before me.
Q. Could McNeil have left the house afterwards without your knowledge?
A. I don't believe he could.

94

Q. Why?

A. I could hear him go out, I believe.

Thereupon it is reported that the Police Magistrate interposed by asking the questions:

Q. Why cannot you answer these questions straight out instead of saying: "I don't believe this and I don't believe that"? Surely you can answer a straight question?

Inspector Urquhart then resumed the role of questioner and the reported examination of Daniel Murphy continues:

Q. Don't you sleep at night?

A. Not until after twelve o'clock.

Questioned as to why this was so witness said he had previously been engaged in work which afforded him only a limited time for sleep.

Inspector Urquhart: Is that not all the more reason why you should sleep when you get the chance?[46]

It is not reported whether Daniel Murphy made any answer to this question. He might well have remained silent preferring not to answer that which we consider to have been a comment rather than a "straight question".

While he was giving evidence at the Magisterial Inquiry, Daniel Murphy was asked by Inspector Urquhart "If you knew or suspected anybody of being guilty of the murder would you give information against him or them?" and he answered "Yes; if it was the highest man in the land I would endeavour to bring him to justice, just as I would the poorest man in the land. If it were the King of England, I would have him brought to justice." At this stage, it was reported, "the witness broke down and began to bemoan the loss of his children".[47]

It might justly be remarked that a thorough examination by the investigating officers produced nothing to suggest that the Gatton tragedy was a "family affair" or that the Murphy family were "keeping something back". There is nothing to suggest that the Murphys would not have done everything in their power to assist in discovering the murderer or murderers. It seems to us to be natural for them, in the circumstances, to have resented suggestions that they were withholding important information or shielding any person. The friction apparent between Mrs Murphy and Inspector Urquhart was, it seems to us, caused basically by a clash of cultures—each was pursuing the same end—a successful outcome to the investigation. But Urquhart and Mrs Murphy had totally different backgrounds. Urquhart had a typical British military background and education. The Royal Commissioners described him as "an officer of cultivated intelligence, but of an impulsive and exacting temperament".[48] Mrs Murphy was a devout Irish Catholic who had not been highly educated. Any fair minded person who has carefully studied the events in which these two persons participated could not fail to hold each of them in the highest estimation. It is not unlikely that Mrs Murphy would have viewed Inspector Urquhart as the epitome of British authoritarianism and have considered herself as protector of her family. The drama of their confrontation before the Royal Commissioners was brought to finality with a dialogue that was quaint but fitting:

Q. (*By Inspector Urquhart*) Were the questions which were put to you, and from which you gathered that I thought you were keeping something back, not put to you in the courthouse in the presence of the Police Magistrate?

A. Yes, at the police court.

Q. And the magistrate was on the bench at the time?

A. Yes; and you were present also, and stiff and bold you were.[49]

The reader will recollect that, earlier in our pages,[50] we referred to Inspector Urquhart's report (which was not made public), and we mentioned that there was one matter which we know *was* mentioned in his report. We said that later we would refer to that matter with considerable satisfaction, and we do so now.

Urquhart, when giving evidence before the Commission, did reveal publicly before the Commission that there were no reasonable grounds for suspecting the Murphy family. Inspector Urquhart did this without invitation—he did it fairly and gladly, and that he did so, is to his very great credit. We feel the accuracy and cogency of his evidence on this score cannot be questioned whatsoever. We feel his assessment is patently a correct assessment and we feel that this part of his evidence deserves to be given the greatest prominence possible. The relevant passage of the transcript reads:

Q. Did you search the Murphys' place?

A. No.

Q. Who did?

A. I do not know that there was any systematic search at the Murphys' place at all. That brings me to a matter that I am glad to have an opportunity of mentioning, and that is that I have never seen any reasonable ground for suspecting the complicity of the Murphy family in this tragedy. I have stated that in my report, and I have stated it all along.[51]

After a careful appraisal of all the circumstances of the matter known to us, we unhesitatingly say that there is not a scintilla of evidence to arouse a suspicion as to the complicity of the Murphy family; indeed every circumstance points to the contrary. Of that we have not the slightest doubt.

THE IMPRINT OF CLOTH AND THE FACSIMILE

This is a most intriguing and fascinating circumstance. It is calculated to excite the greatest interest and curiosity. So far as we have been able to discover, it has never before been alluded to in any published article. It was not referred to at all at the Magisterial Inquiry. Indeed, there was, at the Royal Commission, a concerted effort to keep news concerning it from being made public. But a careful reading of disjointed parts of the transcript of evidence taken at the Commission has enabled us to bring it to notice now.

We call the reader's mind back to 27 December 1898, when, at the Brian Boru Hotel in Gatton, Sub-Inspector Galbraith examined the clothes the victims were wearing at the time of their deaths. He also examined the bodies. In his evidence before the Commission he said "I found certain peculiarities."[52] On the following morning Inspector Urquhart arrived in Gatton and inspected the clothing of the victims. It will be remembered that, in his evidence before the Commission, Urquhart said "I inspected the clothing, and saw things there which were gone into afterwards, but unfortunately with no successful result. There is one very striking matter, which I do not think should be made public even now", whereupon one of the Commissioners said, "Very well, don't mention it."[53] Both these officers had noticed, we feel no doubt, the "imprint of cloth and the facsimile".

To present this evidence clearly it is necessary now to turn to parts of the examination of other witnesses. Let us turn first to the evidence of Dr von Lossberg before the Commission on 14 October 1899. The doctor was being examined by one of the Commissioners, Mr Dickson, concerning his examination of the body of Michael Murphy. The transcript at this juncture reads:

Q. Tell me what you found on his left wrist?
A. I found a purse in his hand, and a strap between the hands. They were laid there—I did not put them there. They were laid as they had been on the ground.
Q. Never mind that. Did you find any marks on his left wrist?
A. That does not belong to a post mortem. If I have no suspicion, it does not belong to my examination.

Q. If there were certain marks found on that wrist, you do not know whether they were there or not? You have no recollection?

A. No.

Q. Did you find anything also on Michael Murphy's left forearm?

A. Nothing to cause death, or anything like that.

Q. Did you examine the girls' clothes?

A. I did, certainly.

Q. Did you find anything on their clothes?

A. I gave all this in my evidence. They were torn and bespattered with blood. I told the sergeant to take care of them.

Q. Did you examine their petticoats?

A. I did.

Q. What did you find on Norah's or Ellen's petticoats?

A. Blood.

Q. Anything else?

A. Hairs.

Q. Anything else?

A. Dirt.

Q. Such as human excrement. Anything else? Did you find any peculiar marks? I hope the Commission will understand I am not asking any trivial questions. Did you find any peculiar marks on the petticoats?

A. Yes; all over the petticoats there were blood, dirt, hairs.

Q. Is that all?

A. Yes.

Q. Would it surprise you to know that on Michael Murphy's left wrist there was the exact width of a strap?

The Chairman: He says he did not look for anything, and did not find it.

Q. (*By Sub-Inspector Galbraith to Witness*) Would it surprise you to know that on Murphy's left forearm and on Norah's thighs there was a distinct impression, and the *facsimile* of that was marked in blood on the petticoat?

The Chairman: The fact is that the doctor told you that the post mortem is not complete.

Sub-Inspector Galbraith: Very well; I will not ask any more.[54]

It would appear that the Chairman, His Honour Judge Noel, preferred to have the matter dropped at that stage.

We must now consider part of the evidence given by Sergeant Toomey before the Commission on 2 October 1899. The Sergeant was being examined in regard to the inquiries he had made concerning a suspect named Thomas Ryan. The relevant part of the transcript reads:

Q. (*By the Chairman*) Were there no firearms to look for?

A. There were, but he had never been seen with any. All inquiries were made in that direction without finding any trace of anything to lead to the belief that he had anything to do with the murder.

Q. (*By Mr Dickson*) You know that the imprints of a certain kind of cloth were found?

A. Yes.

Q. Would it not be well if you could find any cloth like that?

A. I believe a good many articles of clothing would make an impression of that description, but it would want to be of a particular pattern.

Q. Would it not be necessary to search for that pattern?

A. I went to the tailor there and asked him what kind of clothing he made, but I could not find it was anything Ryan had worn.

Q. I don't suppose that tailor makes all the clothes worn there?

A. No; but in a country place like that anybody else knows what another person wears.[55]

Dr Andrew William Orr M.D., the analyst, gave evidence, it will be remembered, before the Royal Commission. During his examination he was asked by the Chairman "The police did not ask you any questions definitely, except to find out whether there was semen on the clothing of the women?" To this question Dr Orr replied "Yes, there were things asked me definitely. When I was told I would be called here, I saw the Commissioner, and he distinctly gave me to understand that there were certain points he does not want mentioned —that he does not want to come out." The Chairman asked "They are still under consideration?" and the doctor answered "They are still, I suppose, under consideration."[56] Having regard to this interchange, we are inclined to believe it very likely that Dr Orr, the analyst, had in fact engaged in tests on the facsimile or imprints on the petticoat or petticoats.

It would seem that the inference which might reasonably be drawn from the imprints on Norah's thighs, the imprint on Michael's left forearm and the "facsimile" imprint on the clothing, is that the murderer, wearing a particular type of trouser cloth, had left a distinct impression on the bodies of Norah and Michael and on the clothing (petticoat) of at least one of the girls. That imprint was, most assuredly, the identifying characteristic of the perpetrator of the outrage. It is fascinating to reflect that here the investigating police officers had actually in their possession the "mark of Cain"—the very signature of the fiend.

How strenuously must those police officers have toiled to identify that imprint, to unearth and proclaim the author of that signature.

Can we not picture that impulsive officer, that restless man, that person "of indomitable energy"—Frederick Charles Urquhart? How frustrating, how tantalising must he have found that imprint, that facsimile! How forcefully must he have striven to—"with Fate conspire/To grasp this sorry Scheme of Things entire."[57]

7
OTHER ASPECTS

We have already referred to the plan devised by the police administration whereby a "Special District" of Gatton in the charge of
Inspector Urquhart was created with Sub-Districts being established
at Laidley, Helidon and Tent Hill, each under the control of a Sub-
Inspector.[1] Camps were set up at these latter centres from which
contingents of mounted police conducted their inquiries and search
operations. It is evident that intensive investigations were carried out
over a wide area with commendable energy and attention to detail.
The whole exercise must have placed very considerable strains upon
the manpower and other resources of the colony's relatively small
police force. Working on the theory that the murderer was most
likely to be a local resident, the police ensured that bills conveying
notice of the Government's offer of £1000 reward were widely dis-
seminated and prominently displayed throughout Gatton and
surrounding districts. A Brisbane newspaper of the time informed
its readers that "Every public building in the district, the corner posts
of fences on the roads, trees at the crossing places of streams and,
indeed, every prominent place bears the notice of reward and
pardon."[2]

The Commissioner of Police, Mr W. E. Parry-Okeden, and the
Chief Inspector, Mr J. Stuart, were active in the direction of the
investigation. They received regular reports from Urquhart, and both
visited Gatton on numerous occasions. The extent to which the
Commissioner was involved in the investigation can be gauged from
the fact that between 1 January 1899 and 31 May 1899, he was at
Gatton for periods totalling twenty-one days.[3]

Much of the work associated with the taking of statements and the
interrogation of persons in and around Gatton was undertaken by
Sub-Inspector Galbraith and Sergeant Toomey, who was a member
of the Brisbane detective force. Percy Galbraith, who was forty-
four years old at the time of the murders, was born in England and had
been educated for a military career, but instead followed his fortunes
abroad. He migrated first to New Zealand, where for five years he

served in the Armed Constabulary, and then he moved to Australia. He joined the Queensland Police Force in 1883 at the age of twenty-nine.[4]

Michael Toomey, at the time of his assignment to the Gatton investigation had been in the Police Force for almost eleven years. Both were experienced investigators.

A strange and distinctive feature of the Gatton murders, and one which certainly frustrated the police, was the absence of any really tangible clue. There was apparently no dominant fact or thing which pointed unerringly towards any identifiable person as a suspect. Nor was there anything (apart from "the imprint of cloth and the facsimile"), which even suggested to the investigators a line of inquiry in any particular direction. Several objects were found, in respect of which the police pursued relentless investigations; but in each case their inquiries came to a dead end. These objects were a shoe, two letters and a piece of paper which had been used as a "pipe stop".

The shoe, which was found in a waterhole at the culvert on the Tent Hill road, was a well worn man's canvas shoe with an almost new brown lace. Initially the police attached much significance to this discovery, which they linked with the suspect Richard Burgess. However, on comparing it later with the boots worn by Burgess, they found it to be of a larger size. The police made extensive inquiries in an endeavour to trace the owner of the shoe, and to find out where the brown lace had been sold, but they met with no success. It was ascertained that a gang of men had been working on the road not far from the culvert a short time before the murders and it was thought possible that the shoe had been discarded by a navvy and thrown into the culvert.[5]

Frank Moran, a farmer, and one of the owners of the paddock in which the murders were committed, deposed at the Magisterial Inquiry that, while returning to his farm from the Mt Sylvia races at about 3 a.m. on 27 December 1898, he heard a loud noise at the culvert like "something rushing into the water or bushes".[6]

In the course of a search made of Moran's paddock shortly after the discovery of the victims' bodies two letters were found which momentarily raised the hopes of the police. These letters were addressed to a man named Loney. Inquiries revealed that Loney, who had at one time lived in an hotel at Gatton kept by relatives of the girl May Cook to whom the "In Memoriam" notice referred, died at an advanced age in the Ipswich Hospital about two years before the Gatton murders. It appears that Loney was possessed of some correspondence concerning money coming to him from a deceased friend abroad, and at the time of Loney's death two of these letters were missing. Despite a close search they were never recovered, until they most mysteriously turned up in Moran's paddock about two years later.

It was ascertained that while in the hospital Loney became friendly with a man named Burke, who was also an inmate at the time and occupied a bed near Loney. The acquisition of this information greatly interested the police because it was known that the name Burke was an alias frequently used by Richard Burgess. However, once again a promising clue proved to be of no significance. It was established that the man Burke was John Burke who had worked for Mr E. McDonald, a hotel licensee at Esk. Strangely enough, John Burke had died early in January 1899, at about the time the police were endeavouring to establish his identity.[7] It was never established how the letters got into Moran's paddock.

The "pipe stop" was also found in Moran's paddock. It had been fashioned from a sheet of the official memorandum paper of the Gatton Agricultural College.[8] In his evidence before the Magisterial Inquiry at Gatton on 6 March 1899, in response to a question in that regard, Daniel Murphy said that he and some of his sons smoked, but Michael and McNeil did not. He never used a piece of paper to stop his pipe.[9]

The police considered carefully every scrap of information they could unearth and followed up every reasonable suggestion and every lead. On 5 January 1899, McNeil passed to the police the pieces of a torn letter which he found "a mile [two kilometres] beyond the Tent Hill post office". When the fragments were pieced together the letter read—

My dear brother,

I am writing you these few lines hoping you are quite well as I am. I have been on the ground of the murder and I can see that the police and black trackers have not been to Campbell's paddock yet. I told them of it.

The letter broke off abruptly at this point and bore no signature. The police searched Campbell's paddock, which was a field of about forty hectares, three kilometres south of Gatton, but nothing of significance was discovered.[10]

A few days after the murders a Mr Walter Hargreaves, an ironmonger in Gatton, reported that he had, a short time before, sold a box of ·380 cartridges. He also claimed that when checking his stock of cartridges he discovered a box of this particular calibre in which two cartridges were missing. The police investigated but apparently their inquiries yielded nothing to assist them.[11]

Another matter into which the police apparently made extensive inquiries was a report that, late on the night of Boxing Day, 1898, two mounted men rode into Helidon, called at the hotel there, where they had drinks, and then rode on. It was said that the horses of these men were "very much heated" and they apparently had been ridden hard. It seems that information regarding these two men was not received until some considerable time after the murders. When asked at the Police Inquiry Commission when he first heard of the matter, Inspector Urquhart replied,

> I heard of it, I think, towards the end of April. I am not quite sure as to the date. It was about that time. I would like to say I got that information some time after I had written the report on the murders. That information has modified the views I expressed in the report to some extent. I will go this far and say that in these two horsemen is the most likely clue which has been struck yet. Of course the matter has been kept very quiet. We kept it so quiet hardly anybody knows about these horsemen and I want it kept quiet.[12]

Evidently the search for the two horsemen proved fruitless. One can only conjecture as to whether they ever existed.

In the gullies of Moran's paddock and of adjacent paddocks there were a number of waterholes and the police thought it possible that one of these might hold the key to the solution of the crime. The firearm used by the murderer was not found at the scene of the crime. Also, a whip belonging to Daniel Murphy which Michael was known to be carrying in the sulky was missing. It was decided to search the waterholes in an endeavour to find the whip, the firearm, a garment, or anything else the killer might have discarded. This represented an arduous task, for each waterhole had to be manually pumped out and then the mud at the bottom dug up. A "double action three inch [*seventy-five millimetres*] pump worked by a lever" was requisitioned and a party of constables and black trackers set to the formidable assignment. The pump, it seems, was hardly adequate for the work, for it frequently broke down, but the police and trackers eventually completed the back-breaking task. Their labours were in vain. With the exception of the canvas shoe found at the culvert, the waterholes yielded only water and mud. To exacerbate the frustration of the police the Press was somewhat critical of the delay in the commencement of the pumping operations and expressed "surprise that such an apparently inadequate pump was sent from Brisbane".[13] Despite an intensive search which continued over a long period of time neither the whip nor the firearm was ever found.

The motive for the murder of the Murphys was a subject upon which there was enduring conjecture. The public, not only in Queensland but throughout Australia, followed the newspaper accounts of the crime, the police investigation and the court proceedings with avid interest, and discussed them endlessly. Everybody had a theory.

1. Mr and Mrs Murphy.

2. A group of some members of the Murphy family. Mr and Mrs Murphy are in the front row with Katie on the extreme right, then Ellen, Norah and Polly.

3. Michael Murphy.

4. The Murphy farmhouse at Tent Hill, near Gatton, 1898.

5. William McNeil.

6. Richard Burgess.

7. The murder scene — Moran's paddock, 1898. Norah's body was found at the base of the large spotted gum on the right. McNeil's sulky can be seen with a broken right-hand shaft and close to the left-side of it are the horse's legs which were removed so that its body could be taken away for boiling down to recover the bullet. Paddy Perkins, the black tracker, is in the foreground; the bodies of Ellen and Michael were discovered lying slightly to his right-hand side.

3.

4.

5.

6.

7.

8. The Tent Hill Road and Moran's sliprails in 1898. A horse-drawn vehicle can be seen passing through the sliprails.

9. The victims' funeral at the Roman Catholic church in Gatton on 28 December 1898.

10. The Murphy children's burial in the Gatton cemetery on 28 December 1898.

11. The Monument to Michael, Norah and Ellen Murphy in the Gatton cemetery.

12. The main street of Gatton, Queensland, in 1898, looking south.

13. W. E. Parry-Okeden, Commissioner of Police for Queensland at the time of the murder enquiry.

14. The main street, Railway Street, in Gatton, Queensland, in 1977, looking south.

15. F. C. Urquhart, head of the Criminal Investigation Branch at the time of the Gatton murders, 1898.

While most believed the circumstances pointed clearly to lust as the motivation, some held that the murderer was basically actuated by a maniacal craving for revenge. In support of this theory they cited the incredible brutality to which the victims were subjected—such as the force of the blows rained upon them, the strangulation of Norah with the hames strap and even the slaying of the horse.

While the motive of lust is certainly the more natural and feasible theory, it is apparent that the police did not entirely discount the possibility that the killer was motivated by revenge. They made careful inquiries into the background of the Murphy family, their business dealings and the extent and nature of their intimacy with their friends. This much is evident from an examination of the newspaper reports of the evidence given at the Magisterial Inquiry. At the Inquiry members of the Murphy family and those witnesses who were acquainted with them were asked if they knew of anyone who bore them ill-will, or had a grudge against them. No one did. Everybody, it seems, liked the Murphys and held them in the highest regard. As has been mentioned previously, the police inquired into Michael Murphy's activities during the ten months he spent in the Mitchell Sub-District as a special constable during the shearing strike of 1891. This was a time when hatreds flared and grudges were forged, but Michael appears to have made no enemies. At the Magisterial Inquiry Daniel Murphy was questioned in relation to this matter and deposed that Michael, on his return from the West, had never said that he had got into any trouble out there and he thought that had Michael been threatened he would have mentioned it.[14]

Mary Murphy was questioned at the Magisterial Inquiry as to whether she knew of any person harbouring a grudge or any ill-feeling against her or her family. She said she did not, but related details of an incident which occurred many years before when the family was living at Spring Creek. The incident concerned a female schoolteacher (whom she named) who was removed from the Spring Creek School after Mrs Murphy had complained of her conduct to the Education Department. Mrs Murphy deposed that "letters were written to the newspapers concerning the matter" and on one occasion the teacher had called at the Murphy home and had tried to get Norah to sign a document. Continuing, Mrs Murphy said that she had quarrelled with the schoolteacher who was "very bitter". She denied that she had heard subsequently that the schoolteacher's brother had said that he "would have revenge even if it were ten years hence" but she deposed

16.   The sliprails in Moran's paddock photographed in 1962. The original posts still stand but the sliprails have been replaced by a wooden gate. In 1976 the area was levelled and today a council depot stands in the vicinity of the former sliprails.

17.   Moran's paddock photographed in 1977. The large spotted gum still stands on the right of the picture. One of the authors, Desmond Gibney, is in the foreground.

18.   The culvert on the Tent Hill Road, Gatton.

105

that she had heard that the schoolteacher's sister had said so.[15]

Mention was made previously, in Chapter 4, of the fact that at 2 a.m. on Wednesday, 28 December 1898—less than seven hours after his arrival in Gatton—Sub-Inspector Galbraith was examining a suspect for the murders. This suspect was a man named Thomas Joseph Ryan, a labourer and drover, who lived in Gatton with his parents.

Soon after the discovery of the outrage a hotel keeper in Gatton named Mortimer suggested that Ryan might have been the murderer. When Galbraith arrived on the evening of 27 December, Sergeant Arrell told him that Mortimer wished to see him.[16] Galbraith went to Mortimer's place, about 90 metres from the railway station. Mortimer told Galbraith that he had not seen Tom Ryan from four o'clock on the afternoon of 26 December, and he had a suspicion that he was the man, as he had threatened Mrs Murphy's, and the girls', lives.[17] Galbraith had Ryan brought to the police station where he interrogated him and "stripped and examined him at his own wish". He then let him go.[18]

It appears that suspicion was cast upon Thomas Ryan because it was known that some years previously he had feuded with Mrs Murphy over his association with her eldest daughter Polly. At the Magisterial Inquiry in Toowoomba on 23 March 1899, Polly McNeil was examined by Inspector Urquhart regarding her association with Ryan and her evidence was reported in these terms—

Q. Do you know Tom Ryan?
A. Yes.
Q. Before you met your present husband there was some sweet-hearting between you and Tom Ryan?
A. Yes.
Q. How was it that did not come to anything?
A. I don't know.
Q. Did you break it off?
A. It died out between us.
Q. Was there not a bit of a row before it died out?
A. We often had those.
Q. Was there not one of your mother's?
A. Yes.
Q. Did Tom Ryan have a "down" on your mother over it?
A. I don't think so.
Q. Did he ever threaten her?
A. I never heard him.
Q. Did anybody in the family ever tell you he did?
A. No.

Q. Is it true your mother gave you a beating for going with Tom Ryan?

A. Yes.

Q. You still went with him after that?

A. Yes.

Q. Did not Ellen carry letters from Tom Ryan to you?

A. I think she did.

Q. And he lent you his horse?

A. Yes.

Q. You kept it at your place without your mother knowing it?

A. Yes.

Q. Was Tom very much annoyed when you married McNeil?

A. I do not think so.

Q. Did not Norah want you to break it off with Tom?

A. Yes.

Q. Did not you tell Tom that your mother, Norah and Ellen were against you?

A. I do not know.

Q. Now you know very well. Try and think. Did not you tell him your mother was against you?

A. He knew that.

Q. How did he know?

A. I told him.

Q. Did not he tell you that Norah and Ellen were also against him?

A. I don't think I ever mentioned their names to him.

Q. How did Tom know Norah was against him?

A. I could not say, I'm sure.

Q. Did he know the whole family was against him?

A. I do not know.

Q. You might have told Tom Ryan Norah was against him?

A. Yes. I might have told him.

Q. Did you ever hear Tom Ryan say he would have Polly in spite of the whole lot of them?

A. Yes he said that.

Q. Did he say it to you?

A. My mother told me he said that he would have Polly in spite of her.

Q. What was the reason they objected to Tom Ryan?

A. Because he was fond of drink.

Q. Did not Michael want to break off the match between you and Tom Ryan?

A. I don't think so. He never interfered with him.

Q. Did he ever speak to Tom about it?

A. No.

Q. Did Michael and Tom Ryan ever have a fight over it?

A. No.

Q. How long had this affair been going on between you and Tom Ryan?

A. About nine or ten years.

Q. Did you tell him you were not going to have anything more to do with him?

A. I don't remember.

Q. Did you ever hear him say he would have revenge?

A. No.[19]

Thomas Ryan also gave evidence at the Magisterial Inquiry. In his evidence taken at Gatton on 10 March 1899, he deposed that he had known the Murphy family for about eighteen years and that about five years previously he had had "a bit of a row" with Mrs Murphy because she had not wanted him to go with her daughter. Ryan said that he did not give up Polly at the time of the row and stated that at the time he had said that when he wanted Polly he would not ask Mrs Murphy. He denied ever saying that he "would have Polly in spite of all" and that he had said he would be revenged on Mrs Murphy for taking Polly away from him. "She did not take her away from me," he said, "so I didn't want to be revenged on her." Ryan also denied that he had once followed Mrs Murphy along the Tent Hill road and that he had on another occasion chased Polly along the road on horseback. He did not know of the Murphys having any enemies and he had no idea who had committed the murders.

Ryan was questioned by Inspector Urquhart regarding his movements on Christmas Day and Boxing Day. He said that on 23 December he went to Esk with cattle, got drunk in Esk and got back as far as Buaraba Station on Christmas Eve. He reached Gatton at about eleven o'clock on Christmas Day and got drunk again. He remembered nothing from then until he found himself in bed on the morning of Boxing Day. He was told that a constable had brought him home the previous afternoon. On Boxing Day he went back to the hotel to look for the horse he had been riding on Christmas Day, but he could not find it. He went home at about six o'clock and did not get up until about eight o'clock the next morning. Inspector Urquhart asked him, "If someone says they saw you out that night, what then?" and Ryan replied, "It would be a falsehood." Ryan said he did not recover his horse until the afternoon of 27 December when the horse was brought up to the hotel. The horse was taken from the hotel on Christmas Day by a man named Paddy Dwyer who, on Boxing Day, had gone to the Burnside races.[20]

At the Police Inquiry Commission both Sub-Inspector Galbraith and Sergeant Toomey were examined regarding the inquiries they had made in relation to Thomas Ryan. Galbraith responded to questions put to him as follows—

Q. (*By Mr Garvin*) Have you told us all that you did up to this point?
A. Yes; without going into details.
Q. Did Ryan satisfactorily account for himself during the whole day and night of the twenty-sixth of December?
A. No.
Q. In what way?
A. Ryan stated that at an early hour on the evening of the twenty-sixth he went back to his own house and went to bed. That was by no means satisfactory to me, considering that it was holiday time, and that he was a man who was likely to take advantage of the privilege it gave. It seemed to me a peculiar explanation.
Q. What time did he say he went to his house?
A. I am speaking from memory now, but I think he said it was about five o'clock in the afternoon.
Q. Could you account for him from time to time until the following morning?
A. No, I could not account for him. I may tell you that I took very great steps to try and account for him, but these steps did anything but account for him—quite the opposite, so that I had a very strong suspicion of Ryan at the time, and for some considerable time afterwards.
Q. (*By the Chairman*) And what dissipated that suspicion?
A. Well, the general surroundings. In a general way Ryan has not cleared himself to me now, but I make no accusation against him, and I am not saying this for my own protection. I do not think he is the man who committed the murder, but, in a general way, unless Mr Urquhart has fuller information, Ryan has never cleared himself.
Q. (*By Mr Garvin*) Was there any other person in Ryan's house besides himself?
A. Yes, his father and mother.
Q. Did you question them?
A. Yes; they were subjected to very severe questioning, and their statements were not consistent with each other.
Q. Did they corroborate the son's statement?
A. They undoubtedly said that he was at home, but a strong piece of evidence against that was that a most respectable woman, Mrs Mortimer, was quite convinced that she saw Mrs Ryan out late at night looking for somebody. Then the father is a man who drinks, and he was drunk.

Q. Did you find out from inquiries made at any of the hotels if he had been drinking there after the time he told you he went home?

A. No. As far as I know myself, and from the close inquiries that I made, we could not get a trace of Ryan after five o'clock, or it might be half past five—I am speaking from memory—except that he and his mother, and I think his father also, placed him in his own house.[21]

The transcript of Toomey's evidence, given three days later, contains these responses—

Q. (*By Mr Garvin*) Did you make exhaustive inquiries throughout the district with a view to ascertaining whether anyone residing in the district had a grudge against the Murphy family?

A. I made a portion of the inquiries. Of course, I pretty well knew all the people.

Q. Could you learn anything?

A. Yes. If you want me to give names I will do so.

Q. You can just tell us what you heard.

A. I heard that a certain person had had a great difference with Mrs Murphy over McNeil's wife.

Q. You can mention his name, as we know.

A. That was Tom Ryan at Gatton.

Q. Did you make inquiries to account for Ryan's time during the whole of the day and night of the 26th of December?

A. I did. At least, I did as far as Gatton was concerned.

Q. What did you find out about him, starting with the morning of the 26th?

A. I believe he was at Buaraba with cattle, and he came home—whether it was on the Sunday or the Monday I would not be sure—but, anyway, he was away and came home, and was drinking about Mortimer's hotel. He was there on the morning of Boxing Day, I think, and went home, and evidently went to bed, or lay down, and came back again in the afternoon. He had a drink or two and went home.

Q. What time was it when he went home that last time?

A. I cannot say without looking up the papers. I do not remember the exact hour. [*Looking at Ryan's statement.*] I do not see it here, but it was some time between five and six o'clock.

Q. Was he sober then?

A. No, he had some drink in him.

Q. Where did he go?

A. He was in the kitchen at Mortimer's hotel, and he was supposed to have gone home. He went into the yard, I think. I may say that I think I know what you want. I have questioned Tom Ryan and the witnesses who stated that they saw him on the night of the tragedy at Gatton, and I think they were mistaken. That was not the night they saw him. They were mistaken as to the night. He said in his statement that Paddy Dwyer came and took his horse away out of Mortimer's yard to some races at Laidley. Ryan came up, and said—cursing—"I wonder where my horse is," and it was a Sunday his horse was taken away, so that I believe it was on the Sunday night that Ryan was there, and not the Monday night.

Q. Not on the Monday at all?

A. He was at the hotel on Monday.

Q. I want you to confine yourself to the Monday. You said he was supposed to have gone home?—Did he live there?

A. Yes; his father and mother lived about 100 yards [*ninety metres*] from the hotel, and he lived with them.

Q. Did he go home, then, between five and six o'clock?

A. Yes.

Q. What was his condition?

A. He had some drink, but was not what you would call drunk.

Q. Do you know whether he left his place that night?

A. We never could ascertain.

Q. Did you question him about it?

A. Oh, yes.

Q. What did he say?

A. He said he did not, and his father and mother said the same thing—that he never left the house that night.

Q. Did you ever show him to the boy Carroll?

A. Carroll and he knew one another intimately; they were residents of the place.

Q. Did you ask Carroll whether Ryan was the man at the sliprails?

A. I did. There is no one who has been suspected for these murders that I did not ask the witnesses who saw the man at the sliprails about.

Q. Did Ryan resemble Day?

A. With the exception of having a large moustache. I should say he resembled Day in height and build and that, to an ordinary individual, but not from my point of view.

Q. Did you ask the boy if he was satisfied that it was not Ryan he saw at the rails that night?

A. I asked the boy, and he said he was satisfied. In fact, I am sure I asked him and he said, "No"; but I never placed any reliance in the boy's story.

Q. However, he said Ryan was not the man he saw at the sliprails?

A. Yes.

Q. Were your inquiries of such a nature as to satisfy you that Ryan was not out of Gatton at the time that these murders would have been committed, or about the time that the man would be seen on the road?

A. I made every inquiry that was possible to be made. There was nobody saw Ryan except that they think he was seen at seven o'clock. Some people thought that, but I believe they were mistaken as to the night; and it would not take him twenty yards [*eighteen metres*] beyond Mortimer's hotel, as far as he is supposed to have been seen.

Q. From the inquiries you made regarding Ryan, have you any reason to suspect him in connection with this offence at all?

A. I cannot say that I have. There has been work done in connection with Ryan nobody knows anything about, with the exception of two or three men told off privately to investigate that part of the case.[22]

It seems virtually certain that Thomas Ryan was not in any way involved in the crime. He apparently came under the surveillance of the police at a very early stage of their investigations solely because of the knowledge of his differences with Mrs Murphy some years previously. That he was at one time a suitor for the hand of Polly Murphy is evident but this appears to have been his only connection with the Murphy family.

It is time now to direct our attention to William McNeil. It was he, of course, who discovered the bodies in Moran's paddock and who contacted Sergeant Arrell and accompanied him back to where they were lying. He then went to impart news of the tragedy to the Murphy family. He drove Mrs Murphy to the murder scene and subsequently brought the corpses of Norah and Ellen into Gatton. Later, at the Brian Boru Hotel, he was one of several persons who helped to lift the bodies of the two girls and Michael into the room where the post mortem examinations were carried out by Dr von Lossberg. According to Charles Gilbert, when McNeil told him of his discovery of the bodies, he (McNeil) was "excited". William Murphy said that McNeil was "much excited" when he arrived at the Murphy farm and told him of the tragedy.[23] When Sergeant Arrell gave evidence before the Commission he was asked whether McNeil seemed much distressed at the time when he was with him in Moran's paddock on the day the bodies were discovered and Arrell replied, "Yes, very much affected." Arrell also indicated that he questioned McNeil closely as to "who he thought would be likely to do it" and said that McNeil answered all his questions in a straightforward manner and he did not hesitate in the least.[24]

Moreover, McNeil was doing everything he could to help the police. He spent a considerable amount of his time in searching for clues. It was reported at the time that "McNeil, the brother-in-law, is working night and day endeavouring to secure some trace of the murderers."[25] Elsewhere it was reported that "W. McNeil appears most anxious to unravel the mystery, and is using his best endeavours to find some clue or other that will lead to the detection of the murderers. Any item of news or slightest trace he can obtain he immediately informs the police."[26] Subsequently McNeil gave evidence at the Magisterial Inquiry and it was published that he "gave his evidence in a straight-forward manner and without hesitation".[27]

In such circumstances, one might reasonably think that William McNeil would be lauded for his efforts. In some quarters he well may have been; but in other circles he became the subject of suspicion. He himself knew that some people suspected him. In mid-January it was reported in a newspaper that "Mr McNeil returned this afternoon from Toowoomba. He said the police are making inquiries about him. The people there would not speak to him, and the girls at the place he was stopping at would not serve him. He is anxious that the police should arrest him if they have anything against him."[28] Later that month it was reported in a newspaper that:

> McNeil, the brother-in-law, has again been interviewed. He said he knew people had suspected him. "I don't blame them for suspecting me at first," he said. "I suppose they could not help it and I expected it; but the death of the girl Norah was like cutting off my hand. She was good and kind to my children and my eldest girl would not rest satis-fied unless she was with Norah."[29]

According to Mr Richard James, the chemist at Gatton, McNeil once told him that "the police were shadowing his movements. He was rather annoyed about it."[30]

At the close of his evidence before the Commission on 2 October 1899, McNeil was asked by the Chairman whether he wished to say anything else and he said, "I want to know about the expense I have been put to over this tragedy. What reason had they for chasing me about in the way they have done?" It would appear from the transcript that the following then ensued:

Q. The police?
A. Yes.
Q. You must ask them for their reason. Do you complain about the police?
A. Yes, I complain strongly. I have been put to a lot of expense for no reason that I can see. A special man was put on to watch me, and my lad left me because he could not stand the police poking about the place.
Q. Your son?

A. No, my brother, who was looking after my place at Westbrook. The police were watching there.

Q. Do you expect the police not to inquire in every possible direction?

A. They might do that, but they should show some reason.

Q. (*By Mr Garvin*) The police are bound to make inquiries.

A. Yes, but they should show some reason for their inquiries.

Q. (*By the Chairman*) They would probably tell you they had a reason.

A. Well, I asked, and they said no. It has cost me a terrible lot, and they kept my cart until about 20th of last month, and would not allow me any compensation for the time they had it.[31]

When giving evidence before the Commission Mrs Murphy said "...it was Urquhart who tried to make me say that McNeil did it. McNeil no more did it than any of you did. He would be the last man in the world to do it."[32]

Constable Joe Murphy (no relation at all of the Murphys of Blackfellow's Creek, Tent Hill), when giving evidence at the Magisterial Inquiry, related what happened when he served a subpoena on Mrs Murphy on 23 March 1899, recalling her to give evidence. He deposed that Mrs Murphy said, "What do they want me again for? I was there often enough. They nearly killed me the last time. The wretches want me to bring something against McNeil who worked hard to help us all the time." She said they thought she was keeping something back and she believed they wanted her to tell a lie.[33]

At the Magisterial Inquiry various witnesses, including Daniel Murphy (senior) and his wife, were closely questioned concerning the movements of McNeil on the night of the murders. Daniel Murphy said that when he was saying his prayers that night between nine and ten o'clock he heard McNeil go into his room.[34] Mrs Mary Murphy corroborated her husband. She swore that McNeil went to bed between nine and nine thirty and said that, at that time, her husband was either saying his prayers or he was on the verandah smoking. She went on to say that, after the clock struck twelve that night she heard McNeil, who was then in his room, laugh as a result of something said by his little girl to the effect that she would not kiss her mother, but she would her father.[35]

It has already been mentioned that, at the Magisterial Inquiry, Sergeant Arrell said he did not see any traces of tracks left by McNeil between the sulky wheel tracks in Moran's paddock when he first went into the paddock with McNeil on the morning of 27 December 1898.[36] Of course, this is evidence of a negative nature—that Arrell *didn't* see them. And he is giving evidence two and a half months after the event concerning which he is being questioned. Having regard to the unsatisfactory evidence generally as to what tracks, if any, were visible in Moran's paddock on that particular morning, we feel that it would be unreasonable, merely from the evidence of Sergeant Arrell in this regard, to draw any inference to the effect that McNeil's tracks were not there between the wheel tracks of the sulky. What is more, there is, of course, the evidence of Mr Richard James before the Commission to the effect that he went to Moran's paddock a day or two after the bodies had been discovered, and he walked along and looked back to see if he could see the impression of his footmarks a second afterwards, but he could see nothing.[37] Bearing that in mind, we consider that, even if we were satisfied that no track marks were in fact visible between the sulky wheels to Arrell or anyone else that morning of 27 December, that would not be sufficient grounds for drawing an inference that McNeil had not gone into Moran's paddock that morning (as he said he did) before accompanying Arrell to the murder scene.

A correspondant of a Brisbane newspaper reported in its issue of 10 January 1899, that he had, at 5 p.m. on Sunday, 8 January 1899, paid a visit to Mrs Murphy and her family at Tent Hill. His report continued:

I feel that the family resent the unfounded charges which have been cast upon William McNeil, her son-in-law ... I know the force of the adage that "he that excuses accuses"; but it is worthy of remark that, in a small building, it would have been difficult for any member of the household to have left the place between nine and twelve o'clock without the circumstances being known.[38]

Concerning McNeil's movements the next morning, the same reporter made the comment:

McNeil knew the cart was a "gimcrack" affair, and scarcely up to the weight of three passengers, and he started in to see if an accident had occurred. I unhesitatingly say that there is not one word of the subsequent story which does not strictly accord with probabilities. One must be here and on the ground to fully appreciate the whole story.[39]

We hasten to say that, from an examination of the available evidence, we are in complete agreement with the remarks of this reporter. From everything we have examined it is evident that all the members of the Murphy family were fond of William McNeil and he also of them. His little girl was extremely devoted to Norah. McNeil was particularly friendly with Michael, who had accompanied him down from Westbrook in the sulky for the Christmas celebrations at the Murphy farm at Tent Hill. Norah was a wonderful help to him and his wife in looking after the little girl since his wife had become partially paralysed.

McNeil was most devoted to his wife—he travelled down from West-brook every weekend to be with her and his children at the Tent Hill farm. He brought Norah a bridle and Ellen a whip for Christmas. He had every motive for liking and protecting his brothers-in-law and his sisters-in-law. When the tragedy occurred he acted in a most helpful way and did everything which an honourable man could be expected to do. His was not merely a case where it could negatively be said that there was an "absence of proved motive". Having regard to the mutual affection between his little girl and her aunt, Norah, one might reasonably contend that, so far as he was concerned, there was a "proved absence of motive".[40]

The truth, we feel sure, is that if McNeil were ever considered a "suspect" by the police, he was only a "suspect" in the limited sense in which Inspector Urquhart used that term. Before the Commission, when Urquhart was asked whether a particular person was "regarded as a suspect", he replied, "No; the word 'suspect' is used more as a name—as a matter of nomenclature. There were people put down as suspects against whom there was no suspicion, but simply because they were mentioned as persons whose movements should be inquired into. The word is used much in the same way as the term 'astrologer's pill'. That is simply a list of quack letters."[41] McNeil, so it seems to us, was under surveillance because someone "suspected" him, but not because of the existence of any objective fact from which even a mere suspicion, let alone a reasonable inference, could be drawn.

From a careful examination of the available material, we are convinced that William McNeil, far from being justifiably an object of suspicion, should be held in very high regard. So far as we are able to discover, he acted at all times very properly, honestly, and with considerable dignity. In all fairness we have not the slightest hesitation in submitting that in every respect his conduct was commendable—as a husband, as a father, as a son-in-law, as a brother-in-law, as a member of the community—and as a man!

In the absence of any really significant lead, the police, so it would appear, reconstructed the whole affair. Some eight years ago, a well known journalist on the staff of a Brisbane newspaper outlined the police reconstruction thus:

> They reasoned that the three had been held at gunpoint half a mile [*one kilometre*] back, at the paddock sliprails. Michael probably had been forced to drive on through the rails to the murder spot, then, at gunpoint, to tie his sisters' hands behind them, then have his own tied by the maniac.
> Police theorised that Ellen and Michael then probably were left lying at the base of the eucalypt, while Norah was taken away.
> The maniac then apparently began tearing off Norah's clothes to rape

116

her. Her screams of terror undoubtedly spurred Michael and Ellen into frantic efforts to free themselves to aid her.

Police reasoned that the maniac then left Norah and returned to the others. Michael was shot and killed immediately, and the horse, too, in case Ellen broke free and attempted to escape.

The police reconstruction was that the killer then returned to continue his attack on Norah. When she continued hysterical screaming, he strangled her with the leather strap, then stove in her head with a heavy piece of timber.

He then returned to eighteen year old Ellen, raped her, then battered her to death.

He then vanished in the night, taking the dreadful secret of his gruesome crime with him.[42]

The investigating police officers determined to unearth this maniac. At one stage their hopes were high that they had been successful—that he was a man named Richard Burgess.

8
RICHARD BURGESS

Very early in their investigations the police made a check of all offenders recently discharged from prison. A certain Richard Burgess immediately claimed their attention.

On 30 November 1898, Burgess had been released from St Helena, an island prison in Moreton Bay where he had served a term of imprisonment for a violent assault upon an old woman named Barry at Leyburn on 5 May 1898. Leyburn is about sixty-five kilometres south-west of Toowoomba. In the course of the commission of this offence Burgess had been shot in the arm by Mrs Barry's son-in-law.[1]

Burgess, a native of America and formerly a sailor, had a long criminal record in the Australian colonies, and appears to have been actively pursuing his nefarious career in south-east Queensland during 1898.[2] On 8 March 1898, under the name of Patrick Burke, he was charged in the Gympie District Court with having unlawfully and indecently assaulted Annie Jane Ray, a widow, at Kilkivan on 11 February 1898. He was charged also with burglary, it being alleged that, at about midnight on that date, he entered Mrs Ray's dwelling, crawled across the floor into her bedroom and endeavoured to get into bed with her. At the conclusion of the evidence for the prosecution, His Honour Judge Miller ruled that no intention to commit a felony on entry had been proved and he instructed the jury to bring in a verdict of "Not Guilty" which was accordingly done, and the prisoner was discharged.

Giving evidence on the burglary charge, the arresting constable claimed that Burgess had said that Queensland was a big colony with a small population and that it was surely able to keep a pauper or two and that if people would not give to him he would take from them.[3] While held in the police lockup at Kilkivan, Burgess behaved in a most violent manner, his language at times being so dreadful that the constable's wife had to leave the building. It is also reported that at Kilkivan he extolled the Kellys (the Victorian bushrangers), saying that he intended launching out in that line of business and adding that when he did start he would give people something to talk about.[4] On another occasion when arrested he commented to police that he was "born to be hanged".[5]

Burgess had been known to the Queensland police for a long time, and they regarded him as a hardened and dangerous criminal.[6] He led a lonely, nomadic style of life and was considered an expert bushman. He worked sporadically at various bush callings including shearing, and at other times lived by cadging or stealing food as he travelled about the countryside carrying his swag. There is no doubt that Burgess was an incorrigible thief and a depraved erotomaniac. From newspaper accounts of his behaviour while in police custody and at the Gatton Magisterial Inquiry, one gains the impression that he was a distinctive character, cynical, impudent, full of effrontery, but with a certain sense of humour.

Early in January 1899, the police engaged in the Gatton investigations received information from a Darling Downs selector named Donovan that Burgess was in the area of the Bunya Mountains some fifty kilometres north-east of Dalby, having come through the bush from the direction of Crow's Nest. In a later court appearance in Toowoomba, Burgess was to say that he had gone to the Bunya Mountains seeking employment from a man named Daly who had a sawmill there. The report of Burgess's whereabouts intensified the interest of the police in him as a suspect for the murders at Gatton because the normal route from Brisbane to the Bunyas was along the main road, through Ipswich and Gatton to Toowoomba and across the Downs. The police moved quickly to detain Burgess, and on 6 January 1899, he was arrested by Mounted Constable J. Gillies in the vicinity of the Bunya Mountains "on suspicion of being implicated in the Gatton murders".[7]

Burgess, who had armed himself with a stick and had filled his billycan with stones which he apparently planned to use as missiles, refused to state his name or to answer any questions put to him by the constable. He violently resisted arrest, but was overpowered and handcuffed by Gillies with the assistance of two civilians. He was conveyed immediately to Dalby where he was locked up in the police cells on the night of 6 January 1899. Here he is said to have spoken freely of the Gatton murders, saying that the eldest girl Murphy was a great flirt, and that it was time she was put out of the road.[8]

In reporting the arrest of Burgess, a Brisbane newspaper commented that "the selectors around the Bunya Mountains were much alarmed and were pleased to see him in the hands of the Police".[9]

Burgess was brought up before Major Fanning, Police Magistrate at Dalby, on the morning of 7 January 1899 and was remanded for eight days.[10] He was brought up again before the Dalby Bench on 9 January. No evidence was offered and the charge was withdrawn by the prosecutor, Sub-Inspector Durham. Burgess was discharged, but was immediately re-arrested on a charge of stealing a saddle and was escorted to Toowoomba that night. At the request of Sub-Inspector Durham, a Dr Fullerton examined Burgess, but found no bruises or scratches which would tend to indicate that he had taken part in the Gatton outrage.[11] It must be remembered, however, that this examination took place two weeks after the murders at Gatton.

Burgess was brought up in the Toowoomba Police Court at 9.30 a.m. on 18 January 1899, before two lay magistrates, charged with the larceny of a saddle. A solicitor, Mr J.V. Herbert, who was in the court, rose and announced that he appeared for Richard Burgess. Apparently the Justices were somewhat taken aback by this unanticipated intrusion, one of them asking by whose authority Mr Herbert appeared and who instructed him. Mr Herbert, not unreasonably, strongly resented these questions, "characterising them as savouring of impertinence". Sub-Inspector Durham, conducting the prosecution, applied for a remand for eight days. This undoubtedly was done to ensure that Burgess would be retained in police custody until the Magisterial Inquiry into the death of the Murphys got under way at Gatton on Tuesday, 24 January 1899. Mr Herbert consulted with Burgess and then requested that the information and previous proceedings, including the evidence already taken, be read. Informed that no evidence relating to the charge had yet been taken, Mr Herbert contended that, at the very least, the evidence of arrest should be tendered and he strongly opposed the prosecution's application for remand. Sub-Inspector Durham then read the information. Burgess was formally charged with stealing one riding saddle in Toowoomba on 22 December 1898, the property of one Patrick McNamara. Burgess asked for a remand to Brisbane but one of the Justices, Mr Galloway, replied that this could not be done as the offence was alleged to have been committed at Toowoomba. Burgess appeared surprised at the reference to Toowoomba, and so, in fact, did everyone in court other than "the authorities", as it had previously been understood that the saddle was supposed to have been stolen in Brisbane and that Burgess was not anywhere about Toowoomba on 22 December.[12]

Burgess was detained in police custody in Toowoomba and his clothing was sent to Brisbane for "microscopical examination by experts".[13] Late on the night of 23 January 1899 he was escorted to Gatton to give evidence at the Magisterial Inquiry.

A newspaper of the time described Burgess's arrival in Gatton.

Richard Burgess has arrived here and as may be expected, he is the sole topic of conversation. The goods train conveying him reached Gatton half an hour after midnight, the prisoner being in charge of Sergeant

Arrell of Gatton and Constables McInerney and Hendle of Toowoomba. There were about fifteen persons on the platform when the train drew alongside, including the Press brigade. Burgess, handcuffed, was assisted out, and proceeded to walk to the station which is a few hundred yards distant, the small crowd following. The latter attention was apparently soon resented, for as he went through the railway gates into the street leading to the police quarters, he suddenly stopped and, turning round to the crowd, muttered something in a low tone. One of his escort touched him on the arm and he again proceeded. On arrival at the Police Station, a policeman was found asleep on the verandah in front of the cell prepared for the prisoner. Burgess took in the situation at a glance and smiling, remarked, "He is down to it. Another sundowner camped eh!"

After he entered the cell, the officers removed Burgess's pipe, tobacco, matches and other articles including an extra pair of boots, but to the removal of the latter he decidedly objected, remarking, "I want them for the court tomorrow; they let me have them in Toowoomba." However, their removal was insisted upon and this seemed to annoy Burgess and in a gruff tone he asked directly afterwards, "Aint I going to have any blankets?" These were supplied and he then asked for a drink which was also supplied. This compliance with his request softened down his acerbity and he smilingly remarked to the constables, "You fellows can go now" and he settled down for the night. The cell was then locked and the constables mounted guard. On inquiry I learn that Burgess did not pass a particularly good night. He was restless, moved about a bit in his cell and talked to himself in a low tone. Once he opened up conversation with the constable on guard and, after a brief silence then remarked suddenly, "It's a——good job there's a wall between us", the constable thoroughly agreeing with him. Later he was heard pacing up and down his cell muttering to himself.[14]

Burgess was the last witness to give evidence on the first sitting day of the Magisterial Inquiry—Tuesday, 24 January 1899. His appearance was described by the reporter of the *Brisbane Courier* covering the Inquiry.

Yesterday and today I had a good opportunity of studying Burgess. His prison description gives his height as 5 feet 6¼ inches [*168 cm*] and his weight at eleven stone ten pounds [*74·5 kg*]. He certainly seems taller and I should say that his weight must be fully twelve stone. [*76 kg*] He is a man thirty-six years of age, of very powerful and athletic mould. His beard is brownish, inclined to be sandy; his eyes grey, deep-set and restless; his nose slightly out of shape, his forehead fairly high and the top of his head almost entirely bald. Just above the forehead there is a light tuft of hair. He is at times very nervous and the sardonic smile so often spoken of is an involuntary twitching of the muscles at the left corner of his mouth. His voice is low and with a peculiar treble quality.[15]

On Burgess coming into court, the people who could not gain

admittance, gathered outside, crowding round the windows of the tiny building. Burgess was dressed in a striped cotton shirt and dark trousers and carried a broad-brimmed, black felt hat. He gave his evidence in a cool, jaunty manner, his countenance bearing a peculiar smile nearly the whole time. He often gave flippant answers to questions and at times laughed outright at the replies he made. He said that he used many aliases and readily admitted that he stole "tucker", commenting, "I am no capitalist", and "I am always in trouble; I never know when I am out of it." He said that he never made acquaintances. He had no friends and never looked for them but he had plenty of enemies.

Burgess was examined by Inspector Urquhart and the witness traced his movements from 30 November 1898, the date of his release from St Helena, until 6 January 1899, the day on which he was arrested in the Bunya Mountains.[16] He said that upon leaving St Helena where he was given seven shillings and sixpence and a new shirt, he travelled by steamer to Brisbane and on the night of 30 November camped in the bush at Toowong. On 1 December he walked along the old Ipswich Road to Moggill and obtained employment on roadwork at the farm of a man named John O'Brien, but stayed only two days as he considered the wages too low. O'Brien, an elderly man, later told the police that he and Burgess quarrelled and that Burgess assaulted him.[17]

Upon leaving O'Brien's, Burgess travelled to Ipswich seeking work as he moved along, but obtaining none. A Mr Cushing of the Oxley Bacon Factory saw him at Oxley on 9 December and at Redbank on 11 December.[18] Burgess said that he "made no purchases, no silk pocket handkerchiefs or anything else", and striking out in a south-westerly direction, passed below Mt Walker and crossed the Dividing Range to Killarney on the Darling Downs. It took "a week or two" to get from O'Brien's place to Killarney. Burgess said that at Killarney he went prospecting for gold for "a couple of days" with a schoolmaster named Mattingly, and at a store in Killarney (later ascertained by the police to be Barnes & Co.), bought a pair of blucher boots for seven shillings out of some money Mattingly had given him. He had worn out his old elastic sided boots which he had been wearing since the police had been running him down at Leyburn and he "couldn't cop the caper on bare feet". Mattingly later identified Burgess at the Toowoomba Police Barracks and corroborated these statements. He said that he had engaged Burgess, who had used the name Joseph Ryan, to assist him and his wife in prospecting for gold at Elbow Valley near Killarney on 15 and 16 December. He discharged Burgess on 16 December, giving him ten shillings.[19] On 17 December, Burgess travelled by train to Warwick and apparently from that date until close to Christmas he wandered about the Warwick-Allora district, although details of his movements during that period are not known.[20]

Burgess said that on Christmas Eve he arrived at the homestead of a selector about twenty-two kilometres from Allora. The homestead was in the bush about two kilometres off the main road to Toowoomba. That night he camped in an outhouse, and on the next morning, Christmas Day, had breakfast with the selector who had two little girls at home and "more knocking about somewhere". This selector, a man named Sparksman, subsequently confirmed Burgess's statement.[21]

Burgess said that he left the selector's place at about ten or eleven o'clock on Christmas Morning and struck off in the direction of Clifton. On the night of Christmas Day he camped on the road between Allora and Clifton. On Boxing Day he went on towards Toowoomba, travelling all day across country. At about eight or nine o'clock that night he called at the home of a selector about thirteen kilometres outside of Clifton where he asked for, and was given, a drink of water at a tank. He described the dress of the selector and said that he "had a stammer in his speech". Burgess said that on the night of 26 December he camped "on the road towards Toowoomba". When pressed by Inspector Urquhart to identify the place where he camped that night, Burgess replied that he could not as there were gaps in his recollection between Christmas and 29 December. He said, "My head aint an almanac altogether"; but he told Urquhart that if the Inspector would accompany him he would show him every place where he had camped.

Burgess deposed that he had never been in Gatton previously and that he had first heard of the murders from a man he met leading a stallion along the road near Helidon. He had crossed the Range from the Downs, and travelled down Flagstone Creek reaching Helidon on or about 29 December. From there he kept picking up information as he went along and he also read about the murders in newspapers. After leaving Helidon, Burgess crossed the Range again and got up to Highfields from where he travelled over the Darling Downs to the Bunya Mountains. Questioned regarding his resistance to Constable Gillies at the Bunya Mountains, Burgess said that he had "rounded on" the constable because he had not told him why he was arresting him, he was dressed in civilian clothes, and "did not know his duty".

On 27 January 1899, while still in police custody in Toowoomba, Burgess made a statement to his solicitor, Mr J.V. Herbert, in which he described his movements from 25 to 27 December. This statement contained greater detail than the vague account given by Burgess in his evidence before the Magisterial Inquiry, and differed from that account in one important particular, namely the date upon which he claimed to have been given a drink of water by the selector near Clifton. At the Inquiry, Burgess stated that this incident occurred on the night of 26 December, the night the Murphys were murdered, whereas in the statement given to his solicitor, he maintained that it took place on the evening of 25 December. The selector, a man named Siebenhausen, who had an impediment in his speech, was interviewed and recalled the incident but, it seems, was uncertain of the date. In different reports in the newspapers, Siebenhausen is quoted variously as stating that the incident occurred on 25 December, 26 December, and "either 25 or 26 December".[22]

The statement made by Burgess read—

On the morning of 25 December I had breakfast at a farmer's about fourteen miles [*twenty-two kilometres*] from Allora near the Range. At about nine o'clock I left there and at about 10 or 10.30 a.m. passed along by a station due west. I came to a house. A man resided there who stammered in his speech. I got a drink of water there. That was about eight o'clock in the evening and I then went five or six miles [*eight or ten kilometres*] towards Greenmount. I camped about ten o'clock that night on a fringe of timber. Coming from the place where I got a drink of water I met a man wearing a white helmet and driving a sulky about four miles [*six kilometres*] from the house. I had dinner on 26th with a Danish woman about five miles [*eight kilometres*] from the last camp due north. I stopped there about an hour and afterwards called at several places. I got a drink of water at one place and spoke to a boy at another for about half an hour. I then went 200 yards [*180 metres*] on to get something to eat at a place where they have a stallion four miles [*six kilometres*] from Nobby. I camped on Boxing Night in front of a big house about two miles [*three kilometres*] from Greenmount railway station. I left that camp next day 27 December. Leaving my swag at the camp I went back to Bell's Hotel at Greenmount and asked several people for work. Among others I asked the Archers who own a thrashing plant. I then went to Allan's farm and got breakfast from Mrs Allan, Mr Allan being away at the dairy with milk. I then spoke to the wife of one of Allan's employees at a house between Allan's and Bell's Hotel. I then went to the camp, got my swag and dressed in a lighter, white felt hat and grey tweed suit.[23]

With this statement Burgess also gave to Mr Herbert a rough map showing the route which he claimed to have taken between Allora and Greenmount on 25 and 26 December. Burgess drew the map in pencil on a piece of blotting paper measuring 584 millimetres by 432 millimetres. The map contained considerable detail and, drawn from memory as it was, indicated that Burgess was well acquainted with the area. He represented the Dividing Range by a mass of figures of eight, and wrote "Station here" which was presumably Pilton. He drew a road due west and wrote the words "This road bearing west I went along to this turn", and he indicated various characteristics of the country with phrases such as "ploughed ground", "hawthorne hedge", "cross road", and "road going mountain". He indicated where he camped on the night of 25 December not far from a "big house like a wool-shed", and showed the place where he met the man in a sulky and also a "humpy" where he called on the morning of 26 December. He then marked a well near which he wrote "Creek. Willows growing here", and following the creek wrote "Big bank" and "a lot of reeds". He then traced his route to a house which he annotated "This is where I got something to eat from the Mrs of the place the day of the 26th", and in front of the house marked a cross road and indicated another house further along at which he also called. Continuing to trace his route on 26 December, Burgess showed where he spoke to a woman whose husband was ploughing, and at another place he wrote "Here they were playing cricket when I went by." Approaching Greenmount he indicated several tracks and houses, a place where he got a drink of water and another where a stallion was kept. He then traced his route by a "big mountain" and showed the railway line, the rail platform at Greenmount, Bell's Hotel and not far away a spot beside which he wrote "Camped here night of 26th pretty late."[24]

Burgess's account of his movements on Christmas Day and Boxing Day as given in his statement and map were largely corroborated. The man in the sulky whom Burgess passed on the road on Christmas Day was the Presbyterian Minister from Allora, the Reverend J. Smiley. Mr Smiley confirmed that at about eight o'clock in the evening on that day while travelling towards Allora he met a swagman on the road walking towards Greenmount. The two met at a point about ten kilometres on the Allora side of Greenmount. Mr Smiley, who at the time was wearing a white helmet, particularly remembered the encounter because his horse shied at the traveller.

The Danish woman from whom Burgess claimed to have obtained dinner on 26 December proved to be a woman named Pierson. Mrs Pierson confirmed that a man carrying a swag and wearing tweed trousers and coat and an old straw hat, called at her house at about 1.30 p.m. He had dinner and asked for work, and she told him there was a threshing plant near Nobby. Mrs Pierson was indisposed at the time, and the man inquired what the symptoms were and named a medicine that would cure her. Mrs Pierson said that the swagman stayed at her place for about half an hour and left in the direction of Irvine's farm, which was about a kilometre away.

A farmer named Forsyth who lived about four kilometres from Mrs Pierson confirmed that a cricket match was played in his paddock on Boxing Day, and some ladies watching the game stated that they saw a swagman going through the paddock at about four thirty in the afternoon.

The boy to whom Burgess said he had spoken for about half an hour was also located. He was sixteen years old Michael Fallon, who resided on his father's farm some distance from Forsyth's place. Young Fallon was chopping wood about milking time on Boxing Day when a man carrying a small swag approached and asked if there were any threshers about. The man talked for about half an hour and at one stage remarked that there would be some boozing at Nobby that night as it was a holiday, and "if a man went over and threw a few of them out and broke their necks a man might get a job in their place".

Burgess's statement that he obtained food on Boxing Day at a place where a stallion was kept was also apparently corroborated. This was at the farm of a man named Beck. It was confirmed that a swagman called at Beck's house at dusk on 26 December and asked for and was given food. He complained of feeling unwell and stated his intention of going into Nobby to the hotel to get some brandy and port wine. He departed in the direction of Nobby.

A number of persons in the vicinity of Greenmount stated that they saw a man answering Burgess's description on the morning of 27 December. One of them, a Mrs Nightingale, who evidently was the woman referred to by Burgess as the wife of one of Allan's employees, said that a man called at her house looking for work at about a quarter to eight that morning. He looked very tired and worn out and when he sat down, appeared to doze off.[25]

In direct conflict with Burgess's account of his movements on Boxing Day were the statements of a number of persons who identified him as being in the vicinity of Gatton at that time. On 23 January 1899, at the Toowoomba Police Barracks, Burgess was placed in a line-up with seven other men. Florence Lowe and Thomas Drew both picked out Burgess as the man they had seen near the sliprails of Moran's paddock on the night of 26 December, and Frank Hallas, aged fifteen years, and his sister Beatrice, seventeen, identified Burgess as a man who called at their father's house at Gatton at about half past six on the evening of 26 December and was given a drink, a boiled egg and a box of matches.[26] If the swagman who was at Beck's farm near Nobby at dusk on Boxing Day was, in fact, Burgess, he could not possibly have been in Gatton at 6.30 p.m. on the same day, as the two places are approximately fifty kilometres apart in a direct line.

On 24 January 1899, at the Gatton Court House, after he had given his evidence at the Magisterial Inquiry, Burgess was placed in a line-up with a number of other men including some railway gang workers who had volunteered their services. A woman named Lizzie Labinsky identified Burgess as a man who, she said, called at her place at Laidley on 23 December. She must have been mistaken as it seems certain that Burgess was in the Warwick-Allora area at this time. Mrs Margaret Carroll and her son, John Carroll, picked out Burgess as having "a strong resemblance" to the man they saw at the sliprails of Moran's paddock on the night of 26 December, and Michael Donoghue (who is also in some reports referred to as "Michael Donohue") thought Burgess "looked like" the man he had seen at the sliprails on the same night, but he could not be sure. David Reisenleuter and Thomas Costick claimed to recognise Burgess as being near Tent Hill "about Christmas Day". Mrs Esther Hodges, Mrs Louisa Berg and Miss Hannah McGuire identified Burgess as being near Helidon on 29 December, and John Neylan, a farmer of Highfields at the top of the Range, recognised him as the man who called at his place on the evening of 29 December and ravenously ate a meal of meat and vegetables which was given him.[27] Burgess readily confirmed the identifications which placed him at Helidon and Highfields on 29 December, but he denied being in Laidley and Gatton as claimed by the other witnesses. With these he got quite angry. In both line-ups which were supervised by Sub-Inspector White, Burgess frequently changed his position in the line and exchanged hats with the other men near him.[28] He evidently was an old hand at this game.

Shortly after Burgess's arrest on 6 January 1899, newspaper reports appeared claiming it was rumoured that Burgess had told the police that on the night of Boxing Day he had camped near the culvert on the Tent Hill road. This culvert is about 485 metres from the sliprails giving entrance to Moran's paddock in the direction of Tent Hill and is about 460 metres west of the spot where the murders took place. Burgess is reported to have stated that while camped there that night he "heard a horse gallop furiously along the road from the direction of Gatton". These newspaper reports also claimed that a party of police "with the aid of a photograph and persistent inquiry" had traced Burgess from the culvert near Gatton in a south-easterly direction to the neighbourhood of Laidley from where he appeared to have doubled back until he reached Mt Whitestone at the head of Ma Ma Creek. From this point, according to the reports, the police tracked Burgess to near the junction of Ma Ma Creek and Lockyer Creek, on to Helidon and then to Flagstone Creek, at which place several of the residents identified a photograph of Burgess as the man whom they had seen in the district about the end of the month.[29]

These reports are not consistent with Burgess's statements regarding his movements on Boxing Day and thereafter made at the Magisterial Inquiry and to his solicitor, Mr Herbert, and as graphically represented in the map which he drew. Burgess admitted being in Helidon on or about 29 December 1898, claiming that he had come down the Range from the Downs, but he emphatically denied being in either Laidley or Gatton.

The police investigation of Burgess appears to have centred mainly around his statements concerning his movements between Killarney and Greenmount during the period from 15 to 27 December 1898, and it would seem that the reports of his alleged statement that he had camped at the culvert near Gatton on the night of 26 December, and of his allegedly having travelled from there to the Laidley area and back to Helidon were without foundation. It is evident that the police made very extensive inquiries in the area between Killarney and Greenmount and that Burgess's account of his movements in that locality was carefully checked out. Newspapers of the time reported that Sub-Inspectors Galbraith and Durham and Sergeant Toomey headed these inquiries, and that police carrying out the investigations established a camp near Greenmount.[30] It would appear that the public followed these investigations with great interest, for one newspaper commented:

> The police may be compared to the ancient Sphinx in the matter of the silence with regard to late developments connected with the Gatton tragedy. The public are in a state of ferment to know the result of Inspector Durham's and Detective Toomey's labours in the Clifton district but nothing from an official source has transpired as far. Notwithstanding this, it is now generally considered that Burgess's account of his travels about Christmas time is fairly correct. The reticence of the police lends colour to this theory because it is alleged that if the police had upset Burgess's story they would let the facts be known.[31]

On 26 January 1899, Burgess was again brought up in the Toowoomba Police Court before three Justices of the Peace on the charge of larceny of a saddle. The proceedings were, to say the least, unusual.

Sub-Inspector Durham offered no evidence on the larceny charge, withdrew it and preferred another of having no visible means of support. Burgess, who was again represented by Mr J. Herbert, when asked to plead said, "Oh, I don't know. I plead not guilty." Constable J. Gillies gave evidence that Burgess had no money on him when he was searched at the Dalby watchhouse after his arrest on 6 January 1899, and that he was not then in employment. Constable McInerney deposed that he was present at the Magisterial Inquiry at Gatton on 24 January when, in his evidence, Burgess had said that he had worked for only four days and received only ten shillings since 30 November 1898, and that he stole food if people would not give it to him.

Mr Herbert asked for a discharge claiming there was no criminality in what the defendant had been doing. His application was refused. The matter then proceeded and subsequently, when Burgess went into the witness box, he said that "Richard Burgess" was the name he went by and that he was in the Dalby district early in January 1899, inquiring for a man named Daly who had a sawmill in the Bunya Mountains. He wanted to see Daly about a job at the sawmill, but he was arrested before seeing him.

Mr Herbert again asked for the dismissal of the charge commenting that the prosecution was an absurdity and he did not know the object of it. He said the defendant's evidence showed he was looking for work and if the charge was not dismissed any man travelling looking for work might be arrested.

Sub-Inspector Durham said that the extraordinary circumstances of the case were special reasons why the court should deal with it, partly in the interest of the defendant, who, if sent out now would have no one to help him. The defendant, while travelling through the country, was causing fear. He therefore asked the Bench to deal with the case exceptionally. Mr Herbert replied "I object. That is not in the evidence" to which Sub-Inspector Durham replied with the remarkable statement that if the Bench would deal with the case it could be reviewed by the Executive. The exchange continued—

> *Mr Herbert:* Who is going to pay for that? If they do as you ask and give an improper verdict, that will be a deliberate insult to the Bench.
> *Sub-Inspector Durham:* Other circumstances must have come to the knowledge of the Bench that would cause them not to deal with the matter as an ordinary one.
> *Mr Galloway, J.P.:* The defendant is sentenced to two months imprisonment in Brisbane Gaol.[32]

Not unexpectedly, there appeared in the Press at this time some expressions of disquiet concerning the treatment of Burgess by the police and the courts. A Sydney newspaper commented—

> The legal proceedings that have taken place so far in connection with the Gatton case are not of a character which will go to increase public respect for the majesty of the law. They can only be justified, if at all, by a very strained interpretation of the always dangerous moral maxim about the end sanctifying the means. The whole energy of the Police Department of Queensland has been exercised for over a month following up mysterious clues which have led to nothing. In the meantime a suspected person has been arrested and submitted to a course of treatment which, whatever the ultimate outcome may be, wears a present appearance which is most difficult to reconcile with the fundamental principles of British liberty. That they suspected Burgess of knowing something about the crime was, however, allowed to transpire at an early stage and the result of this suspicion was his arrest on an apparently trumped-up charge of stealing a saddle. While held in custody on this charge, he was put into the witness box to give evidence about the Gatton outrage in connection with which he was at the time under suspicion. He there had to submit to cross-examination on a matter concerning which endeavours were being made to build up a capital indictment against him. As a result of the admissions thus wrung from him, he was then charged with vagrancy and sentenced to two months gaol. The evidence upon which this conviction was made is the same as might be given against any of the thousands of "sundowners"

who carry their swags about the country. But it was claimed by the Police that there were "other circumstances" which should influence the Court in sending the man to gaol. That is to say that rumours not then before the Court in evidence, but presumably known to it in other ways, should be considered. And the Court considered it as suggested.

No disguise was made of the fact that it was because of these rumours and not of the evidence that the police wanted to have Burgess imprisoned while further investigation was made into them. All these proceedings therefore simply amount to a series of manoeuvres to deprive Burgess of the benefit of the Habeas Corpus Act and enable the authorities to keep him in durance without giving him an opportunity to answer the real charge upon which he is held. Thus we have a man virtually under arrest, but not under committal, put in gaol on a bogus charge while the police work up their charge against him. No matter who Burgess is or what he has done, this is all the same a violation of the spirit of fair play which is instinct in British law. Until he is proved guilty he is entitled to all the rights and liberties of a man who is innocent, and without prejudice to any subsequent proceedings in which he may figure, these he should have. There was either sufficient ground to justify the arrest of Burgess in a fair and above board way or there was not. If there was he should have been so arrested; if there was not then there was no justification for the sort of proceedings that have been taken. After having thoroughly located the man, it should have been an easy thing to have prevented him escaping without straining the law for the purpose of putting him under lock and key. With all their secretiveness however, it appears that they made their spring before they were ready. And hence the necessity of following it up by irregular means. If all ends well, that may condone everything but it is, nevertheless, dangerous to experiment where the sacredness of individual liberty is at stake and this is an experience which, it is to be hoped, will act as a warning of what to avoid, rather than a precedent to be followed in dealing with suspected persons.[33]

Burgess was escorted from Toowoomba to Brisbane on 28 January 1899, and was lodged in Boggo Road Gaol. During February portion of his sentence was spent in travelling with a party of police headed by Sub-Inspector White over the route he claimed to have taken from the date of his discharge from St Helena up to 28 December 1898. This expedition was undertaken with a view to verifying or disproving Burgess's statements regarding his movements during this period and in particular his account of his whereabouts on Boxing Day.[34] A young Queensland public servant named Arthur Hoey Davis accompanied the party as official shorthand reporter. Under the pseudonym "Steele Rudd", he was later to achieve fame as one of Australia's best known writers.[35] It would seem that after this exercise, which was the culmination of a most intensive investigation of Burgess, the police were of the opinion that he had established an alibi and they had no, or insufficient, evidence to connect him with the murders.

Shortly after he had served his two months sentence Burgess left Queensland and moved south.[36] The Queensland Police enjoined the police of the other colonies to keep an eye on him and he was subsequently arrested in Melbourne and charged with attempted rape. He was convicted on 19 July 1900 and was sentenced to seven years' imprisonment which he served in Pentridge goal. He boasted that he was the Gatton murderer. He was released from Pentridge on 27 April 1907 and later went to Western Australia, was imprisoned and died there.[37]

In 1924, in his book *Studies in Australian Crime*, J.D. Fitzgerald wrote—

> Burgess may have been the murderer; but the people in the district who ought to have known some of the circumstances, never took his arrest seriously. They thought there was another explanation of the crime, touching profounder depths than those fathomed by the passions of a vulgar tramp with a sexual mania.... The murderous tramp theory seems the more natural and feasible. At the same time, one of our greatest Australian jurists, now dead, was profoundly convinced from an intimate acquaintance with the case that the crime had tragic analogies with the "Oedipus" and the "Lear".

After a careful examination and appraisal of all the information available to us in relation to Richard Burgess we are inclined to the view that it is most unlikely that he was the perpetrator of the Gatton outrage. Apart from the fact that his account of his movements on the fateful Boxing Day approximately fifty kilometres from the scene of the crime was apparently corroborated, thus establishing for him a complete alibi for the crime, his innate character and previous criminal *modus operandi* suggests to us that a preconceived crime of such magnitude and audacity, and involving such a degree of premeditation was not within his capabilities. Burgess appears to have been of an impulsive disposition and his crimes were committed spontaneously with little regard to the risk of detection. He had a proclivity for attacking people who were particularly vulnerable and whom he could easily worst in a physical encounter—women alone, and elderly and feeble persons.[38] (The woman attacked by Burgess at Leyburn in May 1898 was sixty years old and the farmer, John O'Brien whom he assaulted at Moggill early in December was reported to be about ninety years of age.)[39]

In our view Burgess was not the type of man to preconceive and carefully and methodically plan a crime, reconnoitre a location propitious to his designs and then pit himself against three victims together, one a strong young fellow in the prime of his manhood.

Nor do we believe that it was in Burgess's nature to act in concert with an accomplice in the commission of a crime. The available evidence appears to us to indicate the validity of the observation of a newspaper reporter who wrote, "Truly is it reported of Burgess that he is a man who abhors company and that he avoids society as much as possible."[40]

9
THOMAS DAY

Thomas Day has already been the subject of reference in this outline of events, throughout which he looms as a shadowy and most mysterious figure. He appeared, it seems, out of nowhere and after a brief sojourn in Gatton, faded again into the obscurity from which he had emerged.[1] He was, in December 1898, about twenty or twenty-one years of age and was described as "a man fully 5 feet 9 inches [*175 cm*] or 5 feet 10 inches [*178 cm*] in height...quite a young, overgrown fellow."[2] He was a stranger to Gatton, having arrived there about eleven days before the murders. Mr Clarke, the butcher, met Day on 15 December 1898, on the Tent Hill road near his butchery. Day told Clarke that he had come from New South Wales and that he came by Laidley to Gatton. He was engaged by Clarke and commenced employment on the following day. He worked for Clarke from 16 December 1898 until 10 January 1899, his work consisting of looking after the coppers at the slaughter yard and carting meat into Gatton township to Clarke's butcher shop.[3]

Shortly after their arrival in Gatton the police became aware that Day was a recent arrival and was in the employ of Clarke. At the Commission, Acting Sergeant Toomey gave evidence of his questioning of Day on the morning of 30 December 1898. Part of his evidence was as follows:

Q. Tell us first about Day. When did you first hear about him?
A. I found out about him myself.
Q. In what way?
A. I called at Clarke's on the morning of the 30th.
Q. Without having heard anything—or any rumours?
A. Without having heard anything at all. I made inquiries to ascertain if anybody was seen about. That is to say, after making a search in the paddock round the scene of the murder in company with a black tracker. I do not know who I spoke to first at Clarke's. I asked if there were any strangers there and was told "Yes; a man had been hired here about a fortnight ago." I inquired where

he was and was told. I went to see him. It was the man Day. I said to him "Terrible affair up here (meaning the murders). Do you know anything at all about it?" "No," he said, "I never heard anything." I said, "Where were you on the night of the murders?" "Well," he said, "I was about; I was in bed. I had tea at seven o'clock. I usually have tea in the evening, at that time. I left the kitchen and went to bed." I said, "Did you not go out after that?" He said "No." I said, "You are supposed to have been seen on the road." He said, "No, I was not." I said, "Who saw you go to bed?" He said, "I do not know anyone did. I am fond of reading. I went into my room. I read for a little and went off to sleep." I said, "Didn't you hear anything at all during the night?" He said "No." I said, "That is very strange. This girl in the house heard screams and reports of firearms."

Q. (*By Mr Sadleir*) The girl Lowe?

A. The girl Thurgoff [*sic*] who was in the employ of Clarke at the time.

Q. (*By Mr Dickson*) How far away would he sleep?

A. About fifty yards [*forty-five metres*]—not that; but it would make a great difference, because she had the back door open and was not in bed. She got up to put some cats out, and she would have every opportunity of hearing what was going on. I inquired where he came from, and he said he came from Brisbane. He came over from Sydney in a boat, but came from Brisbane by road. He got hard-up, and Mr Clarke employed him. He said he thought he was not going to stay there long. I said, "How is that?" "Oh," he said, "Clarke is a man who never keeps anyone long, I am told, and I do not care for the place." I said, "Would you mind me having a look through your room?" He showed me into his room. I looked through everything. There was very little—just a singlet or two, two blue jumpers, I think two pair of pants, a couple of straps, and a blanket. I looked through his clothes, and examined them very carefully. I found that, just about here [*pointing to a spot on the inner side of the arm, near the elbow-joint*], on the right sleeve of a blue jumper, a patch of blood. The blood was perfectly dry. It did not appear to me to be very recent—any way, at the time. I never said anything, but passed it over, until I had everything examined. I turned the sleeves of the jumper inside out to see if there was blood inside, and I found none. I said, "How did you get this blood on your jumper?"

Q. What size was the patch of blood?

A. Quite small; it would not be an inch square [*twenty-five mm square*] by any means. I said, "How do you account for this blood?" and he said, "Well, I was down at the yard one day, and got wet, and I only have two jumpers. I put on that one, and I then took meat into Gatton and I must have got it off the meat." So I said, "Who saw you wearing this jumper on that day?" and he said "Mr Clarke did." I then made a thorough search of the premises where he was, and of the lofts overhead, underneath, and a boiler, all round the place, and under the boards, and found nothing that would arouse my suspicions in any way, with the exception of this one patch of blood, and I thought that was a very natural thing for a butcher to have on his clothes. I then went and saw Mr Clarke, and said to him, "Is it a fact that this man was wearing a new jumper?" In fact I brought Day with me, and the jumper, which I took away again after showing it to Clarke. I said, "Do you remember Day wearing that jumper any day last week?" and I think I mentioned Friday or Saturday. I said, "Do you remember Day getting wet and changing the jumper which he had on?" He said, "Yes, I do remember he was wearing it at the slaughter yard." I said, "Was he taking meat into Gatton that day?" and he said, "Yes." I did not take possession of the jumper. I did not think there was any need. In fact I do not think so now. I then said to Clarke, "What clothes did Day bring with him?" and he said, "I saw him when he came. There was only a swag, and I think he had only a singlet or two, a shirt or two, a couple of pairs of trousers, and a couple of jumpers, as far as I could see, but I think he got a few articles in Gatton since then." He said he had given him some money and he had bought a few little articles in Gatton. I then asked Clarke what kind of a man Day was, and he told me he appeared to be a very quiet fellow. I asked him if there were any firearms in the place that would carry a ·380 cartridge, and he said, "No." I asked him if Day had any firearms, and he said, "No"; and in fact I made every possible inquiry to satisfy myself.

Q. Did you ask Day who he associated with?
A. He told me he had no associates.
Q. Did he talk about Cox?
A. Cox was not there at the time.
Q. (*By Mr Garvin*) Was he cool and collected?
A. Perfectly cool and collected.
Q. There was nothing to indicate that he was insane?
A. Oh, no: nothing whatever.[4]

Toomey was then asked three questions by a member of the Commission. His answers thereto reflect the disarming frankness of another age:

Q. (*By Mr Dickson*) You said to Day, "You are supposed to have been seen on the road"?

A. That is what a man in my line of business would say. I wanted to get a clue.

Q. Did you tell him anyone had seen him on the road?

A. No. In fact, nobody had seen him as far as I then knew. I tried to get him on the road.

Q. You had not been told that he had been seen on the road?

A. No. I had heard nothing of his being on the road, but a man in my line of business has often to tell a lie.[5]

The members of the Commission then further questioned Toomey in regard to the investigation of Day:

Q. (*By the Chairman*) Did Day tell you where he was born?

A. I never asked him.

Q. Or why he came there?

A. I never asked him.

Q. You made no inquiry into his antecedents?

A. All he told me was that he had come from Brisbane, and had swagged it along the road. I was perfectly satisfied after what Clarke had told me; the blood on the jumper was natural enough, he being a butcher.

Q. (*By Mr Garvin*) Did he appear to be in any way frightened?

A. No, he was perfectly cool and collected and quiet.

Q. (*By Mr Dickson*) Did he tell you he had been working for a man named Wilson, in New South Wales?

A. That was some time after. I was present when his statement was taken, and heard that.

Q. Was his statement correct according to what he had told you before?

A. Yes; but I did not ask him if he had been working for a man in New South Wales.

Q. (*By Mr Sadleir*) Was there anything inconsistent with his former statement?

A. There was nothing inconsistent about it.

Q. (*By Mr Garvin*) When did you first hear that he was supposed to be the man at the sliprails?

A. On that very afternoon.

Q. Go on and tell us.

A. I do not know who told me; but, however, I was told that afternoon that young Carroll saw a man—that he and his mother were near the Murphys when they passed the sliprail, saw a man as they passed by, and had a good view of him. I saw young Carroll that afternoon. Asked, "Were you at the Mount Sylvia races?" He said, "Yes." I said, "What time did you come in?" and he told me. I said, "Did you see the Murphys?" and he said, "Yes, we passed them." I said, "Did you see a man when you passed the sliprails?" and he said. "Yes." I said, "Can you give a description of him?" and he told me his height and the hat he was wearing, but he said he did not see his face, so I said, "Did your mother see him?" and he said, "Yes." I said, "Do you think he was anything like Clarke's man?" I mentioned the man to him at the time, and he said, "Yes; I told my mother that I thought it was Clarke's man." I think if you turn up my statement you will find that I mentioned the matter to him, but he never said anything to me about the man being Clarke's man until I mentioned it.

Q. (*By Mr Dickson*) Did the description of the clothes he was wearing correspond with the clothes that Day was wearing?

A. I asked him how the man was dressed, and he said he might have been wearing a shirt, or he might have been wearing a coat, or he might have been wearing a jumper. I said, "Was he wearing a jumper like the one Clarke's man had on?"

Q. Did you mention the colour?

A. Yes; I told him a blue jumper, and he said he thought it was a blue shirt or a blue jumper.

Q. (*By Mr Garvin*) Did you ask him if he could identify him?

A. Yes, and he said he could not. I would have been only too happy at the time if he could have given me a clue.

Q. (*By Mr Dickson*) Did he say what sort of trousers he had on?

A. He did not.

Q. Did he say what kind of a hat?

A. Yes, a grey slouch hat.

Q. Did that correspond with Day's hat?

A. Day had a hat of that description.

Q. Did you ask him about the trousers?

A. He said he did not know.

Q. (*By Mr Garvin*) Was it immediately after they passed that he said to his mother, "That is Clarke's man"?

A. That is what he told me.

Q. Did you ever hear that that boy had said on the ground before the bodies were removed, "The man I saw at the sliprails on the night of the twenty-seventh was Day."

A. No, I did not. I may state that this boy is a boy who, I believe, will tell a yarn as other boys will. He might tell a civilian whom he met in the street that it was Clarke's man, or some other man, he saw at the sliprails, but when he came to be tested by the police he would not say in any shape or form that it was Clarke's man.

Q. Did you question Mrs Carroll?

A. Yes.

Q. What did she say?

A. She said she did not know the man, but that her son had told her that he thought it was Clarke's man.

Q. She could not describe the man or give any idea of his age?

A. No; I tried her very hard on that point.

Q. (*By the Chairman*) If the boy was right, Day lied when he told you that he was in bed?

A. If the boy was right, certainly.

Q. (*By Mr Garvin*) Could the boy in any way be deceived in the two men, Day and Burgess?

A. I cannot possibly see how he could, for Day and Burgess are as different from another as chalk is from cheese.

Q. Were they different in height?

A. Yes.

Q. And in other respects?

A. Yes, Day was a different man altogether, a man fully 5 feet 9 inches [*175 cm*] or 5 feet 10 inches [*178 cm*] in height.

Q. Was he a young man?

A. Yes.

Q. What age would he be?

A. About twenty or twenty-one; he was quite a young, overgrown fellow.

Q. What sort of a fellow was Burgess?

A. He was a man of over forty years of age.

Q. What build would he be?

A. He was thick set, and about 5 feet 6½ inches [*168 cm*] high.

Q. (*By Mr Dickson*) Had Day a beard when you saw him?

A. No, he could not grow a beard; he had only what is called "cat's hair" on his face; nothing more.

Q. Did you find out that he had bought a razor, and had had a shave?

A. Yes, I heard all about that—that he bought a razor at Smith's, at Gatton.

Q. Was it necessary, do you think, for him to shave?

A. Of course, a man having a little overgrowth of hair on his face might do anything with it.

Q. (*By Mr Garvin*) You say he left Clarke's shortly afterwards?

A. It was some time after.

Q. How long after?

A. I cannot say exactly, but it must have been ten days after.

Q. Do you know where he went after that?

A. He went to Toowoomba by rail. He told me he had had a row with Clarke, and was going to leave him. I asked him where he was going, and he said he was going up the line looking for work.

I asked him if he would call at Toowoomba and see if he could identify Burgess as the man he had seen between Brisbane and Gatton. He said he would, and I spoke to Inspector Urquhart about him, and got him a free railway pass for that purpose.

Q. Where did he go after leaving Clarke?

A. To Toowoomba.

Q. How long did he stay there?

A. I don't know.

Q. Did he eventually join the military?

A. I heard so.

Q. You cannot say of your own knowledge?

A. No.

Q. You had long conversations with him?

A. I had.

Q. And you questioned him on all those occasions?

A. I spoke to him about nothing but the murder every time I met him.

Q. You were satisfied in your own mind that he had nothing to do with the murders?

A. Yes, and I will go further, and say that after the boy Carroll had made that statement, although he would not say it was Day he had seen at the sliprails, yet we did not fail to examine the matter thoroughly. Sub-Inspector Galbraith, Sergeant Johnson, myself, and another man went out and watched Day's hut at night. We remained about four or five hours, and we took him by surprise between one and two o'clock in the morning. He had on a portion of his clothes when we entered the room; I think he slept in his pants. We told him that we required him to go to the police station. He said, "What for?" We told him in connection with the murder. He said, "All right." He seemed quite cool and not a bit flurried. We brought him into Gatton, and he conversed all the way. We kept him at the station till the following morning. I may tell you here that at the time I first visited him I examined him so far as his hands and face—that is, the visible portions of his body—were concerned, to see if there was any scratch or mark on him, and saw only just a little scratch on his arm. At the station he made the statement which has been referred to in this inquiry, and we had him stripped and examined, but found no signs of any marks on him.

Q. When did you first show him to the boy Carroll?

A. Carroll saw him every day and knew him well.

Q. You gave him an opportunity of having a good look at Day?

A. Yes. I was with Carroll one day when Day was passing with some meat to the shop. I said, "Here is Day now." He said,

"Yes." I said, "What do you think of it?" He said, "Look here, I could not say."

Q. Well?

A. Of course, I was testing him every time I came across him to see whether he would come to the conclusion that it was Clarke's man he saw at the sliprails, but I did not press him, as I did not want him to mislead me.

Q. (*By Mr Unmack*) Did it not strike you that the boy might have been put up to denying the identification of the man, so that he should not be mixed up in a matter of that kind in a small place like Gatton?

A. No, I think the boy would have come forward and told us if he had known the man, as the mother was so anxious about the matter, and was a great friend of the victims.

Q. (*By Mr Garvin*) Did you ever ask him whether he had said to his mother that it was Clarke's man?

A. I did, and he said it struck him that it was Clarke's man.

Q. (*By Mr Dickson*) But he still persists in saying that he thinks it was Day?

A. He does, but I do not know how he can after picking out Burgess.

Q. Still he does say so?

A. I have related to you what he stated to me. If he had said that he was pretty certain, or pretty sure, or strongly believed that it was Clarke's man, I should not have missed the opportunity, but he would not say that in any shape or form.

Q. (*By Mr Garvin*) Did you ask him if he knew McNeil?

A. I did, and he said "No."

Q. Did you ever point McNeil out to him?

A. No, I did not; but I think he must have seen him, because McNeil was about the road and in Gatton every day.

Q. Did you ever on any occasion ask this boy if he had seen McNeil at all?

A. Oh, yes.

Q. What did he say?

A. I asked him if it was McNeil he saw at the sliprails, or was the man anything like him, and he said he could not say.

Q. Did he say he would know McNeil if he saw him?

A. No, he did not.

Q. Did you ask him that question?

A. I asked him so many questions that I could not say.

Q. Could the boy make a mistake between McNeil and the man Day?

A. I do not think he could make a mistake in the two men.

Q. I mean, could he mistake the one for the other?

A. I do not see how he could. He never could tell who the man was he saw at the sliprails.

Q. However, you put it point blank to him if it was McNeil?

A. I am certain I did.

Q. And he said "No"?

A. Yes. I may also say that I examined at Clarke's place thinking anything would be burned or done away with. There was a boiler there, and I rooted out the ashes with a stick and examined them. I went down to the slaughter yard and examined everything where the cattle had been killed. There was also a revolver there, hanging up on the verandah of Clarke's house, but it was ·340 bore. I asked Clarke whether he had any cartridges, and he said he had. He brought out the box, and I got him to count them. He did so, and said that he did not think any were missing. I think he also had a double-barrelled breech-loading gun.

Q. (*By the Chairman*) What were the cartridges?

A. ·340 bore, I think.[6]

At the Magisterial Inquiry, Day, of course, did not give evidence. He left the Gatton district soon after terminating his employment with Mr Clarke on 10 January 1899. The interest in Day at the Commission was, to a large extent, stimulated by a police witness, Constable Robert George Christie. Christie read to the Commission a report dated 24 April 1899 which he had addressed to Inspector Urquhart, but which he had not submitted. The relevant part of the transcript reads:

Q. (*By the Chairman*) I understand you want to give us some information with regard to the Gatton murders?

A. Yes. With your permission I would like to report of certain facts which came to my knowledge during the course of my inquiries into the Gatton murders.

Q. Tell us when you got there and how you came to be connected with it at all?

A. I went to Sydney, New South Wales, to escort a prisoner to Queensland. I arrived in Brisbane in March last, and got a fortnight's holiday. I spent my holiday at Gatton, and on the 7 March Inspector Urquhart employed me to make inquiries with reference to the Gatton murders.

Q. Then are you not in the Queensland Police Force?

A. Yes; but I am doing plain-clothes duty at Gatton at present.

Q. Were you first employed on plain-clothes duty on the 7 March?

A. Yes. "Headquarters Gatton Special District, 24 April 1899, *re* Clarke's man, Thomas Day—"

Q. (*By Mr Unmack*) To whom is that addressed?

A. Inspector Urquhart.

Q. What is the date of the report?

A. 24 April 1899.

Q. Is that among the papers?

The Secretary: That has not been sent in.

Witness: I will give my reasons why I did not send it in: I was afraid to send it in. [*Witness then read his report as follows:*]

[*Re Clarke's man—Thomas Day.*]

Headquarters, Gatton Special District,
24 April 1899.

Constable R.G. Christie, D44, reports that on the 24th instant he interviewed Mr A.G. Clarke, butcher, of Gatton, with reference to a man named Thomas Day, who was in Clarke's employment at the time of the Gatton murders. Mr Clarke informed the constable that on the 15th of December last he met Day on the Tent Hill road, near his Clarke's shop, and employed Day, who commenced to work for Clarke on the following day, the 16 December. Day told Mr Clarke that he came from New South Wales, and came by Laidley to Gatton. He worked for Mr Clarke from the 16 December until the 10th day of January last. His work consisted of looking after the coppers at the slaughter yard, and carting meat into Gatton to Mr Clarke's butcher shop, which is situated in the township. Day slept in a skillion-room adjoining Mr Clarke's stables, adjacent to the main road and not far from the scene of the murders. Mr Clarke informed the constable that during night-time, whenever he had occasion to go to Day's room he always found Day with his clothes and boots on, and lying in bed on top of the bedclothes and always easily awakened. The least knock at the room Day would hear it and come out, and he always kept the door and window open at night. Mr Clarke considers Day was a bad character, and after the Gatton murders Clarke distrusted Day, and while working about the boilers at the slaughter yard Clarke had an impression that Day would throw him into the boilers, and on account of this Mr Clarke used to send Day to do other work away from the boilers, and kept his eye on him. On Boxing night Mr Clarke was letting off fireworks from eight o'clock to a quarter to 9 p.m. Since then, Clarke thinks it strange that Day did not put in an appearance to see the fireworks going off; in fact, Mr Clarke did not see Day from dusk on that evening until the following morning. Clarke states that he is sure Day was not deaf. It appears that a day or two after the murders the police brought Day into Gatton and took a statement from him. About this time Mr Clarke saw bloodstains on a blue jumper belonging to Day, and said to Day, "You had better not wash that jumper; the police might want to see it again." Day took no heed to this warning, but a day or two afterwards washed and boiled the jumper twice, and scrubbed it with a scrubbing-brush. One day afterwards Day said to Clarke, "You ought to join the force—you would make a better detective than any of them." and gave Clarke great abuse. Mr Clarke said in his opinion the bloodstains in question were not caused by carrying meat, as they were distinct spots or splashes and shiny appearance. On the 5th of January, Day gave Clarke one week's notice that he was going to leave, and on the 7th he abused Clarke, and wanted to get away, and on the 10th he again asked to let him go, and began to abuse Clarke, and used bad language to Clarke's children, and Clarke let him go, and that was one day before the notice had expired. The constable interviewed Florrie Lowe, who states that she did not know Clarke's man, Day, previous to the murders. The constable also interviewed Mrs Carroll, of Gatton, who stated that on the night of the Gatton murders she was coming into Gatton from the Mount Sylvia races in a spring cart accompanied with her son John, who is about sixteen years old; when passing Moran's paddock, about 8.30 p.m., the three Murphys—Michael, Norah, and Ellen—were driving in a trap about ten or twelve yards [*nine to eleven metres*] in front of her, going in the direction of Gatton; when near the sliprails leading into Moran's paddock she saw a man walking along the road towards them; he passed by the Murphys' trap quite close, and when passing her cart she said to her son John, "This is a footman coming." "Yes," John replied as the man passed the cart; "that is Clarke's man, mother." The constable has been informed by Mr Burnett, fruiterer, Gatton, that when he was coming along the Tent Hill road at night-time, between the 15 and 26 December, he had on two occasions met Day on the road near Moran's paddock and spoke to him, but Day made no answer. Day was a stranger in the Gatton district, and if he arrived in Brisbane from New South Wales in the early part of December probably he is the swagman that passed Wilson at Oxley on the 10th of December last.

R.G. CHRISTIE, Constable No. 503.

Inspector Urquhart, Police Station, Gatton.

Q. (*By the Chairman*) You say you did not send that report in?
A. No, sir.
Q. Why?
A. I had my reasons for not sending it in.
Q. Did you show it to Inspector Urquhart?
A. No.
Q. (*By Mr Unmack*) Tell us your reasons for not sending it in.
A. On the 24 April last me and Sergeant Arrell had a conversation with Detective Head. Head says, "How is things now, Christie?" I said, "In my opinion there is only one man in it—Clarke's man." He said, "What rot." Sergeant Arrell says, "Well, it looks very suspicious." Next morning I was sitting in the police office. Detective Head came in and said to Inspector Urquhart, "I want to speak to you, sir." Inspector Urquhart said, "Very well," and went out into the police yard with him. They had a conversation, and Head then went away. Inspector Urquhart said to me, "Where

143

is Sergeant Arrell, Christie?" I said, "He is inside, sir." He said, "Tell him I want him." Sergeant Arrell came into the courthouse, and Inspector Urquhart said, "You've got a lot to say about this man Day, Arrell. If I hear any more about this, out of this you go—out you go." He said, "The idea of you criticising the work of better men than yourself!" I had then just completed my report which I have just read, and I walked up the street, and a short while afterwards Inspector Urquhart followed me up the street. He said, "Look here, Christie, I don't want you speaking about this man Day." I said, "I have simply made inquiries about him, sir. I spoke to Detective Head about him last night, and that is all I have been talking to about him. I do not see there is any harm in speaking to the detectives." He said, "Well, If I hear any more about this, Christie, I will make it hot for you if I get you talking about this man." He said, "You are a strange man; you have a lot of ideas in your head." I said, "Well, sir, I do not work on a one-man system; I work on several; and I consider that man is in it." And I explained several points which were in my report. He said, "What rot, Christie; he is only a mere boy; he could not commit that crime; he is a beardless boy." I said, "If he is only a beardless boy, Bob King, at Clarke's place, told me he was thirty years old, and weighed between thirteen and fourteen stone [*eighty-two and eighty-nine kg*]." Inspector Urquhart said, "Bob King is a damned liar if he told you such a thing." I was afraid to send in my report through him threatening me.

Q. (*By Mr Garvin*) Why did you not send it to the Commissioner?
A. Because I thought I would get into trouble.
Q. You could have sent it to the Commissioner?
A. Not direct—it is against the rules. I consider that I would have got into serious trouble if I had sent it direct to the Commissioner. I was working direct under Inspector Urquhart, who was in charge of the Gatton special district at the time.
Q. Did you ever express a wish to send this information to the Commissioner?
A. No, because I thought I would get into trouble if I wrote such a thing. I considered that they had made a blunder, and wanted to hush it up. The detectives made a blunder in the first place, and wanted to throw cold water on it. That was the reason for trying to keep me from making inquiries in the matter. The detectives were all against me making inquiries against this man.
Q. That is what you mean by making a blunder with regard to Day?
A. Yes. I say they made a blunder. They did not have his jumper analysed; and Bob King, who works at Clarke's place, told me it was saturated with blood, and there were distinct spots and

splashes all over the jumper. Detective Toomey said it was only on the sleeve, but Bob King told me it was all over the body, and in his opinion it did not appear as if he got it off the cattle. Besides, he never had anything to do with killing the sheep or cattle; he was only employed pottering about the boilers.

Q. (*By Mr Sadleir*) Were you still continued in the same employment by Inspector Urquhart in plain clothes?

A. I am working under Sub-Inspector Galbraith and Inspector Urquhart. I am stationed there to make inquiries *re* the Gatton murders. I do not know whether—I have not got any definite instructions whether I am to go in uniform or plain clothes.

Q. Are you a single man?

A. Yes.

Q. Had you mentioned to Mr Galbraith anything of the substance of that report?

A. No.

Q. You are supposed to give him all the information you collect?

A. Yes. I made a report to Galbraith.

Q. To what effect?

A. About certain information I collected.

Q. About the Gatton business?

A. I thought it might refer to that.

Q. Did you report to Galbraith that you still suspected Day?

A. No; because I was afraid to mention that to him for fear that I would be dismissed, if I did so.

Q. I am speaking of Sub-Inspector Galbraith. Did you mention that to him?

A. No.

Q. You are under the impression that Day was concerned in this murder?

A. Yes; but I had no opportunity of informing Galbraith of this. When I am attached to a station, I must submit everything to the sub-inspector. It was only last month that I was transferred to Gatton.

Q. (*By Mr Dickson*) Under what sub-inspector were you working?

A. Sub-Inspector Galbraith, since 1 September.

Q. You are working under some authority at Gatton?

A. Yes; Sub-Inspector Galbraith.

Q. Do you not take any notice of Sergeant Arrell?

A. He sees all my reports.

Q. Have you spoken to him on this matter?

A. Yes, and he is of the same opinion as myself.

Q. You spoke to Arrell in September?

A. Yes, and we decided to let the matter drop—we were frightened

145

to make a report on it; but when I saw the Royal Commission was appointed I thought I would have a good opportunity to ventilate the matter.

Q. (*By Mr Sadleir*) It appears to me that you are running on one line—that Day is the man?

A. Yes, I came to that conclusion.

Q. He is the only man you wished to sheet the crime home to?

A. Yes. On the morning of the discovery Day went into a shop kept by Annie Smith, and asked for a razor. He took the razor and put it in his pocket, without asking whether it was a good one, and he had a clean shave.

Q. What sort of a beard had he?

A. A stubbly beard.

Q. Why did he shave?—To disguise himself?

A. Probably.

Q. What did he want the razor for?

A. To commit suicide if he was charged.

Q. That is your opinion?

A. Yes.

Q. (*By Mr Garvin*) How long have you been in the Police Force?

A. Six years.

Q. (*By Mr Sadleir*) That's your idea of the evidence—that Day intended to commit suicide?

A. Yes.

Q. Do you wonder at Mr Urquhart swearing at you, when you gave him information of that sort?

A. I never expressed myself to Sub-Inspector Urquhart in this way. I only came to this conclusion a few days ago.

Q. (*By Mr Dickson*) Sub-Inspector Urquhart spoke to you?

A. I had several conversations with Sub-Inspector Urquhart.

Q. Had you spoken to Sub-Inspector Urquhart about Day?

A. Yes.

Q. And to Sergeant Arrell?

A. Yes.

Q. What did you tell Mr Urquhart?

A. That I considered Day was connected with the crime.

Q. (*By Mr Garvin*) Did you give any reasons?

A. Yes; because blood was found on his clothes.

Q. (*By Mr Dickson*) Was Day's shirt taken possession of and examined?

A. As far as I know, it never was. I learned that they took a mere statement from Day, and they never traced him up. He was never traced, and he might have been the murderer.

Q. On the 24th of April, the day you wrote this report out, did you know where Day was?

A. No.

Q. Have you found out since where he was?

A. No.

Q. (*By Mr Garvin*) Why do you think this man was concerned in the Oxley murder?

A. Simply because I have learnt he arrived in Brisbane from New South Wales on the 6th of December, and the Oxley murder was committed on the 10th. Seeing he stopped a day in Brisbane, it would just leave him time to get into Oxley on the 10th or the night of the 10th. He arrived at Gatton on the 14th and informed Mr Clarke, when he employed him on the road, that he was camped in the show ground, pointing to the Gatton show ground.

Q. What would be his object in murdering this boy?—Did you come to any conclusion as to what his object was?

A. I did not say he ever murdered the boy.

Q. How did you connect him with Oxley?

A. There is a swagman supposed to be passed by Wilson at Oxley on the 10th of December, and he was supposed to have handed him something. It was probably a revolver.

Q. You think Wilson handed the swagman something?

A. It might have been a revolver, as the cartridge corresponded both at Oxley and Gatton. Both cartridges corresponded with each other.

Q. Did you make inquiries at Gatton whether this man had been seen with a revolver?

A. Yes, I did. No one knew anything about him. He never associated there with anyone. He hardly spoke to the man who was working along with him.

Q. Did you inquire if he had been seen out?

A. Yes, I did.

Q. What was the result?

A. They said he was seen. The man appeared to be a bad character.

Q. Have you thought what would be his object in committing these murders?

A. For lust.

Q. For lust?

A. Yes.

Q. Are you not aware he met the girl Miss Lowe at the sliprails single-handed before these people came up?

A. Yes.

Q. Why did he not attack her?

A. He knew two men had passed, and he would not get off. They might catch him up.

Q. Do you not think he ran a terrible risk in tackling a big man like Murphy?

A. He might leave her, and take the chance of someone else coming along and getting a better opportunity.

Q. Do you not think he ran a terrible risk in stopping a trap having in it a big, strong, able man like Murphy, if lust was his object?

A. He could decoy them in. He could pretend he had a mate 'possum shooting and the gun exploded, and decoy them down to convey the man up. He might have said, "You can leave the ladies here; it is all right," and it is only natural the girls would say, "We will go down and see what we can do with the poor fellow."

Q. That is your theory?

A. Yes, and when he jumped out he would say, "Here he is," and when he stooped down to see he would shoot him. The girls would be frightened and run away, and he would knock them over the head, and he would have them to himself.[7]

The man Wilson, mentioned by Constable Christie, was variously referred to as Edward Linton Cairns Wilson and as John Edward Liton Carns Wilson. He was an Englishman and in 1898 was a schoolteacher in Ipswich. Wilson was charged in the South Brisbane Police Court in April 1899 with the murder of a boy named Alfred Stephen Hill at Oxley on 10 December 1898. Hill, who was fifteen years old, had left his home at Nundah, a Brisbane suburb, on the morning of 10 December 1898 to visit his uncle at Redbank Plains. He never arrived at his uncle's house and was reported missing by his father. Police ascertained that young Hill was last seen near Oxley at about 5 p.m. on 10 December. On 7 January 1899 his decomposed body and the carcass of the piebald pony he had been riding were found in the bush at Oxley about 350 metres off the main Brisbane-Ipswich road. Both had been shot through the head and nearby was found a live ·380 cartridge and a spent ·380 cartridge case. It seemed that the motive for the crime was the concealment of an unnatural offence committed on the boy.

Wilson had left Ipswich on the morning of 10 December 1898 and walked towards Brisbane pushing a cart in which was his crippled eleven year old son Claude. In his evidence at the South Brisbane Police Court on 13 April 1899, Claude Wilson deposed that at Ipswich his father had shown him a revolver and cartridges in a leather case. He said that as he and his father approached Oxley on the afternoon of 10 December 1898 he saw a boy riding a piebald horse in the bush beside the road. He said that his father left him sitting in the cart while he climbed through a fence and went into the bush. After some time had elapsed he heard the report of a revolver and soon afterwards his father came out of the bush and told him he had shot a hawk. Continuing his evidence, Claude Wilson said that he and his father then proceeded on towards Brisbane and, when approaching the Oxley Hotel, they met a swagman with whom his father conversed in low tones for some time. He said that he saw his father pass something to the swagman and that he and his father then went on to the Oxley Hotel where they stayed for the night.[8]

Edward Wilson was arrested at Albany, Western Australia, on 10 January 1899 aboard the steamer *Yarrawonga* which was bound for South Africa. He emphatically denied any knowledge of the crime and eventually the Crown did not proceed against him.[9]

Constable Christie apparently believed that Wilson had shot the unfortunate boy Hill at Oxley late in the afternoon of 10 December 1898 and shortly afterwards on the same day passed the revolver to a swagman whom Christie believed was Thomas Day. According to Christie's theory, Day then used the revolver in the Gatton outrage sixteen days later. Christie may well have been right. Certainly a ·380 calibre firearm was used in each case, although revolvers and rifles of that bore were in common use at the time. It is interesting to note that at the scene of both murders a spent ·380 cartridge case was found. Was the same revolver used in both murders? And could it have had some defect in the firing mechanism which made the reloading of the chamber necessary or desirable for the firing of a second shot? Undoubtedly this possibility would have occurred to the police investigating both murders; but in 1898 they had none of the technical and scientific aids which are so extensively used today in the solving of crimes. The comparison microscope (an instrument which enables a person to see two bullets simultaneously, magnified many times, as a composite image) was to provide forensic ballistics with a really reliable foundation. But the comparison microscope was not invented until 1924 (by Philip O. Gravelle)—so it was unheard of at the time when intensive investigations were being made into the Oxley and Gatton murders.

Christie's theory is an interesting one, which certainly cannot be dismissed out of hand. It accounts for Day having access to a firearm during the period he was in Gatton. If the theory be accepted then it would follow that Day, unknown to anyone, could easily have had the revolver secreted in his swag and subsequently disposed of it in a creek or elsewhere immediately or shortly after the commission of the Gatton murders.

Constable Christie, it will be remembered, referred to Day, on the morning of the discovery of the murders, going into Smith's shop and purchasing a razor. In this regard the evidence given before the Commission by Andrew Stevenson Smith, a storekeeper and baker at Gatton, is short but interesting:

Q. What do you want to tell us?

A. Just a few words in reference to this man Day. On the morning of the murder this man came into my store and bought a razor. A few hours afterwards he came back shaved and in clean clothes, and he paid a quarter's subscription to the School of Arts, which my daughter was looking after. Within two or three days after this I was speaking to Carroll in reference to the man he saw at the sliprails. I said, "John, who did you take the man to be?" and he said it was Clarke's man. Of course I told detectives Toomey and Head, and Sergeant Arrell.

Q. Did they take action?

A. I expect so. I have no complaint to make against them.

Q. The police knew about it?

A. Yes.

Q. You did not complain that they did not pay any attention?

A. No.[10]

William Burnett, a general dealer at Gatton, gave evidence before the Commission:

Q. (*By the Chairman*) What is your occupation?

A. I am a general dealer at Gatton.

Q. You knew Day?

A. Yes.

Q. Did you associate with him?

A. No.

Q. But you knew him?

A. I used to serve Clarke with vegetables and fruit.

Q. I understand you want to say something with reference to him. Did you ever give the police any information with regard to him?

A. Yes, I told several of them.

Q. Do you remember whom?

A. I told Detective Toomey and Detective Head.

Q. When?

A. After the murder.

Q. Soon after?

A. Yes.

Q. What did you tell them?

A. I told them I met Day on the road.

Q. On the night of the murder?

A. Before the murder.

Q. You met him on the road?

A. Between Clarke's and the sliprails.

Q. What was he doing?

A. Walking down towards the sliprails.

Q. Was he smoking?

A. No.

Q. You have heard the evidence that sometimes he used to go out strolling up and down the road smoking at night?

A. He was not smoking when I came up. I generally go home on Wednesday night. I usually do that round on Wednesday. I said "Good night" to him, but he never answered me. He was quite close to the cart.

Q. Did you give any other information?

A. No, that is all.

Q. What sort of a man was he?

A. He was dark—about the build of Christie here.

Q. Somewhere about that build?

A. Somewhere about the build of Christie—a man of about fourteen stone [*eighty-nine kg*].

Q. (*By Mr Dickson*) About fourteen stone?

A. Well, between twelve stone [*eighty-two kg*] and fourteen stone I should take him to be.

Q. You really gave the police no information about Day other than the fact that you saw him near the sliprails one night?

A. No, I met him twice.

Q. Before the murder?

A. Yes.

Q. (*By Mr Sadleir*) It is only a very short distance?

A. It is between 200 and 300 yards [*180 and 270 metres*] from Clarke's to the sliprails, I suppose.[11]

At the Commission Day's employer, Mr Arthur George Clarke, butcher, gave evidence.[12] The manager of his butcher shop at Gatton, Mr Robert King, also gave evidence. The evidence of each of these witnesses is worthy of close scrutiny—for they were able to observe Day throughout a period of almost four weeks. A significant feature of their evidence is that it is in conflict with that of Acting Sergeant Toomey in regard to blood stains on Day's jumper. Actually the evidence of Clarke is in conflict with that of King in regard to the number of blood stains. Clarke was asked how many blood spots were on the jumper and he said "I should say there were near a dozen." He went on to say "Some of them would be the size of a shilling; and others not larger than No. 3. shot." King, on the other hand, when asked the number of blood stains, said there were "fifty or sixty" and he described them as being "from about the size of a two shilling piece down".

The evidence of Clarke and that of King can best be appreciated by considering the whole of it. Indeed, a careful reading of the transcript of the evidence of these witnesses enables us to conjure up a mental image of each witness. The transcript of Clarke's evidence before the Commission is as follows:

Q. (*By the Chairman*) Your occupation, Mr Clarke?
A. Butcher.
Q. At Gatton?
A. Yes.
Q. I understand you wish to give us some information with regard to this man Day, who was in your employ at the time these murders were committed?
A. I have no information to give.
Q. I understood that you desired to give information?
A. No, I never desired to give information. Day was in my employ.
Q. Did you form any opinion of the man while he was with you?
A. I cannot say I formed a very bad opinion of him.
Q. With regard to this blood-stained jumper, you have heard what Christie has said?
A. I did not hear all he said. I heard my name mentioned.
Q. Well, he said you objected to Day washing his jumper, and in defiance of or contrary to your wishes he not only washed the jumper but boiled it?
A. Yes, I warned him. I cautioned him against washing his clothes. I told him to leave the stain in; that he should not wash anything of that kind, because they might be of some service. I thought the blood would have been analysed. In face of that he washed them, although I could not say he boiled them; and he used a scrubbing brush, soda, and water.
Q. Contrary to your wishes, and contrary to your advice?
A. Yes.
Q. Did you see the stains?
A. Oh, yes.
Q. What were they like?
A. It is very hard for me to say, because I am not a professional at that sort of thing.
Q. Were they spots or smudges?
A. It is hardly likely, with the work that man did for me, that he would get such bloodstains on him—not the way they were placed.
Q. How were they placed?
A. On his sleeve and on his breast.
Q. Were they smudges or spots?
A. They were both. There was a clot of blood and spots. There was no real smear. If he had been carrying beef he would have got a smear.

Q. You say there was no smear?
A. Not to my idea.
Q. But you did notice the other?
A. I did.
Q. And did you inform any member of the Police Force of what you had noticed?
A. I had a conversation with Detective Toomey, but that was afterwards.
Q. How long after?
A. I cannot say. I suppose it must have been three weeks after.
Q. But not before that?
A. No, not before.
Q. Then all the washing and scrubbing had taken place?
A. Oh, yes; all the stains had been taken off.
Q. Can you say whether any member of the Police Force saw this jumper before it was washed?
A. None except Toomey. He was the man who brought the jumper to me and asked me if I recognised it.
Q. Then you contradict Toomey when he says there was only one smear on the jumper?
A. I said there was no smear.
Q. Then he is not correct when he says that was the only mark?
A. It might have been there, but I did not detect it.
Q. He says that was the only mark. You are certain there were spots of blood on the breast?
A. Yes, on the left sleeve and on the breast there was a fair amount—more than he usually had.
Q. (*By Mr Garvin*) About how many spots?
A. I should say there were near a dozen.
Q. What would be the size of them?
A. Some of them would be the size of a shilling; and others not larger than No. 3 shot.
Q. When did you first notice these spots on the jumper?
A. It was Detective Toomey who brought the jumper to me and asked me if I knew the man had such a jumper.
Q. Can you remember the date?
A. I cannot.
Q. You remember the day of the murders, the 26 December, the day of the races. Do you know if Day had the jumper on that day?
A. That was the Monday.
Q. Yes?
A. No, we had not killed on that day.
Q. When was the last date you saw the jumper on him prior to seeing the blood?

A. The only day that I can remember seeing the jumper on that man was on the previous Saturday. That would be the 24th.

Q. What time of the day was it when you saw him?

A. In the morning, about ten o'clock.

Q. If these blood spots had been on the jumper then would you have noticed them?

A. I think so.

Q. But you never saw any blood spots on the jumper until Detective Toomey showed it to you?

A. No, because I never saw the blood spots before Toomey brought the jumper to me.

Q. Were the blood spots fresh?

A. They certainly were not old.

Q. As they got old they would become black?

A. They were not very black; they were inclined to be shiny.

Q. And you know from experience that blood as it gets older gets black. Did you notice if the blood was quite old?

A. It was blackish.

Q. (*By the Chairman*) What conclusion did you come to as to the age of the blood?—Did you come to any conclusion?

A. That is more than I can say.

Q. You did not come to any conclusion?

A. I did not come to any conclusion.

Q. I understood you to say that the nature of Day's employment would not produce any blood spots at all?

A. The work that he did for me was carrying. He merely had to lift pieces of beef.

Q. He had to lift pieces of beef only?

A. Yes, and carcasses of sheep. He did no killing; he was no butcher.

Q. The lifting of those would not have put spots of blood on his jumper?

A. It is possible.

Q. (*By Mr Garvin*) Did you ever see him lifting beef with his jumper on him?

A. No.

Q. What was his usual practice in lifting beef—had he his jumper on or off?

A. He only lifted small joints, and he would put them on his shoulder.

Q. Would he lift them with his jumper on, or in his shirt sleeves?

A. Usually in his shirt sleeves.

Q. Do you think, from your examination of that jumper, that the lifting of beef or sheep could have caused those spots in the way they appeared on the jumper?

A. It is possible.

154

Q. (*By Mr Dickson*) When Day went to bed every night did he keep his boots on?

A. I cannot say that he did.

Q. Did you tell Christie so at any time?

A. I have gone down at three o'clock in the morning to call the man, and I have found him lying on the bed dressed, but that was only occasionally.

Q. Had he his boots on?

A. Yes.

Q. Did you give a display of fireworks on Boxing Night?

A. I did.

Q. At what time?

A. Between eight and nine o'clock. I know that, because I looked at the clock at ten minutes to nine, and called the children in.

Q. Was Day there?

A. No.

Q. Do you know where he was then?

A. No, I do not.

Q. Had you seen him before that?

A. Yes, having his tea.

Q. About what time?

A. I cannot say exactly, but it was about half past six.

Q. Were all the others connected with the house at the fireworks?

A. Yes.

Q. Was Day the only one who was not there?

A. Yes, that is all.

Q. (*By Mr Garvin*) How long was Day in your employment?

A. A little over a fortnight.

Q. What was his general conduct during that time?

A. Very fair; I had nothing to complain of.

Q. Was he at all eccentric in his behaviour?

A. Well, he was a quiet, reserved kind of man; that is the only thing. He would talk about nothing at all.

Q. Did you notice any peculiarity about him?

A. I cannot say, except that he was very reserved.

Q. (*By Mr Dickson*) Did Day deliver meat to the Murphys at any time?

A. No.

Q. While Day was there did the Murphys come to your shop?

A. I cannot answer that question; it is possible they did.

Q. Were they in the habit of calling at your shop?

A. No, because the meat was delivered at their place, but they did occasionally call at the shop for meat.

Q. Do you know whether either of the girls called at your shop that

155

week?

A. No.

Q. Do you know the Murphy family very well?

A. Very well, indeed.

Q. Did you know the girls very well?

A. Very well, indeed.

Q. Did you know with whom they associated?

A. Yes.

Q. Do you know whether Norah or Ellen Murphy had sweethearts about Gatton?

A. I do not know that they had.

Q. (*By Mr Garvin*) Do you remember the morning of the discovery of the bodies?

A. Yes.

Q. Did you see Day that morning?

A. Oh, yes.

Q. Did you have any conversation with him in reference to the murders?

A. That morning he took sheep in, and he was the man who came and told me about the murder.

Q. What did he say, as nearly as you can remember?

A. He asked me if I had heard of the dreadful accident.

Q. Tell us what he said in his own words?

A. He asked me if I had heard of the dreadful accident. I said, "What accident?" He said, "I hear that one of the Murphys is killed." I asked him how it happened, and he said, "The horse bolted." I asked, "Where?" He said, "In Moran's paddock." I said, "I would not believe it, because Murphy's horse is quiet." That is all I know about it.

Q. Did you ask him who told him?

A. No, I did not.

Q. (*By the Chairman*) What time was that?

A. I cannot remember what time it was.

Q. Well, about what time?

A. I cannot remember, though I have been trying to remember ever since.

Q. (*By Mr Garvin*) He only spoke of it as an accident, then. When did you hear it was a murder?

A. I should say about ten o'clock.

Q. Did you have any conversation with Day after you heard of the murders?

A. No.

Q. Why?

A. Because it was a thing he would never talk about.

Q. (*By the Chairman*) How do you mean he would never talk about it?

A. If you mentioned the thing to him he would not answer you back; he would not discuss the matter at all.

Q. (*By Mr Garvin*) You say he told you that he had heard of an accident. When you heard that it was not an accident, but a murder, did you go to him and say, "Those three people have been murdered"?

A. No, I do not think I did, because there were lots afterwards came to the shop, and I do not think I spoke to Day of it afterwards.

Q. Do you remember any other person having a conversation with Day?

A. No.

Q. How, then, did you come to the conclusion that Day would not talk about the matter?

A. Because I mentioned the subject to him, and he would only say "Well," or something like that, and turn away; he would not enter into a discussion at all.

Q. Did you notice, when you were speaking to him about the murder, any peculiarity in his manner?

A. Only a perfect state of indifference. He did not seem to interest himself in the matter at all.

Q. Was that his general demeanour?

A. I think so.

Q. Even prior to that?

A. He was very reserved. He would say "Yes" or "No," and that was all. I never saw him enter into a conversation with any person. My man says the same thing of him now.

Q. (*By the Chairman*) What man?

A. King.

Q. (*By Mr Garvin*) Did King ever tell you that he had had a conversation with Day about the murders?

A. No; he says what I say—that Day would never enter into a conversation, or say anything.

Q. You saw him pretty early on the morning of the 27th; that is the morning of the discovery of the bodies?

A. I know I sent sheep into town that morning, and it must have been pretty early, but I cannot say what time it was.

Q. Did he go about his work that morning in the usual way?

A. Yes.

Q. (*By the Chairman*) Do you know what clothing he was dressed in that morning?

A. If I remember rightly, he had only his shirt and trousers on; I am pretty well certain he had no jumper on that morning.

157

Q. (*By Mr Garvin*) Do you know where he kept his clothes?

A. As far as I know, he kept them in his bunk.

Q. Had you ever occasion to go into his room?

A. No, I never went inside his room until Toomey came to me.

Q. What date was that?

A. I cannot tell you; I suppose it must have been the day the murder was discovered.

Q. Did you look at the jumper that day?

A. That was the day Toomey brought it up, I think. I cannot remember the dates now, it is so long ago.

Q. (*By Mr Dickson*) Had you formed a bad impression of Day?

A. No, I cannot say I formed a bad impression of him.

Q. Had you ever any reason for removing him from the work at the coppers?—Used he to work at the coppers before this?

A. No, he never worked at the coppers.

Q. You did not remove him from that work, then?

A. His work was simply driving the cart about.

Q. (*By the Chairman*) He simply did labourer's work?

A. That is all.

Q. (*By Mr Sadleir*) We were told that you said you removed him from the boilers, fearing that he would throw you into the boilers?

A. That I was afraid he would throw me into the boiler?

Q. Yes?

A. That gets into rather an outside subject altogether. I would rather not go into that.

Q. Is it a fact that you said so?

A. Well, I suppose you want to know the rights inside and out of that too. This is a matter I don't care about talking about. If you wish to know I will tell you. When the wife was alive she advised me to have nothing at all to do with this man. She had a very bad opinion of him, and told me to be careful, that it was quite likely he might knock me on the head. He is a very powerful man, and a big man, too.

Q. (*By the Chairman*) He is?

A. Yes. That is how that originated that yarn about the coppers.

Q. Your wife had expressed distrust of this man to you?

A. Yes. You see that is how that originated.

Q. (*By Mr Sadleir*) Was this before or after the murder?

A. After, most decidedly.

Q. I want you to go back to the 24th, the day Day wore the jumper that Toomey showed you?

A. Yes, that would be the 24th.

Q. What work was Day doing on the 24th?

A. He took a lot of bones and offal down to the yard, and that morning it was raining—a slight shower. He went down and made up the fires and came back. That, I think, is about the extent of his work that day. Of course he cleaned up the shop, you know.

Q. Would he get his jumper soiled by any work he had to do that day?

A. No; he had no killing to do that day.

Q. But he had some meat to carry?

A. No, I don't think so. To the best of my belief he had no meat to carry that day.

Q. Detective Toomey saw the jumper before it was washed?

A. Yes, before it was washed.

Q. Was Florence Lowe employed by you while Day was with you?

A. No.

Q. When—before or after?

A. After.

Q. Do you know whether she knew Day?

A. I think not. I am not certain; but I think not. Possibly she saw him, but I am certain she was not there at the time Day was employed.

Q. You cannot say whether she knew him or not. Did she have any opportunities of seeing Day while he was in your employment?

A. Yes; because she passed the place.

Q. Was she ever at your place while Day was there?

A. I am not sure of that.

Q. You have spoken to her since, have you not?

A. Yes.

Q. Did she say anything at all as to whether she knew Day while he was at your place?

A. Well, she said she saw him.

Q. At your place?

A. Yes.

Q. Did she say anything to you about the man she had met at the sliprails?—Did she ever speak to you about that?

A. No.

Q. Did you never hear it?

A. Of course, I knew very well the girl had to go to Toowoomba, and that sort of thing; but so far as any conversation about the man at the sliprails—I don't know.

Q. You did not know she had seen a man at the sliprails?

A. Yes, I knew that.

Q. How long have you known it—a considerable time?

A. I really cannot tell you how long.

Q. Did you know she had seen a man at the sliprails while she was in your employment?

A. Yes.

Q. Did she ever describe him to you?

A. No.

Q. Did she ever connect Day with him in any way?

A. Not to my knowledge.

Q. Did she say anything about knowing this man she saw at the sliprails?

A. She never said anything to me. It is only what I saw in the papers. She never spoke to me about it.

Q. Were Day and yourself on very good terms while he was working for you?

A. Well, up to the day he gave me a week's notice.

Q. (*By the Chairman*) Did he ever while in your employment express dissatisfaction with the nature of his work?

A. No.

Q. He gave you notice, then, for no apparent reason?

A. He complained of the food, not of the work.

Q. That was his reason for going—the kind of food?

A. Yes.

Q. (*By Mr Dickson*) Had Day a beard?

A. No.

Q. Used he to shave while at your place?

A. All except his moustache.

Q. Had he a razor at your place?

A. I cannot say. I believe he had, because he shaved.

Q. Did he shave before the murders?

A. Yes, he came to my place shaved.

Q. You do not know whether he had a razor at your place before the murders?

A. I am not sure.

Q. Had he any firearms?

A. Not that I know of.

Q. Had you any firearms about your place?

A. Yes.

Q. What firearms?

A. A revolver and a gun.

Q. What sort of a revolver?

A. A six-chambered revolver. I think they call it a "Tranter".

Q. What bore?

A. ·450.

Q. Had you any rifle at all?

A. No.

Q. Were there any other guns about there that you knew of?

A. Not in my place.

Q. How did you kill your cattle?

A. By "pithing".

Q. Were none ever shot?

A. No.[13]

The evidence of Robert King, before the Commission, was as follows:

Q. (*By the Chairman*) What is your occupation?

A. I am a butcher, managing the branch for Mr Clarke at Gatton. I just wish to make a statement. It was in the month of December last Mr Clarke employed a man named Thomas Day—on the 15th of that month, and he started to work on the 16th. I then told Mr Clarke the first time I saw him that I did not like his appearance. He told me he would only keep him until he could get another man—he would do for a while. I did not like him; he seemed to me to be a bad character from the start. I never liked him.

Q. (*By Mr Garvin*) What led you to form that opinion of him?

A. He seemed to me to be a bad looking man.

Q. How long have you been working for Clarke?

A. For ten years. Clarke has had a lot of men during that time, but he never had any man I had a greater dislike to.

Q. (*By Mr Dickson*) Were you Clarke's boss man?

A. Yes, I manage the shop in the township for him.

Q. (*By Mr Garvin*) Do you remember the day the bodies were found?

A. Yes.

Q. It was on the 27 December?

A. Yes.

Q. Did you see Day that morning?

A. Yes.

Q. What time in the morning?

A. About half past six. I had had a sheep to kill. I went out from the township to kill a sheep.

Q. Where did you see him?

A. About the yard.

Q. How was he dressed?

A. He had on a singlet, a white handkerchief round his neck, and dark trousers.

Q. When did you see him after you heard of the finding of the bodies?

A. After Mr Wilson came up the street.

Q. What time?

A. After nine or about that. I did not take particular notice.

Q. Do you remember when you saw Day after that?

A. I saw him in the evening when I went out to kill a bullock.

Q. Was that the first time you saw him after hearing of the murders?

A. No; he was at the shop.

Q. What time?

A. About nine o'clock.

Q. Did you have any conversation with him?

A. He went pretty well straight away after he heard it; he did not say anything to me about it at the time.

Q. Who told him about the murders?

A. He was there when Wilson told me.

Q. Did he make any remark?

A. No.

Q. How was he dressed then?

A. The same as I told you when I saw him at the yard in the morning—dark pants, singlet, white handkerchief round his neck.

Q. Did you have any conversation with him that day about the murders?

A. I would like to read some notes I have here. [*Witness reads.*] Between the 16th and the 26th, the day of the Gatton murders, Day assisted me twice to kill, and I then noticed that he was a stronger man than myself in pulling a bullock into position for skinning. He had a blue jumper and a big slouch hat. When at work I only saw him wear the jumper on one rainy evening. This was no killing day, and there were no bloodstains on it then. The next time I saw this jumper was in Day's room on the 28 December. I noticed that it had blood spots on it on the sleeves and the breast. On the 29th the police took him in about 11 p.m. that night to the court-house. Next day I saw him at the slaughter-yard. We had a conversation about him being examined by the police. I asked him what they said about the blood on the jumper, and he made some reply and said he would "wash the bloody thing". I advised him not to wash it, but he said he must.

Q. (*By Mr Sadleir*) Could he have got that blood on his jumper when killing with you?

A. No. He wore that jumper not on killing days.

Q. Did he wear it on the 28th?

A. No. I saw it in his room on the 28th.

Q. (*By Mr Garvin*) Describe the blood marks that you saw on the jumper on the 28th?

A. It was on the sleeves and over the breast—on both sleeves—from about the size of a two shilling piece down.

Q. Were they all over the sleeves—big spots down to small ones, on the jumper?

A. Yes.

Q. Are you quite sure?

A. Certain.

Q. Did you examine it carefully?

A. I did. That was about the first man that entered my head after I heard about the murder on the 27th. I heard this boy Carroll mention this man, and I heard others also.

Q. Did those bloodstains appear to be fresh?

A. They were fairly fresh; I did not take particular notice to see if they were really fresh; but he had only come down on the 16th, and he wore it on one occasion that was a killing day.

Q. Did you take the jumper down and examine it when you saw it in his room?

A. I did. He was the first man I thought about.

Q. (*By Mr Dickson*) Do you think the stains might have been caused by simply carrying meat?

A. He never carried any meat.

Q. The detective said there was merely a smudge on the arm?

A. They were spots.

Q. (*By Mr Garvin*) Could any person be deceived with regard to those bloodstains—whether they were smudges—did they look like splashes, or what?

A. That is what I took them for to be—splashes or spots.

Q. Was Day in the room when you examined the jumper?

A. No.

Q. When did you speak to him?

A. On the 30th.

Q. Did you ask him whether there was blood on the shirt?

A. Yes, and he said: "Wash the bloody things."

Q. How many bloodstains were on the shirt?

A. Fifty or sixty.

Q. You never saw Toomey examine the coat?

A. No.

Q. (*By the Chairman*) Did you give any of this information to the police?

A. Yes.

Q. At what time?

A. A short time after I got the information.

Q. Did you speak to Toomey about the bloodstains?

A. Yes, and Toomey told me to shut up, and that Day was innocent.

Q. (*By Mr Garvin*) On what day did Toomey say this?

A. I can't say.

Q. (*By the Chairman*) After Day had gone away?

A. Yes. I can get a witness to this conversation with Toomey.

Q. (*By Mr Garvin*) Did you ever ask Day where he was on the 26th?

A. No.

Q. (*By Mr Dickson*) Who is the witness you refer to?

A. My wife.

Q. Is she here?

A. No.

Q. (*By Acting Sergeant Toomey*) Are you a good judge of character?

A. Yes.

Q. Well, don't you think, after looking at Day, that he was a quiet man?

A. Yes, but he had a bad look in his eyes.

Q. As far as you thought?

A. Yes.

Q. Do you remember me coming into your shop and asking whether Day wore a jumper?

A. Yes.

Q. What date would that be?

A. Some time before Christmas.

Q. Do you know what Day was doing when he was wearing the jumper?

A. He was employed in my shop.

Q. Did he bring any meat into your shop?

A. No.

Q. Do you remember telling me that you were not sure that Day wore a jumper?—Speak the truth like a man!

A. I don't remember that.

Q. What were Day's duties?

A. Just getting in wood and looking after the horses.

Q. Had he any experience in killing?

A. No.

Q. He never handled the meat?

A. No, I did that myself.

Q. What did I ask you with regard to the blood on the jumper?

A. You only asked me if Day was wearing a blue jumper.

Q. Was that all?

A. Yes.

Q. Did I not refer to blood being on the jumper?

A. No.

Q. Are you quite sure about that?

A. Yes.

Q. Don't you remember me asking you if there was blood on the jumper?

A. No.

Q. Then what was my object in coming to you?

A. I don't know. You were talking about the shot.

Q. You are one of the men who have been blowing this business up about Day?

A. Yes, because I had my suspicions about the man.

Q. Did you tell me that you suspected another man?

A. No.

Q. Was the jumper hidden when it was found?

A. No.

Q. (*By Mr Garvin to Witness*) Did you see any firearms in Day's possession?

A. No.

Q. Did he appear to be a sane man?

A. Yes.

Q. (*By Mr Dickson*) Did Day associate with anybody?

A. No.

Q. What were his habits at night?

A. I never saw him much after six o'clock. Six o'clock would be the latest I saw him at night.

Q. (*By Mr Garvin*) You suspected this man from the start?

A. I did, according to those who saw him on the road. That is what I went by. He answered to the description.

Q. What motive do you think he would have for committing an offence of this kind?

A. That is a question I cannot answer. What motive would anyone have?

Q. (*By Mr Dickson*) You heard he had been seen on the road?

A. I did.

Q. When did you hear it first?

A. Some time after.

Q. About how long; have you any idea?—A month or a week?

A. About a fortnight or so.

Q. Who told you this?

A. I heard of it from Carroll and Mr Burnett.

Q. Young Carroll?

A. Yes; Johnny Carroll.

Q. (*By Mr Garvin*) Before you heard that, had you formed any opinion yourself?

A. Not before I heard that. As soon as I heard from a number who saw the man on the road that night I did. After that I got it really into me that he was the man.

Q. (*By Mr Sadleir*) That is very interesting. You know the girl Florence Lowe?

A. Yes.

Q. Was she there the same time as Day was at Clarke's?

A. No.

Q. Do you think she ever saw him there?

A. I do not think she did.

Q. Mr Clarke said she was at his place while he was there?

A. She was there on the morning he left. He left Clarke's on the 10th of January.

Q. What time?

A. Some time in the morning. He was in Gatton a little after ten o'clock, and she went to work that day.

Q. Did she see him before the murders?

A. Not to my knowledge. She may have been there at the shop, but I cannot say.[14]

It would seem that the Commission did not treat the evidence of Constable Christie lightly. Indeed, one member of the Commission described Christie's evidence as "very valuable evidence".[15] By September and October 1899, quite a few people suspected that Day had committed the outrage. In her evidence before the Commission Mrs Murphy said that she had "thought over the matter a great deal" and she "came to the conclusion that only Day could do it. The one hand struck the three blows; anyone who saw them could tell that."[16] Sergeant Arrell, in his evidence before the Commission, said "I have had a strong opinion that Day had a hand in it—I will admit that."[17] Daniel Murphy junior also suspected Day. At the Commission he gave evidence to the effect that he did not think Day gave a satisfactory account of himself. He also stated that Mr Clarke "told me what sort of a man he was, and that the police ought never to have let him go".[18]

From Constable Christie's evidence before the Commission it is apparent that he considered "the detectives made a blunder in the first place and wanted to throw cold water on it". He considered that as being the reason for their trying to keep him from making inquiries into Thomas Day. When Inspector Urquhart gave evidence before the Commission it was very evident that he was under pressure from members of the Commission for eliminating Day from consideration as a suspect. The Commissioners made a most searching inquiry from Urquhart as the following excerpt from the transcript will show:

Q. (*By the Chairman*) Did you make any arrests?

A. No.

Q. Did you cross-examine any people as to their doings and their whereabouts?

A. Yes.

Q. That is all in your report?

A. Yes.

Q. (*By Mr Dickson*) Did you find out anything about Day?

A. Yes, I found out all there was to find out.

Q. Did you find out what he had been doing?

A. So far as we could get an account of what he was doing on that particular night, it rests on his own account of himself. He made a statement under examination.

Q. Did you find out whether Carroll had seen a man like Day?

A. I heard of it in the course of the first few days, and I got young Carroll down to the office and examined him, and he said, as regards Day, that he could not recognise the man he saw at the sliprails. I closely questioned him about that. I said, "Did you know the man you saw?" He said, "No, I did not." I said, "Did you think he was like anybody?" He said, "Yes, I thought he was like Clarke's man." I said, "Why did you think so?" He said, "He seemed about the same height, and I thought his clothes were the same." I said, "Can you say it was Clarke's man?" He said, "No, I cannot." Very well, that was at the beginning of the matter.

Q. About when would that be?

A. I can get the exact time. But later on—contemporaneously with this examination of Day and Carroll—I had instructed Acting Sergeant Toomey in the matter, and he had made, unknown to Day, a thorough search of Day's place of abode—the hut he occupied at Clarke's.

Q. When?

A. I cannot give the exact date without looking it up; it was early in the business. He made a thorough search, and Galbraith and several men were told off to watch Day in his hut. That was done by order of the Chief Inspector. They watched him, and paid surprise visits and found him lying in his bunk reading *Rienzi*. Then I made further inquiries. I wanted to know if Day had ever been known to have any firearm or access to any firearm. We could not discover that he ever had any firearm in his possession, or had ever been seen with one, or spoken about one; and we have discovered that the only firearm he could have had access to was an old revolver that hung on Clarke's verandah, and which had not been fired, apparently, for about half a century when we looked at it.

Q. Did you find out whether Clarke kept a rifle about for shooting bullocks?

A. They had a rifle—a gun, I think—for killing. I am not sure about that. He had not access to that.

Q. How used Clarke to kill his bullocks?

A. I think he shot them. I am not sure.

Q. That was all inquired into?

A. Yes.

Q. Day gave evidence or made a statement?

A. He made a statement.

Q. Did Clarke corroborate his statement?

A. Yes, to an extent.

Q. Was Clarke called?

A. No, but a statement was taken from him by Toomey, who inquired into the matter.

Q. Was that ever put into writing?

A. It is in the form of a report from Toomey.

Q. (*By the Chairman*) Were any inquiries made as to Day's history?

A. Only from himself. Of course, we could not get confirmation.

Q. Could you not have traced him?

A. He came there as a stranger.

Q. But he came along a road, I suppose?

A. He came in the train, he said.

Q. A good many efforts were made to trace Burgess; why not Day?

A. There was no suspicion against Day.

Q. Why not?

A. That seems to have been the habit all through—

Q. (*By Mr Garvin*) Was he not subsequently found?

A. Day never was lost.

Q. (*By the Chairman*) They knew nothing about him. Where did he come from?

A. His statement was that he came from New South Wales.

Q. Did you ask him to give you particulars?

A. Yes.

Q. Did you make inquiries?

A. No, because there was no reason to doubt the man. There was no suspicion against him. There never has been until lately.

Q. (*By Mr Dickson*) Where is the statement of Clarke about it?—I could not see it.

A. It is in the report of Acting Sergeant Toomey, who interviewed Clarke on the subject.

Q. Did you find out if he had any associates?

A. He had no associates. There is the man Cox.

Q. Yes, there was Cox.

A. He was not an associate.

Q. He was on friendly terms?

A. He was in the same employ, also worked for Clarke.

Q. Did they find about his habits—walking down past the sliprails occasionally?

A. He admitted he occasionally walked along the road smoking before he went to bed. You have seen the position of the place where he lived, and it was a perfectly natural thing for him to do.

Q. Did they find out that he bought a razor and got shaved?

A. Yes.

168

Q. On the day of the murder?

A. Yes.

Q. You reported he bought it before the murder?

A. I did not report it. I know what I said. I said, "If my memory served me right, it was before the murder."

Q. (*By the Chairman*) The man who sold it says it was after the murder.

A. So I see. It was not of the slightest consequence, because when I saw him two or three days after he was not shaved.

Q. (*By Mr Dickson*) You say, "He bought a razor and paid a quarter's subscription to the School of Arts; but this was before the murder, if my memory is correct"?

A. Yes, but it is not correct.

Q. Your memory is not correct?

A. I wrote it in the office, away from the papers altogether, only the other day. That is why I put this in.

Q. (*By the Chairman*) You made no inquiries to verify his statements about himself?

A. I told you what I did about it.

Q. You did nothing?

A. I did.

Q. You asked him if he was the murderer?—He is not likely to say, "I am the murderer".

A. I put Acting Sergeant Toomey on to find out all he could get and report. He searched his hut, searched his clothes, had conversations with him, and made every possible inquiry. He reported there was not the slightest hope of connecting him with the murder in any way—nothing to point to the fact that he could be in any way concerned in the matter. I had several conversations with Day, and he made a statement to me. They all tended the same way. The man is a young man, and could not possibly have been a hardened criminal or anything of the kind. His behaviour all through was most satisfactory. He came down to me before he left Gatton and said, "I have had a disagreement with Clarke, and I am leaving Gatton. Have you any objection?" I said, "No. Where are you going?" He said, "I am going to Toowoomba." At that time Burgess was in custody in Toowoomba, and I said, "If you are going through Toowoomba, go to the police station and have a look at this man they have got, and let me know if you have ever seen him. Inform the police if you have ever seen him about Gatton." He went to Toowoomba, and called at the police station and told them he had never seen him before. I do not know where exactly he went to from Toowoomba. He was absent for a little time. Then he passed down through Gatton again, which was duly reported to me. He came to Brisbane, and went to the battery and joined the Permanent Artillery in his own name.

Q. Then he deserted?—Is there not a warrant out for him now?

A. There is a warrant for him for desertion from the Permanent Force. We have not been able to find him. There is another man who deserted at the same time who cannot be found. There are three men who deserted from the same force. There are warrants out for them. They cannot be found.

Q. (*By the Chairman*) What do you wish to say?

A. I stated on Friday that the boy Carroll said that he did not recognise the man as Day, but he thought the clothes of the man resembled those worn by Day. I afterwards got a statement from Carroll, and questioned him closely. Afterwards various tests for identification were carried out under the superintendence of Mr White in the courthouse at Gatton, because he had similar tests to carry out in Toowoomba, and it was considered better that one officer should carry out the whole of the tests. It was reported to me by Mr White that Carroll had picked out Burgess as the man he saw at the sliprails.

Q. Was Day amongst the men when Carroll was brought in to make the identification?

A. No.

Q. (*By Mr Garvin*) Had the boy seen Day in the presence of the police?

A. I don't know.

Q. (*By the Chairman*) What was the note that Mr White made with regard to this identification?

A. Mr White has his own notes.

Q. (*By the Chairman to Sub-Inspector White*) What was the note you made?

A. (*Sub-Inspector White*) John Carroll identified Burgess.

Q. You noted that as a fact?

A. (*Sub-Inspector White*) Yes.

Q. You did not note down what Carroll said?

A. (*Sub-Inspector White*) No.

Q. Day was not there?

A. (*Sub-Inspector White*) No.

Q. (*Mr Garvin to Witness—Sub-Inspector Urquhart*) What was the date of this?

A. 24 January.

Q. (*By the Chairman*) Was there any resemblance between Day and Burgess?

A. Not the slightest. The next step was that Carroll gave evidence at the Magisterial Inquiry on oath, where he stated he could not recognise the man.

Q. (*By Mr Sadleir*) He said he could not identify anybody?

A. Yes. He said he could not identify the man at the sliprails as anybody.

Q. (*By the Chairman to Sub-Inspector White*) Carroll still stuck to Burgess as being the man at the courthouse?

A. (*Sub-Inspector White*) Yes.

Q. (*By Mr Garvin*) That was on 24 January?

A. (*Sub-Inspector White*) Yes.

Q. (*By Mr Garvin to Witness—Sub-Inspector Urquhart*) When was it that the police first showed Day to Carroll after the murder?

A. I don't know; he may have seen him in the presence of Acting Sergeant Toomey. I would like to read the report from the *Courier* of 11 March of the evidence given by the boy Carroll on 10 March. It states there that—

John Carroll, son of the last witness, aged thirteen years and nine months, corroborated his mother's evidence. He also said he noticed Michael with a whip, and that the man they passed had a grey slouch hat on; also that he wore a blue coat or shirt. He said he had recognised a man at the courthouse on 24 January as like the person he saw near the sliprails, but he could not swear positively he was the same.

Q. (*By the Chairman*) The boy said, "As like the person"?

A. Yes. When the tests took place Carroll picked out Burgess as the man.

Q. Sub-Inspector White did not take down Carroll's words?

A. No. Mrs Carroll also picked him out, and said he looked like the man.

Q. It seems to me that the word "like" makes all the difference?

A. Yes.

Q. But you say the word "like" absolutely excluded Day, because he was absolutely unlike Burgess?

A. I do not go as far as that.

Q. How far do you go?—The boy thought it was Clarke's man, because of the clothing; he could not see his face sufficiently.

A. Yes. There is another point to be brought into that. The man at the sliprails was seen by another witness—a girl named Florence Lowe, who passed close to him on horseback. The man stepped forward and spoke to her. She, in describing that man, said he wore a dark coat rather long in front—came round in front. Of course we made inquiries with reference to Day being possessed of such a garment—of ever having been seen with such a garment —and he had not. He never had.

Q. There is nothing to preclude two different men being at the sliprails at different times?

A. Oh, no.

Q. Both may be right—the boy and the girl Lowe?

A. Yes, of course. It is within the bounds of possibility they saw two different men.

Q. If there were two or more men engaged in this business, it might have been one was on the lookout at one time and another on the lookout at another time?

A. Yes.

Q. There is nothing to preclude that?

A. There is nothing to preclude that.

Q. (*By Mr Dickson*) Did you know, at the time of the examination, that the boy Carroll said to his mother, as they passed the sliprails, "That is Clarke's man"?

A. I think I did hear it. I do not know that it was officially before me. When the boy made his statement he did not say so.

Q. You knew he had said so?

A. Yes.

Q. (*By Mr Garvin*) Did you know that when you took his statement?

A. I knew he had said so.

Q. Was that not a matter that you should have pressed him on, that he said to his mother, "That is Clarke's man"?

A. Yes.

Q. That would be very important?

A. I pressed him very particularly on that point.

Q. That he was sure it was Clarke's man?

A. Yes, but he was not.

Q. (*By the Chairman*) Did you press him in such a way as to frighten him?

A. No.

Q. (*By Mr Garvin*) Did you ever hear that the boy said, on the ground, after viewing the dead bodies, to McNeil that the man whom he saw at the sliprails when they passed on the night of the 26th was Clarke's man?

A. That he said to McNeil on the ground?

Q. Yes, on the ground?

A. No. I have never heard that before. I do not think McNeil has ever informed anybody. It has never come to my ears.

Q. He informed McNeil?

A. It never came to my ears until this moment.

Q. (*By the Chairman*) You told us on Friday that you were so satisfied yourself that you never made any inquiries into Day's history. Would you be surprised to hear that when joining the Permanent Artillery he gave a false birthplace?

172

A. I am aware of that. I am not sure it is false.

Q. You are not?

A. No. I know he said his birthplace was Cunnamulla.

Q. You did not, I believe, trace his previous record?

A. What previous record?

Q. That there is no trace there of a man called Thomas Day? He either gave a false name or a false birthplace.

A. He gave the same name as at Gatton.

Q. And tells a lie about the reference?

A. No.

Q. That he had a reference from Clarke?

A. No. He named Clarke as a person whom the Permanent Artillery authorities might refer to if they so desired. He did not say he had any reference. I did not understand it so.

Q. Do you not think it is of great moment a man travelling under a wrong name or lying about his birthplace?

A. I do not know that it is. Hundreds of men do it.

Q. Supposing a man is a possible murderer, and you find out he was lying either about his name or birthplace, do you not think it of importance to, at any rate, thrash it out to the end?

A. But it was not found out until quite recently.

Q. You made no inquiries. If you made inquiries, you could have found out.

A. As soon as—

Q. Did you ask him where he came from?

A. Yes.

Q. What did he say?

A. New South Wales.

Q. Did you make inquiries?

A. I do not think we made inquiries in New South Wales.

Q. You accepted whatever he said?

A. We accepted it because there did not appear reasons for testing his statement any further.

Q. If you suspect a man, I think every statement he makes requires confirmation or verification.

A. As a matter of fact, after the inquiries at Gatton, I did not suspect him, and I do not suspect him now.

Q. Tell us why you suspected Burgess, and tried to make the facts fit him?

A. I did not. I absolutely deny that I did anything of the sort.

Q. Why did you suspect Burgess?

A. Because he was identified beyond doubt as the man at the sliprails.

Q. In your opinion beyond doubt?

A. At that time.

173

Q. Is that the only ground on which you suspected him?

A. That was the principal ground. There is his known character, and the fact of his having been found by the police—not found, but seen—in the near neighbourhood of Gatton on the 27th of December.

Q. Near neighbourhood. Where?

A. Helidon.

Q. How far from Gatton is that?

A. Twenty-seven miles [*forty-three kilometres*].

Q. That is on the 27th of December?

A. Yes.

Q. (*By Mr Dickson*) By whom was he identified beyond doubt?

A. What was then apparently beyond doubt by Hallas' children as having been at Gatton at six o'clock, and various people said he was at the sliprails.

Q. Who said he was at the sliprails—I have only Mrs Carroll?

A. Remember the evidence given at the inquiry was taken long after the identification had been made.

Q. You say she identified him positively, and others identified him positively?

A. Here is her identification form. It is the same as was used for those who were going to identify Burgess or anybody else. [*Witness here read form, which he said was signed* "Mr Carroll".] There is a note by Sub-Inspector White. [*Witness read note.*]

Q. (*By the Chairman*) But you had let Day go long before this?

A. Yes. This had nothing to do with Day.

Q. You had eliminated him?

A. Yes, before this formal identification, we had knowledge that they would not identify him as the man at the sliprails.

Q. (*By Mr Sadleir*) Who else at the sliprails identified him?

A. Wait a bit. I wish to point out that the woman pointed out Burgess without the slightest hesitation. Then there is the identification of the boy John Carroll. [*Witness read the identification form of the boy John Carroll.*]

Q. (*By Mr Dickson*) When was that statement taken?

A. On the same occasion—24 January, at the Gatton Court House.

Q. It differs from his evidence. He says, "Amongst those men I picked out one, and I said, 'He is like the one I saw. I would not say whether he was or not.'"

A. Actually he definitely picked him out.

Q. Are there any others?

A. There is Florrie Lowe. [*Identification statement of Miss Lowe read.*]

Q. In her evidence did she depart from that?

A. I must look it up and see. [*Miss Lowe's evidence read.*]

Q. (*By the Chairman*) When you asked young Carroll about the matter did you at the same time ask Miss Lowe?

A. No.

Q. Why not?

A. They were not together.

Q. Why could you not bring them together?

A. We could have done so, but I did not think it necessary. They did not say they were together when they saw the man.

Q. Do you not think it is advisable in a case like that to compare testimony?

A. Yes. I had the testimony before me in writing to compare it, and I did compare it very carefully.

Q. (*By Mr Dickson*) She simply says he was like the man?

A. She picked him out as the man, and in her evidence she says he was like the man.

Q. (*By Mr Garvin*) Was Miss Lowe shown Day?

A. I think she knew him. She was working at Clarke's herself. I cannot say for a fact if she was working there at the same time.

Q. (*By the Chairman*) Is there anything to show that she did know him?

A. I should have to look up the evidence and see.

Q. (*By Mr Sadleir*) Was she working at the same time and place?

A. I am not sure about the same time, but she was working at Clarke's and knew Day.

Q. (*By the Chairman*) That would influence you in eliminating Day —the fact that Miss Lowe knew him and did not recognise him?

A. Yes, and the other girl knew him, Louisa Tharna [*sic*].

Q. We want to know why you should exclude Day so quickly as being a possible participator in the offence?

A. Yes, but you do not know what steps were taken.

Q. Well, we want to know. That is what we are here for.

A. Remember that I did not conduct these things personally.

Q. Half-a-dozen men were conducting it, is that it?

A. No, nothing of the kind. I had the supervision of the case, but I had nothing to do with the actual work of searching. I sat in the office and received reports.

Q. And can you not remember the salient features of the case?

A. Of course I can, but you ask me for details.

Q. No, I do not. I want to know why a possible murderer was so quickly eliminated from the list of suspects and allowed to go away?

A. Well, there was no ground for detaining him—absolutely none. His place was searched first without his knowledge and then in his presence. He was brought into the presence of Clarke, his employer, and questioned most closely by Sergeant Toomey, and all his clothes were overhauled.

Q. You acted on Toomey's reports?

A. Yes, which were conveyed to me verbally every day, and in writing to a great extent, but we had not time, of course, to write everything down, although we kept a pretty good record. I saw the man myself, to try and discover whether there was any reasonable ground for detaining him, and I could find none.

Q. And looking back on all the circumstances do you still think you acted with wisdom in letting him go?

A. I do, because I had absolutely no reason for detaining him. I have arrested a man since for murder, who had far more against him than Day ever had, and the row about it has been something frightful.

Q. (*By Mr Dickson*) After hearing Mrs Carroll's evidence and young Carroll's evidence the other day, if you had had that before you at the time, would you have detained Day?

A. I did not have it before me.

Q. But if you had?

A. Possibly I might, but I do not know that I should, with the knowledge I have of the way in which public opinion in Gatton is formed. I do not think I should attach so much importance to that evidence as a stranger might, but I was a stranger to Gatton at that time.

Q. As a matter of fact, you put Day down on your list as one of the suspects?

A. No; only in this way: At one time, when the story was fresh, and if the girl had recognised him, he might have been fairly regarded as a suspect.

Q. But he was regarded as a suspect?

A. No; the word "suspect" is used more as a name—as a matter of nomenclature. There were people put down as suspects against whom there was no suspicion, but simply because they were mentioned as persons whose movements should be inquired into. The word is used much in the same way as the term "astrologer's pill". That is simply a list of quack letters.

Q. If you put a man on that list is it not an indication that you required him to clear himself of all suspicion?

A. Well, I think the time at which a suspect on that list would be cleared would be when there was nothing further against him, and there was nothing to justify me in regarding Day as a suspect.

Q. (*By the Chairman*) At any rate, you know now nothing about Day's history?

A. I know as much as it was thought necessary to know.

Q. And that is nothing?

A. I do not know why you should jump to that conclusion. What we knew about him will be found in the papers.

Q. (*By Mr Dickson*) He gave evidence, and his evidence was very meagre?

A. Where did he give evidence?

Q. I read it somewhere.

A. He did not give evidence at the inquiry. He made a statement to me. I had him under examination for two or three hours.

Q. (*By Mr Sadleir*) Is that statement written in full?

A. It is here with the papers.

Q. Can you put your hand on Day's statement?

A. Yes; here it is. [*Witness hands in document.*]

Q. How was this statement taken—in shorthand?

A. No; it was taken in longhand. I may say that the statement taken from him and the information collected about the place were not all recorded at that time, because we had no clerks there; but every officer in Gatton was satisfied about the matter at the time. The Chief Inspector, Mr Galbraith, and myself were there, and we could not see anything against the man.

Q. Didn't the fact that these three people—Mrs Carroll, her son, and Florence Lowe—identified Burgess greatly hamper your work?

A. Yes, taken in conjunction with the identification by the Hallas children, boy and girl.

Q. What were their ages?

A. The girl was seventeen and the boy about fifteen, if I remember rightly. Beatrice Hallas, the girl, stated that she attended at the Toowoomba Police Barracks on the 23rd of January and identified Burgess from among seven other men as the man she had seen at her father's house at Gatton.

Q. (*By Mr Garvin*) On what date was that statement made?

A. On the 24th of January. Frank Hallas made a similar statement.

Q. (*By Mr Sadleir*) Both those statements were taken down on the 24th of January?

A. Yes.

Q. But were the facts not substantially known to you all along?

A. Of course they were; this is the formal ratification of things we had previously got.

Q. And had been acting upon?

A. No.

Q. (*By Mr Dickson*) That evidence only goes to show that Burgess was in Gatton; there is any amount of evidence to show that

Day was in Gatton also?

A. Of course; but Day was not on the same footing as Burgess.

Q. We do not know anything about Day previous to that; he said he came from Wagga?

A. Yes.

Q. And you do not appear to have wanted to know anything about Day's previous career?

A. I have not suggested anything of that kind.

Q. (*By the Chairman*) Neither did you want to know anything about Burgess, apparently?

A. That is an unreasonable conclusion.

Q. (*By Mr Sadleir*) Didn't the fact that these statements were known to you turn you from any further pursuit of Day?

A. For the time it turned me on the pursuit of Burgess completely.

Q. And away from Day?

A. And away from Day, or anybody else, but not altogether. I issued instructions to the officers not to disregard any other clue on account of the scent on Burgess being hot.

Q. Did Burgess on his arrest at once relieve himself of suspicion?

A. No, he did not; he absolutely declined to do so.

Q. How long did that last?

A. Down to the time of the Magisterial Inquiry. When he was put in the box he would not account for himself.

Q. What date was that?

A. The inquiry was held on the 24th of January.

Q. You sent out police to make inquiries and endeavour to trace Burgess in his wanderings before that?

A. Yes.

Q. Had their inquiries been concluded at that time showing that he could not possibly have been at Gatton on the night of the murder?

A. No.

Q. So that you still had reason to believe that Burgess was probably the murderer?

A. Yes, that is so.

Q. And all your inquiries in regard to any other person—Day or anyone else—were conducted with that feeling in your mind?

A. At that time, yes; but at no time were the inquiries of the police confined solely to Burgess. And, as a matter of fact, there was not a soul in Gatton at that particular time who did not think as I did.

Q. (*By Mr Garvin*) But you only came to that conclusion with regard to Burgess about the 20th of January?

A. Well, no; I had suspicion of Burgess before that. My conviction—

well, I cannot call it a conviction—but my suspicion was strengthened very much; and at one time, I admit freely, I thought Burgess was the man. What, I suppose, you may call the zenith of my suspicion was after these identifications.

Q. But the identifications did not take place till about the 24th of January?

A. No.

Q. That would be about twenty-five days after the murder?

A. That is the formal identification.

Q. I understood that in reply to Mr Sadleir you said that on the 24th of January you only looked for Burgess?

A. No, no.

Q. That you discharged Day?

A. Oh, no. I think I can make that clear to you. What you apparently wish me to say is that but for Burgess I would have pursued Day, but I tell you that I would not have pursued him.

Q. Then I want you to tell us why you gave up following Day between the date the bodies were discovered and the 24th January?

A. Because there was nothing to follow; there had been no suspicious circumstances against Day.

Q. (*By the Chairman*) Had he not blood on his arm?

A. Yes; he was a butcher, and had been carrying meat on his arm. Mr Clarke told us that.

Q. What sort of a stain was it?

A. It was a smudge on the sleeve.

Q. (*By Mr Garvin*) Do you know whether the persons who identified Burgess had seen Day—whether they were shown Day?

A. I do not know; I do not think they were.

Q. (*By the Chairman*) Did anybody suggest to you that you should have the blood on Day's sleeve analysed?

A. No.

Q. And you did not think of it yourself?

A. No, I did not; and I do not think it would have been of any use if we had had it analysed.

Q. Why?

A. It would simply have been pronounced to have been mammalian blood.

Q. But analytical chemists can go further than that?

A. They can't here.

Q. I am told that there are several chemists here competent to do so?

A. They won't swear absolutely.

Q. But they will say probably?

A. But it can be done absolutely in some places.

Q. Did it not strike you as a reasonable inquiry to take possession of the man's coat and have it analysed?

A. No.

Q. His employer says now that he boiled his coat—I do not know whether he told you that at the time?

A. He did not. I have the statement here taken by Acting Sergeant Toomey, who interviewed Clarke. He was also supposed to have killed a sheep and burnt it on the top of his clothes, and several other little things. I might have arrested every butcher in the country and called him to account for blood on his clothes as reasonably as Day.

Q. The arrest of a butcher at Normanton would not have been a reasonable arrest?

A. I mean about Gatton.

Q. (*By Mr Garvin*) But there was a reason given why this man's clothes should have been microscopically examined.

A. What reason?

Q. The mere fact that he was seen washing his clothes after he was spoken of as a suspect.

A. All these men wash their clothes occasionally.

Q. That is all very well, but in this case it was a reason why his clothes should have been taken possession of.

A. I do not think the washing of the clothes was mentioned till long, long afterwards.

Q. Of course it would be a different thing if you did not hear that till long afterwards?

A. It was never mentioned till it was mentioned by Sergeant Arrell about two months afterwards. That was the first I heard of it.[19]

Who was this introspective and unsociable man who called himself Thomas Day? What was his real name and where did he come from? What sort of a man was he—this youthful swagman who was fond of reading? What ultimately became of him after he left Gatton in 1899? The answer to all these questions is "Regrettably, we do not know."

All that is known is that, shortly after leaving Gatton, Day came to Brisbane and joined the Queensland Permanent Artillery, from which he soon deserted.[20] The Brisbane contingent of this force was "A" Battery stationed at Victoria Barracks, and it was probably in this battery that Day enlisted. The report of Major R.A. Anderson, Officer Commanding "A" Battery for the year ended 30 June 1899, contains the information that, during the year, nineteen men deserted, of whom twelve were Australian. Of these deserters the Major comments:

The unusually large number of deserters during the year is due to the large number of recruits who have been enlisted to make up the increase of establishment. Of the nineteen men who deserted, sixteen had less than six months' service. It is in the early period of his service that a man is most likely to desert, when the work and discipline are strange to him, and it has been found that very few men desert after they have completed six months' service.[21]

We have endeavoured to find in the Queensland Archives records of persons serving in the Queensland Permanent Artillery in 1899; but it seems that no such records are now in existence. In the issue of *Smith's Weekly* of 11 June 1927, it was reported that Day "left the district. Later he drifted to Brisbane, and joined the Permanent Artillery, from which he deserted and went to South Africa, where he was killed during the Boer War." No authority is given for this statement that he was killed at the Boer War, and we have been unable to discover any other reference of such a nature. Nor have we been able to discover any further information regarding the man called Thomas Day.

The man Thomas Day is, we consider, a worthy subject of close examination. We are of the view that, very thorough though the police investigation was in all other respects, insufficient investigation was made in relation to this man and his background. Indeed, it is possible that had as searching an examination of Day as that of Burgess been made, the Gatton mystery might have been solved. Day was one of the first persons questioned by the police; but he did not, in the early stage of the investigation, arouse the suspicion of the investigating officers. He then left the district of Gatton and, when suspicion had begun to centre upon him some months later, it appears the authorities were unable to trace him. It would seem that the knowledge that Day had washed and scrubbed his jumper with such thoroughness, against the instructions of his employer, was not gained by the police till several months after the event. But the police, at a very early stage of the investigation, knew that Day was a stranger and a recent arrival in Gatton. They also knew that, even on his own account, he was, at the time of the murders, very close to the murder scene. That is, they knew that here was a stranger to the district who at least had the opportunity to commit the crimes, in the sense that he was near the place where the victims were found, shortly before their deaths. They also knew that he had, on at least two previous occasions, been seen on the Tent Hill road, near the sliprails, at night. In the light of this knowledge it is difficult to understand why Acting Sergeant Toomey did not thoroughly question Day as to his antecedents and as to his movements before arriving in Gatton.[22]

The police devoted considerable effort and time in an endeavour to establish that Burgess was in Gatton on the evening of 26 December 1898—that is, that he had the opportunity to commit the crimes. But

181

here was Day—a man who was within such a short distance of the sliprails at all material times—a man who at least had the opportunity to commit the crimes. It is, we submit, surprising that his whole background, previous history and previous movements were not most thoroughly checked.

In the circumstances, we can well understand His Honour Judge Noel, the Chairman of the Commission, saying to Urquhart "A good many efforts were made to trace Burgess; why not Day?"[23] We are able to appreciate why the Commissioners said in their Report, "We are of opinion that sufficiently exhaustive investigation and inquiry were not made in every instance as regards suspects."[24]

10
AN ASSESSMENT

A good many crimes are proved by *direct* evidence, that is to say, either by the evidence of an eyewitness, or eyewitnesses, who perceived the criminal act, or by means of a confession obtained from the actual perpetrator of the act. But in many cases direct evidence is not available. It has very truly been pointed out that:

> In a great portion of trials, as they occur in practice, no direct proof that the party accused actually committed the crime is or can be given; the man who is charged with theft is rarely seen to break the house or take the goods; and, in cases of murder, it rarely happens that the eye of any witness sees the fatal blow struck, or the poisonous ingredient poured into the cup.[1]

In the case of the Gatton crimes, no testimony was available from eyewitnesses, or from the murderer or murderers themselves, as to who committed the murders and raped the girls. There being no *direct* evidence, the investigators were obliged to found their investigation upon *circumstantial* evidence. The term circumstantial evidence is commonly used in contradistinction to direct testimony. An argument from circumstantial evidence is based on a number of facts or circumstances, any one of which alone may be insufficient for proof, and taken by itself, may have little evidential force or value, but all of which, taken together, constitute a body of evidence which is often as cogent and convincing as the direct testimony of credible witnesses. Therefore, it is no derogation of evidence to say it is *circumstantial*. Nor is it proper to consider each circumstance separately—the circumstances should rather be considered together and in their totality. If this be done they may lead to a conclusion unsupportable by each circumstance considered by itself. Guilt may be sufficiently proved if it be a natural inference which reasonable men would, beyond reasonable doubt, unhesitatingly draw from the cumulative effect of the facts proved. The cumulative effect of circumstantial evidence was beautifully described by Baron Pollock in 1866 in the case of *Regina* v. *Exall*:

> Thus it is that all the circumstances must be considered together.

It has been said that circumstantial evidence is to be considered as a chain, and each piece of evidence as a link in the chain, but that is not so, for then, if any one link broke, the chain would fall. It is more like the case of a rope composed of several cords. One strand of the cord might be insufficient to sustain the weight, but three stranded together may be quite of sufficient strength.

Thus it may be in circumstantial evidence—there may be a combination of circumstances, no one of which would raise a reasonable conviction, or more than a mere suspicion; but the whole, taken together, may create a strong conclusion of guilt, that is, with as much certainty as human affairs can require or admit of.[2]

The cogency and efficacy of circumstantial evidence depend upon its being incompatible with, and incapable of explanation by any thing other than the fact or hypothesis which it is adduced to prove. It is therefore not enough that a particular hypothesis will explain and coincide with all the facts. Before the hypothesis advanced can be said to be proved it must harmonise with and satisfactorily account for all the facts, *to the exclusion of every other reasonable hypothesis*. If the circumstances are equally capable of explanation by any other reasonable theory, then it is clear that the hypothesis advanced is not established, but remains a matter of uncertainty. It is only when no other supposition will reasonably account for all the facts that the hypothesis advanced may legitimately be adopted. Wills, in his work, *Circumstantial Evidence*, puts the matter thus:

> *In order to justify the inference of guilt, the inculpatory facts must be incompatible with the innocence of the accused, and incapable of explanation upon any other reasonable hypothesis than that of his guilt.* This is the fundamental rule, the *experimentum crucis* by which the relevancy and effect of circumstantial evidence must be estimated.[3]

Circumstantial evidence is usually drawn from one or more of several well defined classes of facts:

1. circumstances which give rise to the motive;
2. circumstances from which the unlawful plan may be inferred, such as threats and declarations of intention;
3. opportunity;
4. preparation for committing the crime, such as, procuring a weapon, tools, etc., or providing the means for effecting the plan;
5. possession of the fruits of the crime, or bearing marks which the perpetrator might reasonably be expected to bear (for example, scratches, blood-spots);
6. unexplained appearances of a suspicious nature and attempts to account for them by false representations and false denials;
7. the suppression, destruction, fabrication, concealment or simulation of evidence;

8. similar facts, that is, misconduct on other occasions (if it be permissible to tender such evidence on the basis that it is relevant for some further reason than its tendency to show bad disposition);
9. concealment or flight after the crime has been committed; and
10. facts which go to establish personal identity, such as, tracks, footprints, fingerprints, features, articles of dress, gait, documents and papers.[4]

In the light of this discussion, what circumstantial evidence did the investigators of the Gatton outrage have for their consideration? The answer is "Not a great deal." Established objective facts and circumstances were most certainly present; but, in the main, they do not appear to assume great significance in the light of the argument from circumstantial evidence.

The investigators, during those crucial weeks of January 1899, were highly suspicious of Burgess and were not at all suspicious of Day. Moreover, although Toomey had noticed what appeared to be bloodstains on Day's jumper, he took no steps whatever to have an analytical test made of the stains; and it was not until "about two months afterwards" that Urquhart first heard that Day had washed this jumper.[5] It would seem that during January and February 1899, the main efforts of the investigators were centred on Burgess. At the time of the commencement of the Magisterial Inquiry on 24 January 1899, the police inquiries into the movements of Burgess had not been concluded and Urquhart believed that Burgess was probably the murderer. Urquhart, as we have seen, said before the Commission, "I had suspicion of Burgess before that. My conviction—well, I cannot call it a conviction —but my suspicion was strengthened very much; and at one time, I admit freely, I thought Burgess was the man. What, I suppose, you may call the zenith of my suspicion was after these identifications."[6]

In answer to a question put to him by a Commissioner, Urquhart said "What you apparently wish me to say is that but for Burgess I would have pursued Day, but I tell you that I would not have pursued him." Urquhart was then asked, "Then I want you to tell us why you gave up following Day between the date the bodies were discovered and the 24 January?", and he answered, "Because there was nothing to follow; there had been no suspicious circumstances against Day."[7] From this, two points clearly emerge—first, Urquhart's suspicions of Burgess reached their zenith after the "identifications" of Burgess; second, up until 24 January 1899 (at least), Urquhart considered "there had been no suspicious circumstances against Day". It would seem desirable, at this stage, briefly to comment upon the "identifications" of Burgess and the circumstances surrounding Day.

We have already referred to the statements made by those who allegedly identified Burgess as being in the vicinity of Gatton on

Boxing Day. Florence Lowe and Thomas Drew were two of those people. It will be recalled that they both picked out Burgess in a line-up and identified him as the man they had seen near the sliprails of Moran's paddock on Boxing Night.[8] There were also the two Hallas children, Frank and his sister, Beatrice; they identified Burgess as a man who called at their father's residence at Gatton at about 6.30 p.m. on Boxing Day. John Carroll, it will be remembered, when passing Moran's sliprails on Boxing Night, told his mother that the man at the sliprails was "Clarke's man". In his evidence before the Commission, John Carroll said that he was still of the opinion that it was "Clarke's man". He also said that he did not identify Burgess as being the man who was at the sliprails. John Carroll testified that he had said that "Burgess looked something like him".[9] When giving evidence before the Commission, Urquhart was asked, "Didn't the fact that these three people—Mrs Carroll, her son, and Florence Lowe—identified Burgess greatly hamper your work?", and he answered, "Yes, taken in conjunction with the identification by the Hallas children, boy and girl." It is obvious that Urquhart placed great weight upon these alleged identifications.

Was Urquhart, at that stage of his career, alive to the great dangers of acting on visual identification? It would be surprising if he were. Many people today are unaware of the number of instances where miscarriages of justice have occurred through erroneous visual identification. It has, with good effect, been said:

> In the investigation of every allegation of legal crime, it is fundamentally requisite to establish, by direct or circumstantial evidence, the identity of the individual accused as the party who committed the imputed offence. It might be concluded, by persons not conversant with judicial proceedings, that identification is seldom attended with serious difficulty: but such is not the case. Illustrations are numerous to show that what are supposed to be the clearest intimations of the senses, are sometimes fallacious and deceptive, and some extraordinary cases have occurred of mistaken personal identity. Hence the particularity, and as unreflecting persons too hastily conclude, the frivolous minuteness of inquiry, by professional advocates as to the *causa scientiæ*, in cases of controverted identity, whether of persons or of things.[10]

In his work, *According to the Evidence*, Gerald Abrahams, M.A. (Oxon), Barrister-at-law, made the pertinent observation:

> To those who lack confidence in circumstantial evidence, and prefer the evidence of eyewitnesses, the case of Adolf Beck should constitute an object lesson to demonstrate their error. For Adolf Beck's tragedy was that circumstantial evidence could have saved him and was not allowed to do so.[11]

The case of Adolf Beck is the classic case of a miscarriage of justice in the English judicial system through erroneous visual identification. It has been said that "it still remains a most remarkable example of the fallibility of human testimony and of human judgment".[12] The Adolf Beck case is a complete study in itself and it has been dealt with in many works. This is not the occasion to deal with it in any depth, but our readers may appreciate how remarkable a miscarriage of justice it was from the following excellent epitome of the facts and brief comments thereon by Dr Glanville Williams, LL.D., F.B.A., of the English Bar—a lecturer and writer on the criminal law of international renown:

It is possible to show how this kind of error has vitiated actual legal cases. The most notorious and instructive is the trial of Adolf Beck. Beck was something of a rolling stone who between 1868 and 1885 was in various States of South America. During this period, in 1876–77, one John Smith committed a number of petty frauds upon women in London. He would pose as a gentleman of means, make an acquaintance with a woman whom he would visit in her home, and make an offer (which was always favourably received) that she should come to live with him as his mistress. He would then obtain possession of a ring or watch from the woman on one fraudulent pretence or another, and would borrow some small change. For these offences of obtaining property, which he repeated a number of times with different women, Smith received a sentence of imprisonment.

Fourteen years after Smith's release, in the year 1895, when Beck was back in London, the frauds on women began again. The method adopted was almost exactly the same as in the first series. One of the defrauded women thought she recognised Beck as the man who had imposed upon her, and upon his arrest he was also identified by other women who had actually been the victims of John Smith. In all, Beck was wrongly picked out in identification parades by no fewer than twelve women who had been defrauded by Smith. Only one of the women who were defrauded at this period by Smith was certain that Beck was not the man who had defrauded her.

The identification evidence was allowed to result in Beck's conviction although there were some circumstances contradicting it. The cheat was said to be very well dressed whereas Beck's clothes were shabby. The women who gave evidence for the prosecution said that the man who had visited them spoke with a foreign or German accent, whereas Beck did not. The man who had cheated them wrote fluently, whereas the evidence of a chambermaid who had seen Beck writing was that he wrote very badly and slowly. On the other hand Beck failed to prove an alibi for any of the meetings with the women with which he was charged. Also, by an unhappy coincidence, he was found in possession of pawn tickets relating to female jewellery, though none of these related to the missing property. The result of the trial was a conviction, and Beck remained in prison for seven years.

The subsequent history is quite as extraordinary. While Beck was in prison his solicitor attempted to prove his innocence by pointing out physical differences between Beck and Smith; but he met with obstruction and stolid indifference on the part of the prison authorities and the Home Office. It is an astonishing fact that the prison records regarded Beck and Smith as the same person, notwithstanding that it was impossible for Beck to have committed Smith's crimes, as Beck's solicitor many times pointed out.

About two years after Beck's release from prison the frauds started again, and Beck was convicted of them in 1904 on the identification evidence of four women, who picked Beck out on the street or in identification parades, and on the evidence of a handwriting expert, who, as is too often the habit of handwriting experts, found no difficulty in declaring that Beck's handwriting in his private pocketbook was the same as that used by the cheat in letters that the latter had written to his victims. After this second conviction Beck's luck turned. While he was in custody awaiting sentence the frauds recommenced, and Smith was arrested. It could no longer be denied that a ghastly blunder had been made. Beck was given a free pardon and a grant of £5000 as compensation.

The Government set up a legal committee to inquire into the case. In its report, the committee stated the important conclusion that "evidence as to identity based on personal impressions is perhaps of all classes of evidence the least to be relied upon, and, therefore, unless supported by other facts, an unsafe basis for the verdict of a jury." These other facts required by the committee must, of course, be facts implicating the accused. It requires some intelligence and care to distinguish between facts that merely corroborate that a crime has been committed, which are useless to support identification evidence, and facts that connect the accused with the crime, and this distinction obviously needs to be explained to the jury. Common sense suggests that it is also necessary to distinguish between the witness who has merely made a brief acquaintance with the criminal and the witness who knows him well. There is all the difference between saying: "I saw the defendant, whom I have known all my life," and "I saw a man I recognised as the defendant, whom I had met once before." The former statement, in ninety-nine cases out of a hundred, is satisfactory identification; the latter, in the absence of corroborative evidence, never is.

One other observation is suggested by Beck's case. Identification seems to be a matter on which personal pride has a strong effect: a witness often resents it when his ability to recognise someone is questioned. The women who wrongly identified Beck became more sure of their identification under cross-examination.[13]

There are two matters which would tend to make one most cautious when evaluating the identifications of Burgess in the Gatton case. First, it is instructive to turn to the evidence of Mrs Carroll before the Commission. Part of the transcript of her evidence reads:

Q. Were you examined before the Magistrate?

A. Yes.

Q. Was the boy examined before the Magistrate?

A. Yes.

Q. Did you identify anyone?

A. I said that Burgess was like the man.

Q. And your son said the same.

A. Yes.

Q. And now you think you were mistaken?

A. Everybody was saying at the time that Burgess was the man, and we thought it must be Burgess.[14]

Second, it would seem not unlikely that, about the time when formal identifications were being made of Burgess, his photograph was being exhibited publicly. He was then in custody (admittedly for another offence), and had been so for over a fortnight. In the English Court of Criminal Appeal in 1925, the Lord Chief Justice of England, Lord Hewart said:

The appellant had already been arrested, and the effect of what was done was to give the witnesses—or certainly three of them—an opportunity of studying a photograph of the appellant before they were called on to identify him. That course is indefensible. It cannot be right that when a witness, or a possible witness, is being called on merely to identify a person who is already arrested, that witness, before the identification, should be shown a photograph of the accused person. One can see that sometimes it will happen that when a person has been shown a photograph to assist in the arrest of a wrongdoer not yet arrested he may later give evidence of identification. That is a different thing from what happened here. In that case the person is asked to identify the accused person, notwithstanding the fact that he has previously seen a photograph. A person who has seen a photograph of the accused person may identify him simply because he has seen a photograph of him.[15]

In this regard it is interesting to observe that a Brisbane newspaper correspondent in 1899 foreshadowed the sentiments of the Lord Chief Justice of England in 1925. In a Brisbane newspaper of 26 January 1899, the comment was made:

The question arises as to the advisableness and the equity of producing in public print the photograph of a suspect and one who has to be identified. For instance, the writer, who has never seen Burgess to knowledge, could point the man out from fifty others. How many more could say the same thing?[16]

There is no doubt that confirmation of the Burgess alibi made obvious the erroneous visual identifications in his case; and concerning him, there were no other incriminating facts.

The salient feature concerning Thomas Day was that he was a stranger to Gatton and he had the opportunity to commit the crimes, that is to say, he was in Gatton on Boxing Day 1898, and, at the time the Murphys went through the sliprails of Moran's paddock he, on his own account, was not very far distant—about 180 to 270 metres away. There is also the evidence of the boy, John Carroll, who, at the time told his mother that the man at the sliprails was "Clarke's man". The boy Carroll, when asked two or three days later whom he took the man at the sliprails to be, again said it was "Clarke's man". It apparently was Day's habit to walk along the Tent Hill road down towards the sliprails at night—he had been seen in that vicinity on two occasions by William Burnett, who had said "Good night" to Day; but Day did not answer him. It will be recalled that Thomas Drew said that his employer, Donoghue, on the night of the murders, said "Good night" to the man who was at the sliprails and that the man made no reply. Is this a mere coincidence? Young Carroll described the man at the sliprails as wearing a slouch hat; it was admitted by Toomey that Day had a hat of that description. Is that another mere coincidence? All the others "connected with the house" attended the fireworks display which Clarke gave between eight and nine o'clock on Boxing Night; but Day was not there. Is this also a mere coincidence?

According to Clarke, Day would never talk about the murders—if they were mentioned to him he would not answer back, he would not discuss the matter at all; it was a thing he would never talk about. Clarke was asked if he noticed any peculiarity in Day's manner when he was speaking to Day about the murders and he told the Commission, by way of answer, "Only a perfect state of indifference. He did not seem to interest himself in the matter at all." Clarke said that, if he mentioned the subject of the murders to Day, he would only say "Well", or something like that and turn away. Is this to be considered unusual behaviour by Day in the circumstances? Is this again a mere coincidence?

According to Clarke, Day was a quiet, very reserved kind of man. He would talk about nothing at all. He did not, of course, even return Burnett's greeting of "Good night". Yet Toomey said that, when he and other police officers surprised Day at his hut between 1 a.m. and 2 a.m. and told him they required him to go to the police station in connection with the murder, he "seemed quite cool and not a bit flurried". Toomey said that the police brought Day into Gatton and he "conversed all the way". No doubt Toomey took this to be evidence of Day's being at ease. But what is to be made of a man who is generally reserved to the extent of being apparently taciturn, suddenly acting out of character by conversing with police officers "all the way into Gatton"? Is his sudden change of demeanour indicative of inward stress and tension—or does it amount to no more than mere coincidence?

Day's fellow employee, Robert King, noticed what were apparently blood spots on Day's jumper. These were also noticed by Day's employer, Clarke. King noticed the blood spots on Day's jumper on 28 December 1898. Clarke told Day not to wash this jumper; but in the face of that he washed it; he used a scrubbing brush, soda and water for the purpose. According to King, Day was also advised by him not to wash the jumper, but Day said he must. The suppression or eradication of evidence is always something which must be considered. Often it is viewed as a powerful circumstance tending to the guilt of a person. However, it has been known for innocent persons to become alarmed at a body of evidence against them which, although false or inconclusive, they feel themselves unable to refute; such persons have on occasions had recourse to the destruction or the suppression of evidence which seems to incriminate them and even to the fabrication of testimony in order to free themselves from suspicion.[17] Are Day's actions here open to a sinister interpretation? Or should they be regarded in the light of an innocent man becoming somewhat alarmed? Or are his actions in this instance again to be treated as mere coincidence?

There is, we have no doubt, in the conduct of human affairs, a point of time at which apparent coincidence ceases to be mere coincidence and becomes a significant pattern of facts. We hold the view that, in regard to Thomas Day, that point of time was reached when his blood-stained jumper was seen by King on 28 December 1898. We hasten to add that we are far from saying that, at that or at any stage, there was sufficient or any *proof* that Day was the criminal agent in respect of any of the crimes committed. But what we do say is that, with the discovery of blood on his jumper, Day ought reasonably to have been the subject of a lively *suspicion*, which warranted a minute examination of his antecedents and a very close checking of his movements, particularly during the week or so before his arrival in Gatton.

From what has gone before, the reader will readily appreciate the dangers of visual identification unsupported by corroborating facts. It should, however, be noted that the identification of Day by the boy Carroll was of a slightly different order from that of the witnesses who allegedly identified Burgess as being in or near Gatton on the day of the murders. These witnesses purported to identify a person whom they claimed to have seen only on one previous occasion. But John Carroll's evidence was to the effect that he had previously seen Day "several times" or "pretty often" driving in the cart. He said that, on the night of the murders, the man at the sliprails "walked right up close to the cart" and he noticed the man's clothes and hat and he knew him by "his figure and his clothes". In such circumstances, we feel it fair to suggest that the boy Carroll, because of his previous knowledge of Day, might make a more reliable identification than those who purported to identify Burgess. We do, however, recognise that Carroll's identification was by moonlight and in a situation where, apparently, he was unable to see the man's face. We most readily concede it would be quite dangerous to act on this evidence of visual identification in the absence of corroborative circumstances.

In cases which depend to a significant degree on visual identification, judges often warn juries that in the past mistakes have occurred in identification, thereby causing miscarriages of justice. Juries are often directed that they must exercise considerable care before coming to a conclusion on evidence as to identification, and that, before they act upon the evidence of a witness who purports to identify an accused, they should be clearly satisfied that the witness was not only honest in the evidence he gave but that his evidence was accurate.[18]

In mid 1976, the Court of Appeal (Criminal Division) in England considered several appeals which raised problems relating to evidence of visual identification in criminal cases. The Court of Appeal was constituted by five judges and was presided over by the Lord Chief Justice of England (Lord Widgery). In its judgement the Court acknowledged that evidence of visual identification in criminal cases can bring about miscarriages of justice and has done so in a few cases in recent years. The Court was of the view that the danger of miscarriages of justice occurring could be much reduced if trial judges were to sum up to juries in the way it indicated in its judgment:

First, whenever the case against an accused depends wholly or substantially on the correctness of one or more identifications of the accused which the defence alleges to be mistaken, the Judge should warn the jury of the special need for caution before convicting the accused in reliance on the correctness of the identification or identifications. In addition he should instruct them as to the reason for the need for such a warning and should make some reference to the possibility that a mistaken witness can be a convincing one and that a number of such witnesses can all be mistaken. Provided this is done in clear terms the Judge need not use any particular form of words.

Secondly, the Judge should direct the jury to examine closely the circumstances in which the identification by each witness came to be made. How long did the witness have the accused under observation? At what distance? In what light? Was the observation impeded in any way, as for example, by passing traffic or a press of people? Had the witness ever seen the accused before? How often? If only occasionally, had he any special reason for remembering the accused? How long elapsed between the original observation and the subsequent identification to the police? Was there any material discrepancy between the description of the accused given to the police by the witness when first seen by them and his actual appearance? If in any case, whether it is being dealt with summarily or on indictment, the prosecution have reason to believe that there is such a material discrepancy they should supply the accused or his legal advisers with particulars of the description the police were first given. In all cases if the accused asks to be given particulars of such descriptions, the prosecution should supply them. Finally, he should remind the jury of any specific weaknesses which had appeared in the identification evidence.

Recognition may be more reliable than identification of a stranger; but even when the witness is purporting to recognise someone whom he knows, the jury should be reminded that mistakes in recognition of close relatives and friends are sometimes made.

All these matters go to the quality of the identification evidence. If the quality is good and remains good at the close of the accused's case, the danger of a mistaken identification is lessened; but the poorer the quality, the greater the danger.

In our judgment when the quality is good as for example when the identification is made after a long period of observation, or in satisfactory conditions by a relative, a neighbour, a close friend, a workmate and the like, the jury can safely be left to assess the value of the identifying evidence even though there is no other evidence to support it: provided always, however, that an adequate warning has been given about the special need for caution . . . When, in the judgment of the trial Judge, the quality of the identifying evidence is poor, as for example when it depends solely on a fleeting glance or on a longer observation made in difficult conditions, the situation is very different. The Judge should then withdraw the case from the jury and direct an acquittal unless there is other evidence which goes to support the correctness of the identification. . . . [19]

In all the circumstances, it must be readily acknowledged that the alleged recognition by the boy Carroll of "Clarke's man" at Moran's sliprails on Boxing Night 1898 was of poor quality in the scale of evidence of visual identification. On the material apparently available, of course, there was no chance of Day or anyone else being brought to trial. Ultimately there was certainly no credible evidence and no justifiable suspicion against Burgess. Nor was there any *evidence* amounting to *proof* against Day; there was merely *suspicion*. Suspicion is far from being proof; much less is it proof beyond reasonable doubt.

There are varying degrees of cogency in the evidentiary scale. First there is *insufficient* evidence, the lowest degree of cogency, where the evidence in support of an issue is so weak that no reasonable person could properly decide the issue as being established. Next, there is *prima facie* evidence, where the evidence in support of an issue is sufficiently weighty *to entitle* a reasonable person to decide that the issue is established, although, as a matter of common sense, that person is not *obliged* to do so. Third, there is *conclusive* evidence. The evidence of a fact is sometimes said to be conclusive when the evidence in support of it is so weighty that the tribunal must find that fact to be proved.[20]

It is quite clear that the ascertained inculpatory features in regard to Thomas Day constitute *insufficient* evidence. Further investigation of him might well have resulted in the available evidence concerning him being augmented to the extent where it could truly be said that a *prima facie* case existed against him.

Day certainly appeared to be an unusual young man. From the little we do know about him our curiosity is aroused. He seems to have been most uncommunicative; it is evident that he had the capacity to instil an intense dislike and distrust in the minds of King and Mrs Clarke. He was fond of reading—when the police paid him "surprise visits" they "found him lying in his bunk reading *Rienzi*".[21] What sort of a young man was this nomad whose taste for reading extended to a work by Lord Lytton? How many butchers' labourers in 1898 would have read Lytton? How many would have ever heard of him? How many educated men today have read *Rienzi*? How many indeed are familiar with any of the works of Lord Edward George Earle Bulwer-Lytton? A reasonable education, one would think, would be a prerequisite for the reading of such a work. Why would a young man, who could read so well as Day obviously could, be travelling along the roads of a colony other than his own in a "hard-up" state? Day told Toomey that he "came over from Sydney in a boat, but came from Brisbane by road. He got hard-up, and Mr Clarke employed him." Was it just possible that this rather unsociable young man had an emotional or personality problem? A thorough check of his antecedents, background and recent movements was, in our view, certainly warranted.

And yet, those investigators in Gatton at the time and close to the events apparently did not see this as we see it—and as the Chairman of the Royal Commission and some other members of the Commission in the latter months of 1899 saw it. Why was this? We think the answer to this question is to be found in the unfortunate intrusion of Richard Burgess into the picture at the critical time. In our view, Burgess was the classical example of the "red herring". He, it seems to us, diverted the police investigation from more pertinent areas—and particularly from the carrying out of an intensive investigation into the background and movements of Thomas Day. We see Burgess as a man, who, because of his previous convictions and bad record, created a "blind spot" in the eyes of the investigators. His previous convictions were, we consider, given an exaggerated importance by those charged with inquiry into the crimes.

It is well accepted that previous convictions and misconduct on previous occasions, if given undue prominence, can cause inaccurate assessments of the matter in hand. This was pointed out by Dr Glanville Williams in his most valuable work *The Proof of Guilt*, in the following terms:

The Exclusion of Character and Convictions

The feature of the English system that most puzzles and intrigues foreign lawyers is that the prosecution are generally not allowed to give evidence of the accused's bad character or previous convictions in order to help establish that he committed the crime in question. Such evidence can in general be given only after conviction in order to determine punishment. In many other countries, on the other hand, this evidence is the very first to be adduced at the trial. On the face of it the English system might seem to be over-lenient to the accused, because we do in everyday life attach importance to the question whether the person whose worth we are assessing has a criminal record or not. One reason for the English rule is that evidence of general evil propensity widens the issues of the trial so immensely as to be unfair to the accused. Even the notorious Judge Jeffreys may be found to say, in Hampden's case, that "to rake into the whole course of a man's life is very hard"; and Mr Justice Withins said on the same occasion: "We would not suffer any raking into men's course of life, to pick up evidence that they cannot be prepared to answer to." This reason would not in itself explain why we exclude evidence of previous convictions, after notice given to the accused of intention to prove them. Convictions can be precisely proved, so that there will rarely be dispute about them. However, there is a second and stronger justification for the rule, which explains why we exclude even evidence of previous convictions, as a general principle. This is the exaggerated importance that a jury, consisting of persons without legal experience, may attach to this kind of evidence; for they may argue: "This man is charged with crime, and the police think he did it, and he is clearly of criminal habits; therefore he must be guilty." [22]

Urquhart acknowledged that one of the grounds that led him to suspect Burgess was "his known character".[23] We would have thought rather that it was apparent from the manner in which Burgess committed his crimes that he was a most impulsive character with a manifestly low "flash point". To us, it would seem that his previous convictions, when weighed in the light of how his offences were committed, would tend to dissociate him from crimes such as the Gatton murders, which were clearly the result of considerable forethought and planning.

Urquhart also, according to Christie, dismissed the idea of Day being responsible for the Gatton murders with the comment, "What rot, Christie; he is only a mere boy; he could not commit that crime; he is a beardless boy."[24] Now Day was described by Toomey as being a man "5 feet 9 inches [*175 cm*] or 5 feet 10 inches [*178 cm*] in height" whose age was "twenty or twenty-one" and who "could not grow a beard" but who had what is called "cat's hair" on his face.[25] Day's employer, Clarke, said of Day "He is a very powerful man, and a big man, too."[26] King said "Day assisted me twice to kill, and I then noticed that he was a stronger man than myself in pulling a bullock into position for skinning."[27] Burnett said Day was "a man of about fourteen stone [*eighty-nine kg*]...well, between twelve stone and fourteen stone [*eighty-two and eighty-nine kg*]".[28] It is difficult, surely, to understand why a man of such an age and such a physique should be thought to be incapable of committing the Gatton crimes. And how anyone of such a description could seriously be described as being "only a mere boy" is equally difficult to understand.

There is, as we have said, no *proof* that Thomas Day was involved in the Gatton outrage. As a result of an incomplete investigation of him and, it would seem, as a consequence of his never having been subsequently located, we are left with no more than a suspicion that he might have been the guilty party or one of the guilty parties. We are left merely with surmises and conjectures rather than those permissible inferences and legitimate proofs which are the basis of any *prima facie* case against a person. In *Caswell* v. *Powell Duffryn Associated Collieries Ltd.* it was stated:

> My Lords, the precise manner in which the accident occurred cannot be ascertained as the unfortunate young man was alone when he was killed. The Court therefore is left to inference or circumstantial evidence. Inference must be carefully distinguished from conjecture or speculation. There can be no inference unless there are objective facts from which to infer the other facts which it is sought to establish. In some cases the other facts can be inferred with as much practical certainty as if they had been actually observed. In other cases the inference does not go beyond reasonable probability. But if there are no positive proved facts from which the inference can be made, the method of inference fails and what is left is mere speculation or conjecture.
>
> In the present case there are, I think, certain known facts which enable some inferences to be drawn. Beyond that point the method of inference stops and what is suggested is conjecture.[29]

And that is the situation, we feel, in so far as Thomas Day is concerned. There is obviously a lack of proved objective facts from which a *prima facie* case could be compounded. A further investigation of Day in addition to the one cursorily made, an intensive searching of his background, a more concentrated questioning of him and, more particularly, a careful examination of his trousers and a close comparison of the weave of the cloth with the "imprint of cloth and the facsimile" might well have carried us from the area of speculation into the area of reasonable inference based on proper evidentiary material. But, as it happened, the clothing of Burgess was sent to Brisbane for "microscopical examination by experts", while Day (and his clothing) disappeared from the scene, and from police surveillance for ever.

In their report of 29 November 1899, the Royal Commissioners said:

> We are of opinion that sufficiently exhaustive investigation and inquiry were not made in every instance as regards suspects.
> Taking all the facts before us in connection with the action of the police in reference to both the Gatton and Oxley murders, we feel bound to say that there was a lack of cohesion and efficient organisation to enable them to cope with serious crimes in such a manner as the people of the Colony are entitled to expect. On the other hand we feel constrained to acknowledge that great mystery surrounds the Gatton murders, and it does not follow that if the police had been in the highest state of efficiency that the murderer or murderers would have been discovered. That there was inertness and dilatoriness at the outset cannot be gainsaid, but after the matter was fairly taken in hand the officers and men acted individually with zeal . . . [30]

So the mystery lives and lingers. Was there one criminal agent or more? How did the Murphys come to be in the spot where they were slain? What firearm was used and how was it disposed of? These and other matters are still the subject of discussion and debate; and well they might be till the end of time. And what of the other remarkable facts—the three bodies appearing to have been carefully laid out, Norah on a nicely arranged rug, the feet of each body pointing due west, the empty purse in Michael's hand, a complete absence of tracks near the bodies, the ground nearby showing absolutely no sign that a struggle had taken place though marks and fingernail scratches on the bodies of the girls pointed to that conclusion? Of what significance were the attendant circumstances—the man at the sliprails on that brilliant moonlight night, the alleged screams of "Father", the "pipe stop", "Loney's letters", the "In Memoriam" notice with the chinstrap of the horse and the curious "imprint of cloth and the facsimile"? What can we gather from such phenomena?

This combination of attendant facts, this concurrence of separate and independent circumstances has bewildered many inquiring minds for over three quarters of a century. Should such a coincidence of particulars furnish a rational explanation to a perceptive and discerning intelligence? Or should it be viewed rather as a concomitance of trivial irrelevance to be treated merely as " . . . a tale/Told by an idiot, full of sound and fury, /Signifying nothing"?[31]

We wonder; but we know not. We do know that, over the years, we have assiduously studied the Gatton tragedy; but to us, it remains a tantalising enigma. Though our interest and our attention have been intensive and persevering, for us the Gatton mosaic has not been pieced; the veil of mystery has not been pierced. We are, in regard to this fascinating obscurity, in a similar state of mind to that of the Persian philosopher-poet who tells us: "There was a Door to which I found no Key:/There was a Veil past which I could not see."[32]

EPILOGUE

One day late in December 1906, some men in the employ of a Mr James Logan of Gatton were cutting firewood in an area known as the Swamp paddock, situated not very far from the spot in Moran's paddock where the Murphys were struck down. In the hollow of a log on which they were working they found an old revolver wrapped in some moleskin cloth. The revolver was very rusty and the cloth perished and in shreds. Inquiries revealed that the log was from a tree which had been felled some months after the murders. Part of it had been split into fence posts and the remainder had lain in the paddock since. It was apparent that the revolver had been placed in the tree before it was felled and the aperture through which it had been dropped into the trunk would have been about six metres from the ground, so that the person secreting the revolver must have climbed the tree.

This discovery excited much interest at the time; but it seems that the police very soon established that the revolver could not have been the firearm used in the murders eight years earlier. From a reading of newspaper reports of the time it appears that the old revolver found in the log was not of ·380 calibre. It was a strange coincidence, however, that the chamber of the revolver contained two cartridges less than the full charge. In reporting the discovery a Brisbane newspaper commented:

> Then comes to the inquiring mind the natural question—why was the revolver hidden away in a tree, the person depositing it climbing up over twenty feet? Students of criminal cases and of the very compromising things done by perfectly innocent persons under the excitement following upon crimes will be aware that there is nothing new in such an action. In Gatton at the time of the tragedy there was much excitement and a nervous person in possession of a revolver at the time would not be acting unnaturally, however foolish he might be, in trying to get rid of it.[1]

Commissioner of Police, W.E. Parry-Okeden, retired from the Police Force in 1905, and died in Brisbane on 30 August 1926, at the age of eighty-six. While on a visit to the Brisbane Royal National Association's annual Exhibition in August 1924, he was knocked down by a motor car in Adelaide Street and suffered injuries which confined him to his bed for the last two years of his life. At the time of his death he was paid a last tribute by his old friend Frederick Charles Urquhart in the following lines:

> Full was the load your constant spirit carried,
> The heat, the burden of the days gone past;
> Long was the waiting for the rest that tarried,
> Now it has come at last.
>
> Through many trials of life's uncertain dealing,
> Though oft times worn, and torn, and tempest tossed;
> Thy kindly ways the gentle heart revealing,
> Were kept and never lost.
>
> Goodbye; good friend and Chief of old respected,
> Now you have reached the traveller's final bourne;
> May you still know the monument erected,
> In these our hearts who mourn.[2]

Chief Inspector John Stuart was superannuated from the Queensland Police Force on 1 March 1900. He died in Sydney on 2 August 1914.

Frederick Charles Urquhart died in Brisbane on 2 December 1935, at the age of seventy-seven years. His friend, Major-General Spencer Browne, wrote of him:

Then, while we were at Gatton, there came a Woolloongabba tragedy, and the murder of the boy Hill near Oxley, and, on the whole of the three crimes, the police were beaten. Urquhart, as head of the Criminal Investigation Department, came in for the bulk of the blame. He was to be the scapegoat; but we had a Home Secretary who did not clamour for the despatch of Urquhart into the wilderness with the police sins of omission on his shoulders. That was Colonel Foxton, C.M.G., V.D. He asked me to see him as I had been at Gatton for about a month, and he questioned me closely about Urquhart. I could confidently say that a keener and more earnest man had never been on a job of the kind, and I put it to Foxton: "Can you suggest that there is a weakness in the department? Do you think that Urquhart has not the ability to work out the mystery of these crimes, or do you think that a chain of adverse circumstance—peculiar coincidences—has not blotted out direct evidence?" As a fact, we knew who murdered the boy Hill and the brute was gaoled for other crimes; and we had a pretty good idea as to the bloody hand behind the Gatton tragedy, and Foxton knew those things also. A searching inquiry did not "whitewash" the police, but re-established the force in public confidence, and Urquhart became Chief Inspector, and then, in turn, took the blue ribbon of the service.[3]

Percy Galbraith, or "Gal" as he was affectionately known to his colleagues, attained the rank of Inspector in the Queensland Police Force. In 1900 he was sent by the Queensland Government to New South Wales with six Aboriginal trackers to assist the police of that colony in the hunt for the notorious half-caste outlaws Jim and Joe Governor.[4] He was retired medically unfit on 1 October 1910 and settled in Townsville where he was employed by a large commercial firm practically up to the time of his death, which occurred on 27 January 1926.[5]

Michael Toomey reached the rank of Senior Sergeant and resigned from the Police Force in August 1911. He died in Sydney on 1 January 1932. Toomey figured in a sensational incident in Sydney in 1901 while he was performing duty at the Commonwealth Celebrations. On the night of 7 January in that year he was standing in Martin Place opposite the Post Office when a man suddenly lunged at him and plunged a butcher's knife into his back. He was in a critical condition for some time but subsequently recovered. Toomey's assailant was a criminal named Joseph Baker, whom he had previously arrested in Queensland. Baker had, only a short time before this incident, been released from prison under an amnesty proclaimed by the new Commonwealth Government. He had been serving a long term of imprisonment for house breaking in Brisbane.[6]

Sergeant William Arrell left Gatton in February 1901, and was retired from the Police Force on medical grounds on 1 May 1908. He died in Brisbane on 5 June 1932.

Mr Augustus Henry Warner Shand, the Police Magistrate who presided at the Magisterial Inquiry at Gatton, died in Brisbane on 18 December 1922, aged seventy-four years. He was born at Antigua, West Indies, in 1848, and came to Queensland as a young man in or about the year 1873, from Liverpool, England, where he was educated. He was, for a time, a partner in a grazing property which was unsuccessful and afterwards he was appointed Clerk of Petty Sessions at St George. Later he was appointed Clerk of Petty Sessions at Ipswich, and was Acting Magistrate there during the early part of 1899. He was subsequently appointed Police Magistrate at Longreach from which appointment he eventually retired or resigned.[7]

Dr Charles James Hill Wray, L.R.C.S. (Edin.), L.R.C.P. (Edin.) died prematurely in 1902. There was an outbreak of bubonic plague in Brisbane in that year and Dr Wray, as a result of his ministrations to those infected, caught the plague himself and died in Wattlebrae Hospital, Brisbane, on 8 May 1902. Besides the appointment of Government Medical Officer, Brisbane, Dr Wray also held the posts of Visiting Surgeon to the Benevolent Asylum at Dunwich and the Lock Hospital, Brisbane, and Health Officer at the Quarantine Station,

Brisbane.[8] At the time of his death, Mr Archibald Meston wrote of the late Dr Wray:

> ... Only those who knew him as the kindly physician or the amiable and sincere friend could know how pure a diamond was enshrined in that somewhat rough and unpretentious matrix...[9]

Mary Murphy died on 2 September 1922, aged eighty years, and Daniel Murphy on 31 May 1927, at the age of eighty-four years. In reporting the passing of the devout and kindly old man, a newspaper commented:

> Time and time again he was urged to move to where fresh associations might relieve the poignancy of his grief and that of his wife but he would not. He was living at Tent Hill when the murders were committed and it was at Tent Hill he died.[10]

Daniel and Mary Murphy lie buried in Gatton cemetery not far from the monument which marks the grave of their beloved children, Michael, Norah and Ellen.

William McNeil in his later years moved to Kingaroy where he died at the age of eighty years on 12 September 1950. One day in 1916 he displayed the horsemanship for which he was renowned when he rescued a three year old girl from a sulky drawn by a maddened horse as it bolted through the streets of Toowoomba. McNeil was driving in the town when he saw the bolting horse with the child alone in the sulky. He took in the situation at a glance, stood up in his own vehicle and, lashing his horse to a gallop, set out after and overtook the bolting horse. Reaching over, he plucked the child to safety. For this notable act of bravery William McNeil was, on 8 February 1917, awarded a bronze medal by the Royal Humane Society.

The last direct link with the Murphy family was broken with the death in Brisbane of Catherine (Katie) Murphy on 21 February 1974.

As late as in 1973, the Queensland Police made inquiries into the Gatton murders following information given to them by two elderly women who resided at Brunswick Heads on the northern coast of New South Wales. In January of that year, sisters Mrs Margaret Rutherford aged seventy-four, and Mrs Violet Russell, seventy-three, reported to police the confession to the murders allegedly made to them by an old man whom they had known for about twenty-five years. The man, who was born in France and came to Australia at an early age, had died towards the end of 1972. The two women claimed that in March 1972, when he was ill and apparently on his death bed, the man had told them that he was the Gatton murderer. According to the two women, the man said that in December 1898 he was working for a butcher in Gatton. He claimed to have "bashed the Murphy boy and shot the girls" and to have shot and mutilated their horse. He said that he had hidden the revolver in the stump of a tree and after the bodies were found, left Gatton and walked to Casino and later went to Melbourne where he married.[11]

The man's claim that he had been employed by a butcher in Gatton at the time of the murders was obviously an attempt by him to assume the identity of Thomas Day. After the Police Inquiry Commission in 1899, it would have been fairly widely known in Queensland that a man who had worked for a butcher in Gatton had come under the surveillance of the police investigating the murders. It is certain, however, that the Frenchman was not Thomas Day and also that, whoever he was, he could not possibly have been the perpetrator of the crime. His statements that he had shot Ellen and Norah Murphy and that he had mutilated the horse did not accord with the facts and were patently false. Detective Senior Sergeant (now Inspector) Evan Griffiths of the Queensland Police investigated the matter which, at the time, received considerable publicity in the media. Inspector Griffiths has informed us that he was able to establish, beyond doubt, the man's identity and antecedents and also procured documentary evidence which showed that in 1898 the man would have been twelve years old.

In December 1976, we interviewed an elderly man who, as a child, saw Thomas Day. He is Mr John Franklin Clarke, aged eighty-six, now resident in Brisbane. Mr Clarke is a son of Arthur George Clarke the butcher who employed Day at Gatton between 16 December 1898 and 10 January 1899. Mr Clarke told us that, although he was only eight years old at the time, he clearly remembers Day and recalled that on one occasion Day lifted him and his brother (later killed in World War I) onto his shoulder and carried them about the paddock near their father's butchery.

Doubtless, the killer of Michael, Norah and Ellen Murphy has by now taken his secret with him to the grave and it seems certain that the Gatton tragedy will remain a mystery forever.

ABBREVIATIONS USED IN NOTES TO TEXT

TC	*Toowoomba Chronicle* (Toowoomba newspaper)
TT	*The Telegraph* (Brisbane daily evening newspaper)
TQ	*The Queenslander* (a Queensland weekly publication)
MI	The Magisterial Inquiry into cause of death of the three Murphys
RCP	Royal Commission Proceedings—*Proceedings of Royal Commission appointed to inquire into the constitution, administration and working of the Criminal Investigation Branch of the Police Force etc.* (Police Inquiry Commission). Its proceedings, together with Appendices and the Report of the Royal Commission are published in QVP 1899 Vol IV–OL.
QVP	*Queensland Votes and Proceedings*
OL	John Oxley Library, Brisbane
QT	*Queensland Times* (Ipswich newspaper published three times weekly)
MC	*Maryborough Chronicle* (Maryborough newspaper)
EO	*Evening Observer* (Brisbane newspaper)
BC	*Brisbane Courier* (Brisbane daily morning newspaper)
Qd.R.	*Queensland Reports*
A.C.	*Law Reports, Appeal Cases, 1875–90*; from 1891 onwards the year was placed before the A.C. thus (1961) A.C.
Curt.	*Curteis' Ecclesiastical Reports,* 3 vols., 1834–1844
Cr.App.R.	*Criminal Appeal Reports,* 1908 onwards

NOTES TO TEXT

Introduction

[1] TC, 29.12.1898, p. 2.
[2] Ibid., p. 3.
[3] TC, 5.1.1899. See also TT, 23.1.1899 where it is stated that "not enough young women had attended to make it successful".
[4] TQ, 25.3.1899, p. 525, reporting evidence of Edward Andrew Chadwick, one of the organisers of the dance, given at the MI on 16.3.1899.
[5] TC, 26.1.1899, reporting evidence of Patrick Murphy, given at the MI on 24.1.1899.
[6] RCP, evidence of Sergeant William Arrell, p. 408, in answering question 12745.
[7] An article entitled "Ghastly Murderer who Went Scot Free", by a reviewer using the title "Murkah" from *The World's News*, 8 April 1936, p. 11.
[8] TQ, 25.3.1899, reporting evidence of Robert Ballantyne given at the MI on 20.3.1899.
[9] TC, 28.12.1898.
[10] RCP, evidence of Inspector F.C. Urquhart, p. 432, in answering question 13616.
[11] RCP, evidence of F.C. Urquhart, p. 433, in answering question 13623.
[12] *Government Gazette*, No. 1, 3 January 1899.
[13] TT, 19.4.1969—an article by Pat Lloyd entitled "The Maniacal Gatton Killer".
[14] TT, 18.1.1899.
[15] TQ, 1.4.1899. The depositions were taken in longhand—they were written and not typed.
[16] TC, 26.1.1899.
[17] The Commission was set up following upon the Oxley murder of mid-December 1898 and the Gatton murders of 26 December 1898. These crimes aroused widespread feelings of dissatisfaction and doubts concerning the efficiency of the Queensland Police Force. The Recital of the Commission commences "Whereas certain serious crimes have recently been committed in Our Colony of Queensland, and the perpetrators of such crimes have not up to the present time been detected and brought to justice: And whereas doubts have in consequence arisen as to the efficiency of the Criminal Investigation Branch of the Police Force of Our said Colony...."

[18] Recourse has been made to the Press reports of the evidence given by the witnesses at the Magisterial Inquiry because the actual depositions are not available at the State Archives of Queensland. According to the "Record of Depositions Taken at Magisterial Inquiries, Received During the Year 1899" (reference "JUS/R.6" in State Archives of Queensland) at p. 110, the depositions taken at the Magisterial Inquiry were received at the Department of Justice on 30 March 1899. But there is a pencil noting against the entry which reads "Depositions lent to Mr Lawson, Police Dept., per Monteith on 27.9.99". It appears that Robert Hazelwood Lawson was chief clerk in Police Commissioner's Office at the time and that William John Monteith was a clerk in such office. (P. 44 of *Queensland Blue Book* for year 1899—QVP, 1899.)

[19] RCP, evidence of William Arrell, p. 408, in answer to question 12745.

[20] The man was Patrick Michael Quinn and he was interviewed by James Gibney in March 1973. He was allegedly born on 22.11.1882. He seemed quite clear in his mind as to the events about which he spoke and said he would never forget them. He said he left his home about six o'clock on the morning of 27 December 1898, to round up two mares which were in a paddock near Gatton and later in the morning had gone to the scene of the murders and assisted with lifting of the bodies of the deceased into horse-drawn vehicles. It is understood that he had, in February 1973, been interviewed by Detective Senior Sergeant Evan Griffiths (now Inspector) of the Brisbane Criminal Investigation Branch and had volunteered similar information.

[21] *Studies in Australian Crime*, John D. Fitzgerald, first series, 1924, p. 131. A copy is in OL.

[22] TC, 29.12.1898, p. 3.

Chapter 1—The Background

[1] Queensland Place Names Board information—letter of 17.3.1976. See also *Lockyer Saga*, Win Davson, p. 7. OL.

[2] *New South Wales Government Gazette*, Vol. XXXVII (Jan. to June 1855), p. 1102.

[3] Queensland Place Names Board—letter of 17.3.76.

[4] *Lockyer Saga*, Win Davson, p. 7. OL.

[5] Qld. State Archives File, M.173. 544/2.

[6] Ibid.

[7] The population of Gatton (Census 1891) was 241 people—see Pugh's Almanac 1898, p. 128A. The population (Census 1901) was 449 people—see Pugh's Almanac 1903, p. 632.

[8] *Pugh's Almanac*, 1899, p. 858.

[9] *Pugh's Almanac*, 1899, "Diary of Events", p. 73.

[10] QT, 17.12.1898, p. 4.

[11] TT, 2.1.1899.

[12] Her eldest daughter, Polly McNeil, admitted under oath at the MI that her mother gave her "a beating for going with Tom Ryan" (a young man of whom Mrs Murphy disapproved)—see TC, 25.3.1899, reporting evidence of Polly McNeil at MI on 23.3 1899.

[13] TT, 2.1.1899.

[14] TC, 31.12.1898.

[15] Ibid. In 1891 the Queensland coalition Government was faced with the critical industrial upheaval known as the "Great Shearers' Strike". There were serious disturbances in the western districts "and it is no overstatement to say that Queensland was on the brink of a civil war". See *Triumph in the Tropics*, Cilento and Lack, p. 396.

[16] In the course of the "Great Shearers' Strike" the Ayrshire Downs woolshed, in spite of armed guards, was burnt down.

[17] TC, 31.12.1898. Also *Studies in Australian Crime*, John D. Fitzgerald, first series, 1924, p. 132. OL.

[18] TC, 31.12.1898.

[19] TC, 31.12.1898.

[20] TC, 29.12.1898, p. 3.

[21] TT, 2.1.1899; see also QT, 31.12.1898.

[22] TQ, 1.4.1899, p. 584, reporting evidence of Mary Murphy at MI on 24.3.1899. In QT, 25.3.1899, this woman is referred to as "Mrs Vanneck".

[23] TC, 31.12.1898.

[24] TT, 2.1.1899; see also QT, 31.12.1898.

[25] Ibid.

[1] TC, 25.3.1899, reporting evidence of Polly McNeil at MI at Toowoomba on 23.3.1899.

[2] TT, 2.1.1899.

[3] Ibid.

[4] TC, 25.3.1899, reporting evidence of Polly McNeil at MI at Toowoomba on 23.3.1899. See also TC, 8.3.1899, where it is reported that, in her evidence at the MI, Katie Murphy deposed that McNeil "was well liked by the whole family".

[5] McNeil's sulky has variously been described and referred to as "a trap", "a single-horse sulky", "a two-wheeled dog cart" and "a dog cart". We have referred to it throughout the text as a sulky.

[6] TQ, 18.3.1899, p. 477, reporting evidence of John Murphy at MI on 9.3.1899.

[7] TQ, 18.3.1899, p. 477, reporting evidence of Jeremiah Murphy at MI on 9.3.1899.

[8] TC, 25.3.1899. reporting evidence of Polly McNeil at MI at Toowoomba on 23.3.1899.

[9] TQ, 11.3.1899, p. 465, reporting evidence of Katie Murphy at MI on 7.3.1899.

[10] TQ, 11.3.1899, p. 465, reporting evidence of Mrs Mary Murphy at MI on 7.3.1899.

[11] TC, 25.3.1899, reporting evidence of Polly McNeil at MI at Toowoomba on 23.3.1899. See also QT 11.3.1899, p. 2, reporting evidence of John Murphy at MI at Gatton on 9.3.1899.

[12] Ibid. In QT, 25.3.1899, Jimmy Ryan's reply is quoted as being "Mick will be there, and if he is not, I will come home with you."

[13] TQ, 11.3.1899, pp. 465 and 477, reporting evidence of William Murphy at MI on 6.3.1899.

[14] TQ, 11.3.1899, p. 465, reporting evidence of Mary Murphy at MI on 6.3.1899.

[15] TC, 25.3.1899, reporting evidence of Polly McNeil at MI on 23.3.1899.

[16] TQ, 11.3.1899, p. 465, reporting evidence of Katie Murphy at MI on 7.3.1899.

[17] TT, 2.1.1899.

[18] TC, 26.1.1899, reporting evidence of Patrick Murphy at MI on 24.1.1899.

[19] TQ, 25.3.1899, p. 525, reporting evidence of Edward Andrew Chadwick at MI on 16.3.1899.

[20] TQ, 11.3.1899, p. 464, reporting evidence of Daniel Murphy at MI on 6.3.1899.

[21] TQ, 31.12.1898, p. 1244.

[22] Mr James Logan selected his holding on 16.7.1869. His son, Mr R.A. (Bob) Logan is still a resident of Gatton and is one of its well-known and well-respected identities.

[23] TC, 26.1.1899, reporting evidence of Patrick Murphy at MI on 24.1.1899.

[24] RCP, evidence of P.D.F. Galbraith, on 29.9.1899, answering question 13252 at p. 421. At Gatton on Boxing Day, 1898, "sunset occurred at 6.48 p.m. The near full moon was at the zenith at 10.42 p.m.": from Certificate dated 1.3.76 from Qld. Dept. of Mapping and Surveying and Office of the

Surveyor-General, File 50/5, 76/01585 MISC.

[25] TQ, 25.3.1899, p. 525, reporting evidence of Edward Andrew Chadwick at MI on 16.3.1899.

[26] *Childe Harold's Pilgrimage*, XXIV, Canto III (The Eve of Waterloo), Lord George Gordon Byron.

[1] TQ, 11.3.1899, pp. 464 to 465, reporting evidence of Daniel Murphy and Mary Murphy given at MI on 6.3.1899.

[2] MC, 11.1.1899, reporting a letter from a special reporter of TT dated Gatton, Sunday, 8.1.1899, in which it is stated that Mrs Murphy made these remarks when interviewed that afternoon "in regard to the awful affliction which has befallen her".

[3] MC, 6.1.1899, reporting an interview had with William McNeil by a reporter from TT.

[4] This interview is reported in TC, 28.12.1898.

[5] TC, 26.1.1899, reporting evidence of William McNeil given at MI on 24.1.1899.

[6] TC, 16.3.1899, reporting evidence of Charles Gilbert given at MI on 14.3.1899.

[7] All of the quoted material in this paragraph is taken from RCP, evidence of Thomas Wilson, pp. 473 and 474.

[8] RCP, evidence of William Devitt, bootmaker, p. 474.

[9] All of the quoted material in regard to Mr James is taken from RCP, pp. 470 to 473.

[10] TQ, 18.3.1899, p. 513, reporting evidence of William Arrell given at MI on 15.3.1899. See also report in TC, 16.3.1899.

[11] TQ, 25.3.1899, p. 524, reporting evidence of William Arrell given at MI on 15.3.1899.

[12] RCP, evidence of William Arrell at pp. 406 to 411.

[13] TQ, 25.3.1899, reporting evidence of William Arrell given at MI on 15.3.1899.

[14] Ibid.

Chapter 4—The Aftermath

[1] RCP, evidence of William Arrell, answer to question 12725, p. 407.
[2] TQ, 25.3.1899, p. 524, reporting evidence of William Arrell at MI on 15.3.1899.
[3] RCP, evidence of William Arrell, p. 407.
[4] Ibid.
[5] TQ, 18.3.1899, p. 477, reporting evidence of Jeremiah Murphy at MI on 9.3.1899.
[6] TQ, 18.3.1899, p. 477. See also QT, 9.3.1899, p. 5.
[7] TT, 2.1.1899.
[8] EO, 6.1.1899.
[9] TQ, 25.3.1899, pp. 561 and 562, reporting evidence of Robert Ballantyne at MI on 20.3.1899.
[10] TQ, 25.3.1899, p. 524, reporting evidence of William Arrell at MI on 15.3.1899.
[11] TC, 28.12.1898.
[12] RCP, p. 409, evidence of William Arrell.
[13] TQ, 25.3.1899, p. 525, reporting evidence of William Arrell at MI on 15.3.1899.
[14] TC, 9.3.1899, reporting evidence of James Skinner at MI on 6.3.1899. See also TQ, 11.3.1899, p. 465, and also 23.3.1899, reporting evidence of Constable Perkins at MI.
[15] RCP, p. 545.
[16] TC, 26.1.1899, reporting evidence of Dr von Lossberg at MI. See particularly his evidence before Commission, RCP, pp. 464 to 470, 533, 534 and 535 to 537.
[17] RCP, Dr von Lossberg's evidence, pp. 464 to 467.
[18] RCP, evidence of Clement Wiggins, p. 547.
[19] RCP, evidence of Alfred Robinson, pp. 545 and 546.
[20] TQ, 25.3.1899, p. 562, reporting evidence given at MI by Mrs Eames and Mrs Selby.
[21] RCP, Report of Commission dated 29.11.1899, p. XXX.
[22] Ibid.
[23] RCP, p. 407, evidence of William Arrell in answer to question 12741.
[24] RCP, evidence of P.D.F. Galbraith, p. 418, in answer to question 13201.
[25] RCP, p. 535, in answer to question 17176.
[26] RCP, Report of Commission, p. XXXI.
[27] RCP, evidence of P.D.F. Galbraith, p. 419.
[28] Ibid.
[29] RCP, evidence of P.D.F. Galbraith, p. 421.
[30] EO, 29.12.1898, p. 5.
[31] EO, 29.12.1898, referring to events at Gatton on 28.12.1898.
[32] RCP, evidence of F.C. Urquhart, p. 432.
[33] TC, 3.1.1899 and MC, 29.12.1898.
[34] TC, 3.1.1899.

[1] The *Quetta*, a vessel of 3540 tonnes, sank at approximately 9.30 p.m. on 28 February 1890, three minutes after striking an uncharted rock in the strait separating Albany and Adolphus Islands, near Cape York, Queensland. The vessel was at the time on a voyage from Brisbane to England. One hundred and thirty-three of the two hundred and ninety-one passengers on board lost their lives. It was Torres Strait's worst disaster.

[2] *A Journalist's Memories*, Major-General Spencer Browne, 1927, pp. 134 and 135. OL.

[3] RCP, evidence of P.D.F. Galbraith, p. 420.

[4] RCP, evidence of F.C. Urquhart, p. 433.

[5] Ibid., p. 440.

[6] BC, 3.1.1899, p. 5.

[7] *Studies in Australian Crime*, John D. Fitzgerald, first series, 1924, p. 136. OL.

[8] QT, 11.2.1899, p. 6.

[9] RCP, evidence of F.C. Urquhart, p. 440.

[10] Per Stable J. in *Geitz* v. *Maranoa Transport Pty Ltd. and another*, 1959, Qd.R. p. 527 at page 537, adopting a dictum of Philp J. in *Gorring* v. *Turner* (1952), unreported.

[11] Per Viscount Simonds in *Overseas Tankship (U.K.) Ltd.* v. *Morts Dock & Engineering Co. Ltd.* (The Wagon Mound) (1961) A.C. 388, at p. 424.

[12] TC, 31.12.1898; see also TQ, 31.12.1898, p. 1244.

[13] An article by Pat Lloyd in TT, 19.4.1969. See also TC, 31.12.1898.

[14] RCP, evidence of Michael Toomey, p. 442.

[15] TT, 2.1.1899.

[16] TT, 18.1.1899.

[17] RCP, evidence of Archibald Meston, p. 548. See also EO, 30.12.1898, p. 5.

[18] EO, 30.12.1898, p. 5.

[19] RCP, evidence of Archibald Meston, pp. 548 and 549.

[20] Ibid.

[21] RCP, evidence of Archibald Meston, p. 549, in answer to question number 17585.

[22] Ibid, in answer to questions numbers 17601 and 17602.

[23] MC, 30.12.1898.

[24] TC, 28.1.1899.

[25] TC, 1.3.1899.

[26] TT, 2.1.1899.

[27] BC, 3.1.1899.

[28] Ibid.

[29] RCP, evidence of F.C. Urquhart, p. 432 in answer to question number 13602.

[30] *Studies in Australian Crime*, John D. Fitzgerald, first series, 1924, pp. 138–140. OL.

[31] QT, 21.1.1899, p. 5.

[32] MC, 21.1.1899, reporting a statement by the Commissioner of Police

reported at Gatton on 20.1.1899.

[33] RCP, evidence of F.C. Urquhart, p. 422, in answer to question 13270.

[34] Ibid, p. 439, in answer to question number 13819.

[35] *A Journalist's Memories*, Major-General Spencer Browne, 1927, p. 135, OL.

213

[1] *Studies in Australian Crime*, John D. Fitzgerald, first series, 1924, p. 132. OL.

[2] See particularly pp. 25–29, 31–33, *ante*.

[3] TC, 5.1.1899.

[4] TC, 3.1.1899.

[5] RCP, evidence of F.C. Urquhart, p. 439, questions 13817 and 13818 and answers thereto.

[6] RCP, evidence of William McNeil, p. 449, questions 14166 to 14172 inclusive, and answers thereto.

[7] TQ, 18.3.1899, p. 513, reporting evidence of Arthur Booking at MI on 14.3.1899.

[8] Ibid, p. 512, reporting evidence of Margaret Carroll at MI on 10.3.1899.

[9] Ibid, p. 513, reporting evidence of John Carroll at MI on 10.3.1899.

[10] RCP, evidence of Margaret Carroll, p. 405.

[11] RCP, evidence of John Carroll, pp. 405 and 406.

[12] TC, 16.3.1899.

[13] TQ, 18.3.1899, p. 513, reporting evidence of Florence Lowe at MI on 14.3.1899.

[14] Ibid, reporting evidence of William Arrell at MI on 15.3.1899.

[15] TC, 26.1.1899, reporting evidence of Patrick Murphy at MI on 24.1.1899.

[16] *Wills on Circumstantial Evidence*, 1902, 5th edition, pp. 382 and 383. The "just remark" quoted by Wills was an observation made by Sir Herbert Jenner, in *Chambers* v. *The Queen's Proctor*, 2 Curt. at page 434.

[17] See p. 10 *ante* and Note [20] to **Introduction**.

[18] See p. 37 *ante*.

[19] RCP, p. 410, evidence of William Arrell, in answer to questions 12858 to 12865 inclusive.

[20] TQ, 25.3.1899, p. 524, reporting evidence of William Arrell at MI on 15.3.1899.

[21] TC, 26.1.1899, reporting evidence of Louisa Theuerkauf and Catherine Byrne at MI on 24.1.1899.

[22] QT, 11.3.1899, p. 2, reporting evidence of James Portley at MI on 9.3.1899. See also a report of his evidence in TQ, 18.3.1899, p. 478.

[23] TC, 9.3.1899, reporting evidence of Katie Murphy at MI on 6.3.1899.

[24] RCP, p. 446, evidence of Michael Toomey on 2.10.1899, in answer to questions 14047 to 14049 inclusive.

[25] Published in QT, 11.2.1899, p. 6.

[26] MC, 17.2.1899, reporting an article by the special reporter of QT at Gatton.

[27] TC, 5.1.1899.

[28] RCP, p. 439, question 13827 and answer thereto.

[29] RCP, p. 530, evidence of Dr C.J.H. Wray on 14.10.1899, questions 17019 to 17022 inclusive and answers thereto.

[30] RCP, p. 531, evidence of Dr. C.J.H. Wray on 14.10.1899, questions 17051 to 17060 inclusive and answers thereto.

[31] RCP, pp. 537 and 538, evidence of Dr Andrew W. Orr, M.D., on 14.10.1899, questions 17248 to 17276 and answers thereto.

[32] RCP, pp. 467 and 468, evidence of Dr W.H. von Lossberg on 5.10.1899, questions 14810 to 14822 and answers thereto.

[33] RCP, p. 531, evidence of Dr C.J.H. Wray on 14.10.1899, questions 17064 to 17075 inclusive and answers thereto.

[34] This interview took place on Saturday 17 April 1976.

[35] Article entitled "Significance of spermatozoa in the penile urethra at *post mortem*" by Professor A.K. Mant, published in the *Journal of Forensic Science Society*, Vol. 2, No. 2 (March, 1962), p. 125.

[36] TQ, 1.4.1899, p. 584.

[37] BC, 25.3.1899.

[38] TQ, 18.3.1899, p. 477.

[39] Ibid.

[40] TQ, 1.4.1899, p. 584.

[41] Section 33 of *The Oaths Act of 1867*. This original section 33 was repealed by *The Criminal Code Act, 1899*, s.3, and the present section 33 was inserted by *The Oaths Act Amendment Act of 1924*, s.2. The present section provides that the person being sworn "shall, if physically capable of doing so, hold a copy of a Bible or Testament in his hand, but it shall not be necessary for him to kiss such copy by way of assent . . . the person taking the oath shall thereupon, while holding in his hand a copy of the Bible or Testament, indicate his assent to the oath so administered by uttering the words "So help me, God"; or the person taking the oath may, while holding in his hand a copy of the Bible or Testament, repeat the words of the oath as prescribed or allowed by law."

[42] MC, 30.12.1898.

[43] RCP, pp. 399 and 401, questions 12339 to 12346 inclusive, 12357 to 12360 inclusive, and 12407 and answers thereto.

[44] See p. 37 *ante*, and TQ, 25.3.1899, p. 562.

[45] MC, 12.1.1899, reporting *Brisbane Courier*'s Gatton correspondent's report of 9.1.1899.

[46] TC, 23.3.1899.

[47] TC, 9.3.1899.

[48] RCP, Report of Commission of 29.11.1899, paragraph 43, p. XXXII.

[49] RCP, p. 401, evidence of Mary Murphy on 26.9.1899, questions 12415 and 12416.

[50] P. 49 *ante*, lines 3 to 6.

[51] RCP, p. 439, evidence of F.C. Urquhart on 2.10.1899, questions 13813 and 13814 and answers thereto.

[52] See pp. 46, 47 *ante*.

[53] See p. 48 *ante*.

[54] RCP, p. 536, evidence of Dr von Lossberg on 14.10.1899, questions 17211 to 17213 inclusive and 17217 to 17228 and answers thereto.

[55] RCP, p. 445, evidence of Michael Toomey, questions 14006 to 14010 and answers thereto.

[56] RCP, p. 538, evidence of Dr Andrew W. Orr on 14.10.1899, questions 17263 and 17264 and answers thereto.

[57] *Rubaiyat of Omar Khayyam*, LXXIII.

[1] See pp. 64 and 65 *ante*.

[2] TQ, 14.1.1899, p. 52.

[3] RCP, p. 691, Appendix 10.

[4] BC, 29.1.1926, p. 6. Obituary of P.D.F. Galbraith.

[5] QT, 11.2.1899, p. 6. See also RCP, p. 446, evidence of Michael Toomey on 2.10.1899, questions 14050 to 14052 inclusive and answers thereto.

[6] TQ, 18.3.1899, reporting evidence of Frank Moran at MI on 14.3.1899.

[7] QT, 24.1.1899, 31.1.1899 and 11.2.1899.

[8] QT, 11.2.1899, p. 6.

[9] TQ, 11.3.1899, pp. 464–465, reporting evidence of Daniel Murphy at MI on 6.3.1899.

[10] TC, 7.1.1899.

[11] MC, 3.1.1899, quoting a report from "*The Telegraph*'s official reporter at Gatton".

[12] RCP, p. 441, evidence of F.C. Urquhart on 2.10.1899 answering question 13887; p. 420, evidence of P.D.F. Galbraith on 28.9.1899, questions 13216 and 13217 and answers thereto; p. 463, evidence of William Arrell on 3.10.1899, questions 14658 to 14665 and answers thereto.

[13] QT, 21.1.1899, p. 5.

[14] TC, 9.3.1899, reporting evidence of Daniel Murphy at MI on 6.3.1899.

[15] QT, 9.3.1899, p. 5, reporting evidence of Mary Murphy at MI on 8.3.1899.

[16] RCP, evidence of William Arrell, p. 410, questions 12848 and 12849 and answers thereto.

[17] RCP, evidence of P.D.F. Galbraith, p. 419, answering question 13215.

[18] RCP, evidence of P.D.F. Galbraith, p. 420, questions 13218 and 13219 and answers thereto.

[19] TC, 25.3.1899, reporting evidence of Polly McNeil at MI at Toowoomba on 23.3.1899.

[20] TQ, 18.3.1899, reporting evidence of Thomas Joseph Ryan at MI on 10.3.1899.

[21] RCP, evidence of P.D.F. Galbraith, p. 421, questions 13234 to 13243 inclusive and answers thereto.

[22] RCP, evidence of Michael Toomey, pp. 444 and 445, questions 13976 to 13998 and answers thereto.

[23] See pp. 27 and 36 *ante*.

[24] RCP, p. 411, evidence of William Arrell, questions 12897 and 12901 to 12903 inclusive and answers thereto.

[25] MC, 5.1.1899, furnishing the report of the "*Courier*'s Gatton correspondent.

[26] TC, 5.1.1899.

[27] TQ, 28.1.1899, p. 185.

[28] TQ, 14.1.1899, p. 52.

[29] MC, 31.1.1899, reporting an item "by telegraph" of 30.1.1899.

[30] RCP, p. 472, evidence of Richard James, in answer to question 14984.

[31] RCP, p. 449, evidence of William McNeil, questions 14174 to 14180 and answers thereto.

[32] RCP, p. 401, while answering question 12413.

[33] TQ, 1.4.1899, p. 584, reporting evidence of Constable Joe Murphy at MI

on 24.3.1899.

[34] TC, 9.3.1899, reporting evidence of Daniel Murphy at MI on 6.3.1899.

[35] Ibid., reporting evidence of Mary Murphy at MI on 6.3.1899.

[36] Pp. 33 and 34 *ante*.

[37] P. 31 *ante*.

[38] BC, 10.1.1899, p. 5.

[39] Ibid.

[40] In *Rex* v. *Ellwood* (1908) 1 Cr. App. R. 181, p. 182, Channell J. observed "there is a great difference between absence of proved motive and proved absence of motive". In the later case of *Abramovitch* (1912) 7 Cr. App. R. 145 at p. 147, he said ". . . it has been well said that absence of proved motive is a very different thing from proved absence of motive."

[41] RCP, p. 437, in answer to question 13753.

[42] Pat Lloyd in an article entitled "The Maniacal Gatton Killer", TT, 19.4.69.

[1] EO, 9.1.1899, p. 5.

[2] QT, 14.1.1899, p. 5.

[3] BC, 17.1.1899, p. 4.

[4] QT, 21.1.1899, quoting a report from the *Gympie Times*.

[5] QT, 10.1.1899, p. 5.

[6] BC, 17.1.1899.

[7] TQ, 14.1.1899, p. 52. All newspaper accounts refer to the charge as being "on suspicion of being implicated in the Gatton Murders". The authors have endeavoured to ascertain the actual charge preferred against Burgess on this occasion. A search has been made at the Dalby police station and the courtesy and helpfulness of Inspector Len Gannon is gratefully acknowledged. The original bench book however was not traced. It might well be that Burgess was arrested on a "holding" charge, it being unlikely that he was actually charged with the Gatton murders. We are, of course, quite unable to appreciate how anyone could be arrested "on suspicion of being implicated in the Gatton Murders".

[8] Ibid.

[9] BC, 10.1.1899.

[10] BC, 9.1.1899. See also TQ, 14.1.1899.

[11] TQ, 14.1.1899, p. 52.

[12] TQ, 21.1.1899, p. 101.

[13] QT, 24.1.1899, p. 5.

[14] TC, 26.1.1899.

[15] BC, 26.1.1899, p. 5.

[16] TC, 26.1.1899, reporting evidence of Richard Burgess at MI at Gatton on 24.1.1899. See also TQ, 28.1.1899.

[17] QT, 2.2.1899, p. 6. See also EO, 30.1.1899, p. 5.

[18] EO, 21.1.1899, p. 2.

[19] TQ, 4.2.1899. See also BC, 30.1.1899 and QT, 28.1.1899.

[20] QT, 28.1.1899, p. 5. See also BC, 30.1.1899, p. 5.

[21] QT, 31.1.1899, p. 5. See also BC, 30.1.1899, p. 5.

[22] BC, 27.1.1899, p. 5. See also TQ, 4.2.1899, pp. 233–234.

[23] TQ, 4.2.1899, pp. 233–234.

[24] BC, 30.1.1899, p. 5. See also TC, 28.1.1899.

[25] Information given by persons corroborating Burgess's account of his movements of 26 and 27 December 1898 was reported in the *Brisbane Courier* of Monday, 6 February 1899, under the heading "Press Investigations on the Downs". It was stated that the report was "abridged from the *Darling Downs Gazette* of Saturday".

[26] EO, 24.1.1899, p. 2. See also TC, 26.1.1899, and QT, 26.1.1899.

[27] Identification of Burgess on 24.1.1899 by the persons referred to was reported in QT, 26.1.1899. See also TC, 26.1.1899.

[28] TC, 26.1.1899.

[29] QT, 14.1.1899, p. 5.

[30] QT, 31.1.1899. TQ, 11.3.1899.

[31] QT, 7.2.1899, p. 5.

[32] BC, 21.1.1899, reporting proceedings in the Police Court, Toowoomba on 26 January 1899.

[33] MC, 4.2.1899, quoting from the *Sydney Daily Telegraph*.

[34] QT, 2.3.1899, p. 5.

[35] In 1905 Steele Rudd wrote a series of stories about this expedition and in 1909 they appeared in book form under the title *For Life*. He resorted to fictitious names for the protagonists in the events described but it purported to be a true account of those events and was laced with humorous anecdotes here and there. This book was republished by the Queensland University Press in November 1968.

[36] TQ, 1.4.1899, p. 614.

[37] *Studies in Australian Crime*, John D. Fitzgerald, first series, 1924, p. 143. OL. Details of Burgess's conviction and imprisonment in Melbourne were obtained from the Public Record Office, Victoria.

[38] Ibid, p. 141.

[39] QT, 10.1.1899, p. 5 and 2.2.1899, p. 6.

[40] QT, 12.1.1899.

[1] Pp. 70–72 *ante*.

[2] RCP, p. 443, evidence of Michael Toomey in answer to questions 13940 to 13942.

[3] RCP, p. 450, report of Police Constable Robert George Christie, dated 24 April 1899, referred to in evidence of Christie before Commission on 3 October 1899.

[4] RCP, p. 442, evidence of Michael Toomey, in answer to questions 13903 to 13912 inclusive.

[5] RCP, p. 443, evidence of Michael Toomey, in answer to questions 13913 to 13915 inclusive.

[6] RCP, pp. 443 and 444, evidence of Michael Toomey, in answer to questions 13916 to 13975 inclusive.

[7] RCP, pp. 450 to 452, evidence of Robert George Christie, on 3 October 1899, in answer to questions 14207 to 14266 inclusive.

[8] QT, 15.4.1899, reporting evidence of Claude Wilson at South Brisbane Police Court on 13.4.1899.

[9] QT, 12.1.1899 and 20.5.1899.

[10] RCP, evidence of Andrew Stevenson Smith, p. 405, in answer to questions 12647 to 12650 inclusive.

[11] RCP, p. 477, evidence of William Burnett, on 5 October 1899, in answer to questions 15200 to 15220 inclusive.

[12] In the "Index to Witnesses" in the RCP, the name of this gentleman is spelled "Clarke". We have also noticed that, in some published articles the name is spelled "Clarke". Right throughout the transcript of evidence, however, at the Commission the name is spelled "Clark". In the narrative, however, we have adhered to the form "Clarke", which we believe to be correct.

[13] RCP, pp. 453 to 456, evidence of Arthur George Clarke, on 3.10.1899, in answer to questions 14309 to 14452 inclusive.

[14] RCP, pp. 475 to 477, evidence of Robert King, on 5.10.1899, in answer to questions 15118 to 15199 inclusive.

[15] See the remark of Mr T.O. Unmack to this effect, p. 545 of RCP, before question 17444.

[16] RCP, p. 400, evidence of Mary Murphy on 26.9.1899 in answer to questions 12386 and 12388.

[17] RCP, evidence of William Arrell, p. 463, in answer to question 14669.

[18] RCP, evidence of Daniel Murphy, junior, p. 403, in answer to questions 12523, 12531 and 12546.

[19] RCP, evidence of F.C. Urquhart, pp. 434–438 inclusive, in answer to questions 13638 to 13802 inclusive.

[20] RCP, p. 435, evidence of F.C. Urquhart, answering questions 13675 and 13676.

[21] QVP, 1899, Volume 1, p. 803. OL.

[22] RCP, evidence of Michael Toomey, p. 443, in answer to questions 13916 to 13918 inclusive.

[23] RCP, evidence of F.C. Urquhart, p. 434, question 13656.

[24] Report of Royal Commission, para. 38, p. XXXI.

[1] By Lord Chief Justice Abbott in *The King* v. *Burdett* (1820) 4 B. & Ald. 95, p. 161.

[2] *Regina* v. *Exall*, 176 E.R. 850, p. 853.

[3] *Wills on Circumstantial Evidence* (1902), 5th edition, p. 262.

[4] These "well-defined classes of facts" are largely those enumerated in an article entitled "Arguments from Circumstantial Evidence" (an extract from *Bell's Principles of Argument*), published in Vol. LXV, *Canadian Criminal Cases*, pp. 316–329.

[5] RCP, p. 438, evidence of F. C. Urquhart, in answer to questions 13801 and 13802.

[6] Ibid, p. 438, evidence of F.C. Urquhart, in answer to question 13781.

[7] Ibid, p. 438, evidence of F.C. Urquhart, questions 13785 and 13786 and answers thereto.

[8] Pp. 125–127 *ante*.

[9] P. 72, *ante*.

[10] *Wills on Circumstantial Evidence* (1902), 5th edition, p. 156.

[11] *According to the Evidence*, Gerald Abrahams, Chapter 10, p. 136.

[12] By Eric R. Watson, LL.B. in his Preface to *Adolf Beck* (Notable British Trials Series) 1924.

[13] *The Proof of Guilt (A Study of the English Criminal Trial)*, Glanville Williams, LL.D., F.B.A., Fellow of Jesus College, Cambridge, and Reader in English Law in the University of Cambridge; of the Middle Temple, Barrister-at-Law, 2nd edition, 1958, pp. 103–106.

[14] RCP, p. 405, evidence of Margaret Carroll, questions 12638 to 12642 inclusive and answers thereto.

[15] In the case of *Rex* v. *Haslam* (1925) 19 Cr. App. R. 59, p. 60.

[16] TT, 26.1.1899.

[17] See *Peacock* v. *The King* (1911) 13 C.L.R. 619, p. 636 per Griffith C.J. citing *Best on Evidence*, 3rd edition, p. 518.

[18] See *Regina* v. *Maarroni* (1970) 92 W.N. (N.S.W.) 757, particularly p. 762.

[19] *Regina* v. *Turnbull and Camelo*, *Regina* v. *Whitby* and *Regina* v. *Roberts* (as yet unreported). Judgment delivered Royal Courts of Justice, Friday, 9 July 1976.

[20] For a full discussion of the varying degrees of cogency in evidence see *Cross on Evidence*, Australian edition (1970), pp. 26–28.

[21] RCP, p. 434, evidence of F.C. Urquhart, in answer to question 13645. *Rienzi* is an historical novel, written in the year 1835 by Edward Bulwer Lord Lytton (1803–1873). The subject of his work is Cola Di Rienzi (1313–1354), an Italian patriot who was born in Rome and called "the last of the Romans". He delivered the city of Rome from the aristocracy and proposed a series of laws for the better government of the community. As tribune of the Roman Republic, Rienzi was invested with virtually dictatorial power. After a reign of seven months the people turned against him and he fled to Naples. After a period of two years of religious meditation he resumed his life as a political reformer and in 1354 he entered Rome and was received with acclaim. But in two months his rule had become intolerable and an

infuriated crowd surrounded him in the Capitol, and put him to death.

[22] *The Proof of Guilt*, Glanville Williams (1958), pp. 181–182.

[23] RCP, p. 436, evidence of F.C. Urquhart, in answer to question 13721.

[24] RCP, p. 451, evidence of R.G. Christie, in answer to question 14217.

[25] RCP, p. 443, evidence of Michael Toomey, in answer to questions 13942 and 13943.

[26] RCP, p. 455, evidence of A.G. Clarke, in answer to question 14410.

[27] RCP, p. 476, evidence of Robert King, in answer to question 15137.

[28] RCP, p. 477, evidence of William Burnett, in answer to questions 15216 and 15217.

[29] *Caswell* v. *Powell Duffryn Associated Collieries Ltd.* (1940) A.C., 152 at p. 169.

[30] RCP, Report of Royal Commission, 29.11.1899, para. 38, p. XXXI.

[31] *Macbeth*, Act V., scene 5, William Shakespeare.

[32] *Rubaiyat of Omar Khayyam*, XXXII.

Epilogue

[1] E0, 26.12.1906, p. 7.

[2] *A Son of Australia—Memories of W.E. Parry-Okeden*, Harry C. Perry, 1928, p. 337.

[3] *A Journalist's Memories*, Major-General Spencer Browne, 1927.

[4] *A Son of Australia—Memories of W.E. Parry-Okeden*, Harry C. Perry, 1928, p. 296.

[5] BC, 29.1.1926. Obituary of P.D.F. Galbraith.

[6] BC, 8.1.1901, p. 5.

[7] These particulars were kindly furnished by the late Mr A.H. Warner Shand's grandson, Mr S.H.W. Shand, a prominent Brisbane solicitor.

[8] *Blue Book of Queensland*, 1901, pp. 52 and 53. See also *Pugh's Almanac*, 1899, p. 197.

[9] BC, 9.5.1902, p. 5.

[10] The report referred to appeared in the edition of *Smith's Weekly*, dated 11 June 1927.

[11] The statements made by Mrs M. Rutherford and Mrs V. Russell were reported in the *Sunday Sun*, Brisbane, on 21.1.1973.

PENGUIN TRUE CRIME

A series of brilliant investigations into some of the most mysterious and baffling crimes ever committed.

Titles published and forthcoming:

Crippen: The Mild Murderer   *Tom Cullen*

The famous story of the doctor who poisoned his wife and buried her in the cellar.

Who Killed Hanratty?   *Paul Foot*

An investigation into the notorious A6 murder.

Norman Birkett   *H. Montgomery Hyde*

The biography of one of Britain's most humane and respected judges.

The Complete Jack the Ripper   *Donald Rumbelow*

An investigation into the identity of one of the most elusive murderers of all time.

The Riddle of Birdhurst Rise   *R. Whittington-Egan*

The Croydon Poisoning Mystery of 1928–9.

Suddenly at the Priory   *John Williams*

Who poisoned the Victorian barrister Charles Bravo?

Stinie: Murder on the Common   *Andrew Rose*

The truth behind the Clapham Common murder.

The Poisoned Life of Mrs Maybrick   *Bernard Ryan*

Mr Maybrick died of arsenic poisoning – how?

The Gatton Mystery   *J. and D. Gibney*

The great unsolved Australian triple murder.

Earth to Earth   *John Cornwell*

Who killed the Luxtons in their remote mid-Devon farmhouse?

The Ordeal of Philip Yale Drew   *R. Whittington-Egan*

A real life murder melodrama in three acts.